Formation for ministry within a learning church

The structure and funding of ordination training

GS 1496

Church House Publishing
Church House
Great Smith Street
London SW1P 3NZ

ISBN: 978-0-7151-4353-7

GS 1496

Published 2003 for the Ministry Division of the Archbishops' Council by Church House Publishing

Copyright © The Archbishops' Council 2003

All rights reserved. No part of this publication may be reproduced or stored or transmitted by any means or in any form, electronic or mechanical, including photocopying, recording, or any information storage and retrieval system, without written permission which should be sought from the Copyright Administrator, The Archbishops' Council, Church House, Great Smith Street, London SWIP 3NZ.

Tel: 020 7898 1594
Fax: 020 7898 1449
Email: copyright@c-of-e.org.uk

Cover design by Visible Edge

Printed in England by The Cromwell Press Ltd,
Trowbridge, Wiltshire

FORMATION FOR MINISTRY WITHIN A LEARNING CHURCH

THE STRUCTURE AND FUNDING OF ORDINATION TRAINING

The report of a working party set up by the Archbishops' Council

	List of abbreviations	v
	Preface	vii
1.	Introduction	1
2.	The issues that have driven our work	15
3.	Some theological priorities	27
4.	Lifelong learning: a better trained clergy	36
5.	A new framework for ministerial education	47
6.	Reconfiguring the Church's training resources: proposals concerning training institutions	68
7.	Financial issues	89
8.	Encouraging and managing flexibility: some further training issues	118
9.	List of proposals and outlook	132
	Map of theological colleges, regional courses and OLM schemes recognized by the House of Bishops	5
	Map of Methodist districts and ministerial training institutions	6
	Glossary of educational terms	54
	Illustrative regional maps 1, 2, 3, 4	85–88

Appendices

1. Terms of reference and membership of the working party on the structure of funding of ordination training 137
2. List of those who contributed to the consultation process 139
3. Total number of ordinands in training 2002/2003 149
4. Sponsored candidates in training since 1970 151
5. Training institutions used by the Methodist Church and numbers in training 152
6. Training institutions used by the United Reformed Church and numbers in training 155
7. A possible structure for Regional Training Partnerships 156
8. Illustrative organizational charts 166
9. College and course budgeted expenditure, fees and estimated subsidies in 2002/03 169
10. Forecast Vote 1 at present 172
11. Reduction to 490 training full-time and part-time numbers stable at 590 174
12. Reduction to 490 training full-time and part-time numbers increase by 112 to 702 179
13. Full-time and part-time numbers stable but reduction by 50 in numbers of people requiring family maintenance 183
14. Reduction of 150 to 390 people training full-time, reduction of capacity by 200 to 415 and increase of 201 in numbers training part-time 187

Notes 191

List of abbreviations

Abbreviations of Church reports referred to frequently in the text

ACCM 22	*Education for the Church's Ministry. The report of the working party on assessment*, ACCM Occasional Paper No. 22, 1987
Beginning Public Ministry	*Beginning Public Ministry: Guidelines for ministerial formation and personal development for the first four years after ordination*, ABM Ministry Paper No. 17, 1998
Mission and Ministry	*Mission and Ministry. The Churches' Validation Framework for Theological Education*, Ministry Division, 1999
Reader Ministry and Training	*Reader Ministry and Training – 2000 and Beyond*, Ministry Division, 2000
Managing Planned Growth	*Managing Planned Growth*, Ministry Division, GS Misc 597, January 2000
Mind the Gap	*Mind the Gap. Integrated Continuing Ministerial Education for the Church's Ministries*, Ministry Division, 2001

Ministerial training institutions

CBDTI	Carlisle and Blackburn Diocese Training Institute		Cranmer	Cranmer Hall (St John's College), Durham
EAMTC	East Anglian Ministerial Training Course		Mirfield	College of the Resurrection, Mirfield
EMMTC	East Midlands Ministry Training Course		Oak Hill	Oak Hill Theological College
NEOC	North East Oecumenical Course		Queen's	The Queen's College, Birmingham
NOC	The Northern Ordination Course		Ridley	Ridley Hall, Cambridge
NTMTC	North Thames Ministerial Training Course		Ripon	Ripon College, Cuddesdon
SAOMC	St Albans and Oxford Ministry Course		St John's	St John's College, Nottingham
SEITE	South East Institute for Theological Education		St Stephen's	St Stephen's House, Oxford
STETS	Southern Theological Education and Training Scheme		Trinity	Trinity College, Bristol
SWMTC	South West Ministry Training Course		Westcott	Westcott House, Cambridge
WMMTC	West Midlands Ministerial Training Course		Wycliffe	Wycliffe Hall, Oxford
WEMTC	West of England Ministerial Training Course		Bangor	Centre for Ministry Studies, Bangor
			North Bank	North Bank Centre for Christian Living
			UTU	Urban Theology Unit, Sheffield

Preface

About three years ago the Archbishops' Council established a working party to continue the work of an earlier working party ('Managing Planned Growth') by considering some questions identified by the earlier group. These included some technical questions concerning the financing of ordination training and also the much wider question about what such training is for, raising a whole range of fundamental issues.

It was no secret to anyone who had followed the history of attempts to reform ministerial education in the recent past that this would not be easy. Our first task was to try to listen to as many voices as possible and get a picture of the strengths and weaknesses of the existing arrangements. Although we were almost overwhelmed by the number of responses and their diversity, the work of the group was immensely helped by the willingness of so many people to help. They included those directly involved in ministerial education, in the continued formation of clergy and Readers, members of congregations, recently ordained ministers, ecumenical friends, Synod representatives and a host of others.

The report itself has emerged from several years' work which produced two preliminary versions, an interim report widely debated during 2002 and a draft final report published towards the end of that year. The comments we received in writing were augmented by a series of regional meetings around the country and many other meetings with individuals and groups with special interests and expertise who asked to talk with us. The Archbishops' Council and the House of Bishops have been kept informed at every stage.

Although it would be too much to hope that any group working on such a sensitive subject would be able to please everybody, we have real confidence that our recommendations can make a major contribution to 'formation for ministry within a learning Church' for many years ahead.

At the very end of the report (9.4) there is a section entitled 'Our hopes for the future'. For anyone wanting a quick introduction to the principles we have tried to embody, there is probably no better place to start that that. A summary of the report is also available.

We believe that the extensive resources and expertise already devoted by the Church to ministerial formation need better coordinating and that this can be best done on a regional basis. We think every opportunity for cooperation with other churches and with the universities and the Church colleges should be taken. We are convinced that good clergy formation both depends on and helps secure learning across the Church as a whole. We know that just as discipleship is lifelong, so too must be our commitment to growing in the wisdom that discipleship requires. Because theology is the Church's own discipline, there can be no substitute for learning within the community of faith. Formation for ministry is a lifelong process and we believe that the initial training of the clergy should be seen as the period from the entry into training to the end of the first training post. Such an extended initial training will take some pressure off the pre-ordination curriculum, enable new patterns of training combining formation, study and practice and be a good platform for continued ministerial development. None of this comes cheaply, but we should do all we can to ensure that precious resources are well spent.

Not surprisingly, many people have asked what will happen to the existing colleges, courses and OLM schemes. These resources are just too valuable to risk, and it is our strong hope that by entering into partnership with each other and with the dioceses our present institutions will be strengthened and make an even more notable contribution to the life of the Church in the future.

Of course, none of this will work unless everyone involved is willing to move into a more collaborative, partnership-oriented way of thinking and working. In several places that is already happening and new energy is being released as a consequence.

One final thought: the working party was set up to investigate the structure and funding of ordination training. We have rightly been challenged as to why we have talked about formation more widely. We hope the answer is obvious from the report itself. Fundamentally, this is a theological issue; it is about the nature of the Church as a single body with many members and an infinite variety of gifts supplied by the Holy Spirit.

✠ John Hind
Chairman of the Working Party
on the Structure and Funding of Ordination Training
April 2003

Chapter 1

Introduction

1.1   The Church and our society rightly have high expectations of the training of ordained ministers. At times these expectations are unrealistically high but all who work in this field are aware that the initial and continuing ministerial education of clergy offers an important opportunity to focus and to give shape to the mission and ministry of the Church under the providence of God. Our working party has been given the task of undertaking a fundamental review of ordination training. It was set up by the Archbishops' Council, with Bishop John Hind as its chair, following a recommendation made by the working party that produced *Managing Planned Growth*.[1] The terms of reference and membership of the working party will be found in Appendix 1.

1.2   From the earliest days of the working party we have understood *both* that we have been entrusted with a task *and* that we can only begin to fulfil it by drawing on the insight and expertise of a far wider range of people and institutions. Thus, we have carried out three large-scale consultation exercises. We are grateful to all those who have taken time and care to offer a full set of responses that have substantially affected the proposals contained in this report. We began our work by seeking the views of many interested parties (the dioceses, training institutions, our ecumenical partners and institutions of higher education) and issued a general invitation in the Church press for individuals and groups to contribute. We received more than 150 responses that helped to shape our thinking. Then, in February 2002 we published our interim report, held a range of consultative meetings on the basis of that report and received about 180 often substantial written submissions in response to it (for a list of those who contributed, see Appendix 2). This led to the production of our draft final report, which we circulated to all interested parties in November 2002, and which was endorsed by the Ministry Division's Theological Education and Training Committee, the Archbishops' Council and the House of Bishops. Finally, we have added detailed consideration of the financial issues in Chapter 7. Thus throughout the process and in preparation for publication and for debate in the General Synod, scheduled for July 2003, we have sought to test our thoughts in the Church and beyond and to draw on a wider wisdom.

1.3   We have interpreted our terms of reference broadly, as we have been encouraged to look from the perspective of the considerable challenges and possibilities facing the Church in the area of training in the early decades of the twenty-first century. In this sense our work has been different from the limited reviews of the early 1990s[2] that led to the amalgamation of some regional courses and the closure of some theological colleges. Thus, we have not interpreted our task as being another routine review or indeed being driven by the immediate need to save money or reduce the capacity of the training institutions. Rather, in line with one main strand of the responses from our first consultation exercise, we detect *an appetite for significant change, albeit change that builds on existing strengths*. The demand for change was expressed in our initial consultation exercise. To give one example:

'We believe that there has to be a fairly radical look at this matter [the structure and funding of ordination training], and that the Church probably has to envisage some far-reaching changes in the pattern of training…'

This desire for change needs, however, to be set alongside the need to build on the current best practice and to develop our training establishment. Many respondents in the consultation exercise on our interim report made this point: any successful plan for change must be evolutionary, rather than revolutionary, where possible building on the best current practice. In the light of this, we have sought

i) to review the Church's requirements in ministerial education for the clergy in the context of a learning Church as a whole;

ii) to develop an approach that combines significant change with the development of the current best practice;

iii) to seek an approach that will enable and encourage the growth of ecumenical partnership in training.

Consequently, we have put forward a series of significant and, in part, bold proposals. We make proposals to *provide high-quality training for the clergy that will equip them to offer vibrant and collaborative spiritual leadership and to empower a vocationally motivated laity – and, thereby, to promote and serve God's mission in the world.*

The current provision of ministerial education within the Church of England

1.4   We turn now to the Church of England's current provision. Ministerial education is of course set within the wider system of vocational discernment and selection for a range of ministries. Candidates for ordained ministry initially explore their sense of vocation with the relevant officers of their own dioceses and are then sponsored for a bishops' selection conference, administered by the Ministry Division. The sponsoring bishop makes a decision about whether to send the individual candidate into training in the light of the advice given by bishops' selectors. The same process is used for the few candidates coming forward for Accredited Lay Ministry, i.e. those who are formally sponsored by a bishop and attend a national selection conference with a view to exercising a nationally recognized lay ministry. Thus, ministerial education is a form of training for those whose vocations to a particular ministry have been discerned on behalf of the whole Church.

1.5   Before describing our current provision it is worth reflecting briefly on the sometimes confusing terminology used in this field. The popular term 'training' is regularly used for the whole process of formation and education leading up to ordination. It carries with it, however, the implication that this is something that *ends* at ordination, as well as, to some ears, inappropriate utilitarian overtones. In more specialist uses, the Church has a range of language:

- Some prefer to speak of 'preparation' for ordination to denote the whole pre-ordination process.

- Others will distinguish between the educational (or academic), formational and training dimensions of the whole process. This is a helpful set of distinctions in that it indicates the complexity of task, involving the intellect, the whole person and relevant skills.

- The term 'formation' has come to mean either the whole process or that part of it which refers to personal, liturgical and spiritual development in preparation for the distinctive role of the ordained.

Introduction

- The term 'theological education' is often used synonymously with initial training for ordained ministry, even though presumably it is hoped that the clergy's theological learning will continue after ordination. The term can also appear to devalue all the theological education that happens that is not ministerial preparation. However, it carries the important point that preparation for ministry involves substantial theological learning.

- This language can be given more precision by speaking of 'initial ministerial education' (IME) as currently understood for the pre-ordination phase and 'continuing ministerial education' (CME) thereafter. In turn the former Post-Ordination Training (POT) has been almost universally displaced by CME 1–4 (the first four years) which is followed by CME (or continuing ministerial education and development, CMED) for the rest of a person's ministry. IME is not itself an unambiguous term – it does not in itself indicate whether the intended ministry is lay or ordained.

- Similarly, the term 'ministerial training' is itself ambiguous as it encompasses training for ordained and lay ministries.

This range of terminology indicates that no one term is adequate to describe all the dimensions of the task. In this report we have normally used the term 'ministerial education', encompassing the formational, educational and training aspects of preparation for ordination ministry, though we also use the shorthand 'training'.

1.6 The Church of England's provision for the education and formation of its clergy is currently made up of IME to the point of ordination and the combination of apprenticeship with a training incumbent in the title parish and the first three to four years of CME. At this point some clergy are deemed ready to take up a post of responsibility, while others will continue ministry in an associate role. (Examples of posts of responsibility would include team vicars, some chaplains, tutors in a theological training institution and incumbents.) For the rest of their ministry, clergy are expected to make use of a range of types of CME to continue their learning and development.

1.7 Within the synodical system of Church government, the House of Bishops has final responsibility for ministry issues, including the training of the clergy. It is the House of Bishops that grants 'recognition' to the institutions that offer ordination training and that decides on all policy matters. The role of the Ministry Division within this area is to advise the House of Bishops on matters of policy and to carry out key functions on behalf of the Church. For example, on the financial side it sets the fees and approves budgets, while on the educational side it approves the curricula offered by the colleges, courses and OLM schemes. Through the Inspections Working Party the House of Bishops carries out inspections of training institutions offering IME every five years.

1.8 Initial ministerial education is provided by a partnership between the House of Bishops, the General Synod, which votes for the funding of training each year, the dioceses, the Ministry Division, the theological colleges, courses and diocesan OLM schemes and their partners in higher education, the universities and church colleges of higher education. Individual training institutions require recognition by the House of Bishops in order to train ordinands for the ordained ministry of the Church of England. This in turn requires approval of the financial and educational proposals by the Ministry Division. Through this work it seeks to ensure that the money allocated by the Church for the training of ordinands is effectively spent and that a good and appropriate standard of ministerial education is offered by all theological colleges, courses and OLM schemes. The map on p.5 shows the theological colleges, courses and OLM schemes recognized by the House of Bishops for the training of Church of England candidates.

1.9   Bishops' regulations for training, available, among other places, in the Church of England Year Book, set out the basic regulations regarding the length of training in years and the mode of training (college, course, OLM scheme) according to categories of sponsorship of candidates, age and theological qualification.

1.10   Candidates for ordained ministry normally are sponsored by a bishop to attend a bishops' selection conference, administered by the Ministry Division. Candidates can currently be sponsored for one of three categories of priestly or diaconal ministry:

i)   stipendiary/non-stipendiary. This category allows candidates to exercise either stipendiary or non-stipendiary ministry, and to move between these types of ministry;

ii) permanent non-stipendiary;

iii) ordained local ministry.

Candidates can also be sponsored for accredited lay ministry (stipendiary/non-stipendiary or permanent non-stipendiary, as above). This category is a nationally recognized form of lay ministry. It is distinguished from other forms of lay ministry by the fact that candidates, like those for ordained ministry, have attended a bishops' selection conference, administered by the Ministry Division, and been selected against the criteria for selection agreed by the House of Bishops. On receipt of the report from the bishops' selectors, the bishop, advised by the diocesan director of ordinands, makes a decision on whether or not to send the candidate into training. As will be seen from the following paragraphs, the categories of sponsorship are important in terms of the access of the candidate to certain types of training.

Theological colleges

1.11   Theological colleges offer two to three years of training in a full-time mode for those candidates who are sponsored for ordained ministry that includes stipendiary ministry, i.e. sponsorship for the flexible category, stipendiary ministry/non-stipendiary ministry. Candidates under 30 normally train in colleges, those over 30 have a choice of college-type or course-type training. In conjunction with their bishop or Diocesan Director of Ordinands (DDO), these candidates choose the colleges (or if over 30, colleges or regional course) to which they will apply. Candidates over 30 and those who are theology graduates are required and enabled to do two years' training while candidates who are under 30 and are not theology graduates will undertake three years of training. The purpose of these regulations is to ensure that all candidates who are presented for ordination are equipped, theologically, spiritually and personally, to *begin* ordained ministry. As noted above, the whole training package includes the training offered by the first parish with a training incumbent and the provision of CME in these years.

1.12   Candidates who qualify for college-type training have a choice of twelve theological colleges, including one in Wales. Colleges offer a range of academic awards from diploma level to Masters level and beyond. Within the range are programmes that include university theology degrees (BA) and ministerial degrees (e.g. BTh) and diplomas. Formation for ministry is offered through the opportunities afforded by full-time study, the worship and

Theological colleges, courses and OLM schemes recognized by the House of Bishops

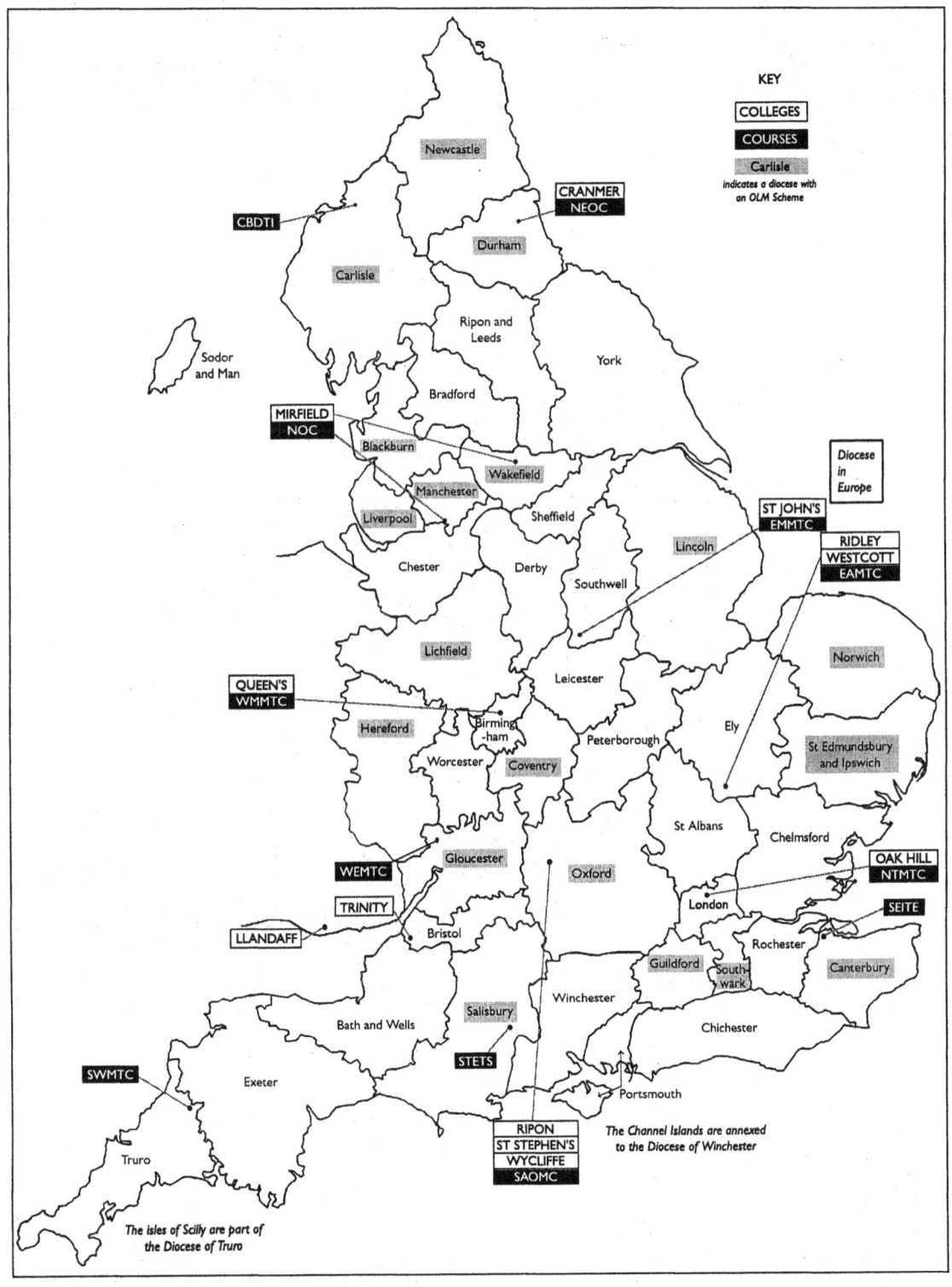

Methodist Districts and Training Institutions

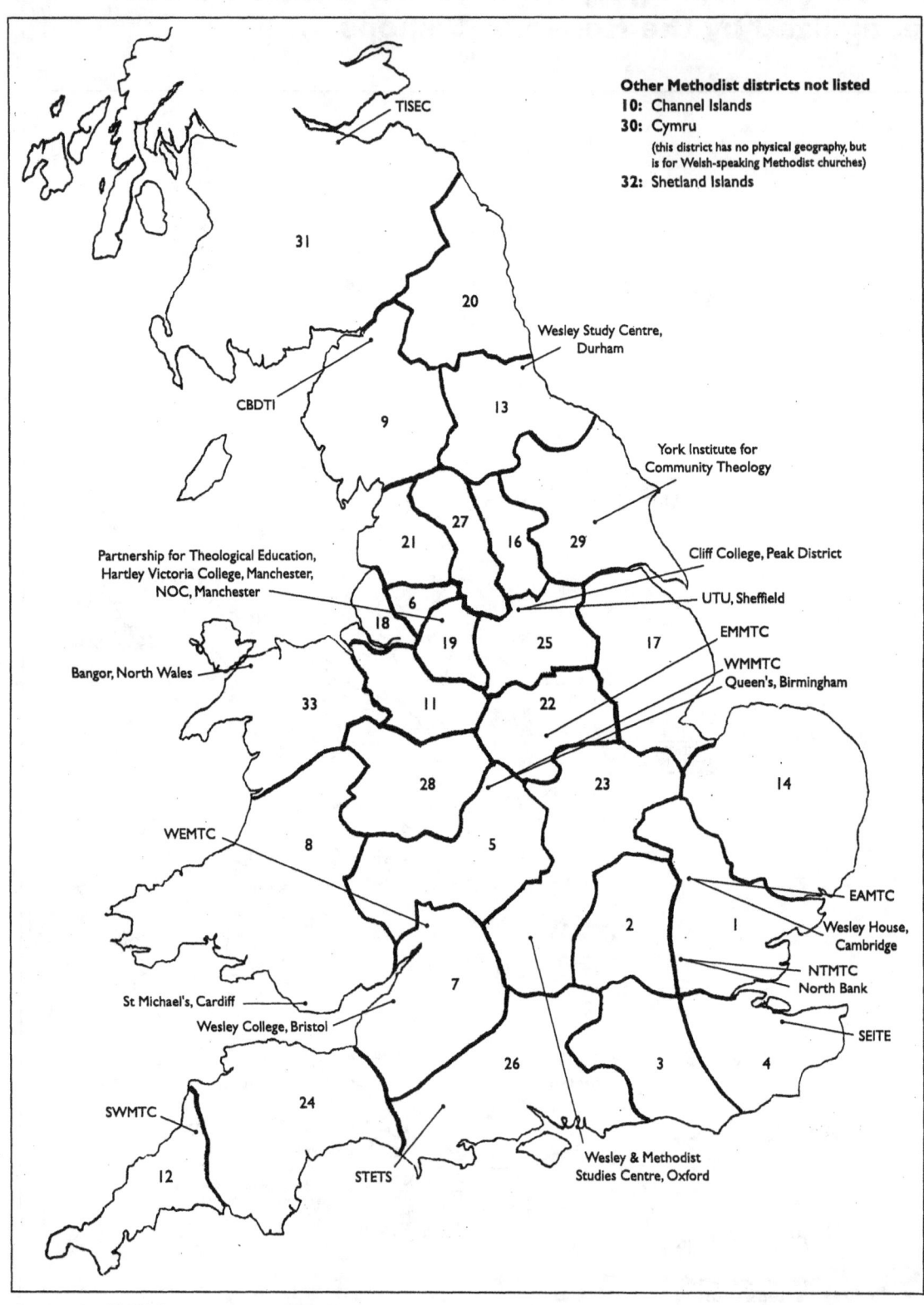

1	London North East	9	Cumbria	18	Liverpool	26	Southampton
2	London North West	11	Chester and Stoke	19	Manchester and Stockport	27	West Yorkshire
3	London South West	12	Cornwall	20	Newcastle upon Tyne	28	Wolverhampton and Shrewsbury
4	London South East	13	Darlington	21	North Lancashire		
5	Birmingham	14	East Anglia	22	Nottingham and Derby	29	York and Hull
6	Bolton and Rochdale	15	Isle of Man	23	Oxford and Leicester	31	Scotland
7	Bristol	16	Leeds	24	Plymouth and Exeter	33	North Wales
8	South Wales	17	Lincoln and Grimsbey	25	Sheffield		

communal life of the college and an extensive range of placements. The numbers of candidates in each theological college is controlled by a quota system known as the Bishops' Agreed Maximum for theological colleges. The quota is revised each autumn for the next academic year in the light of the projected numbers in training.

Regional courses

1.13   The twelve theological courses are organized on a regional basis and offer for most candidates a three-year initial training programme in a part-time mode for candidates over 30. They train candidates sponsored for permanent non-stipendiary ministry and candidates over 30 sponsored for stipendiary ministry/non-stipendiary ministry who opt to train in this way. As with college training, the purpose is to equip candidates to *begin* ordained ministry, with the title parish and the first three to four years of CME completing the initial training. These courses are each sponsored by a group of dioceses. Candidates from these dioceses will normally be expected to train on their regional course. All the courses now have university validation for their basic programmes, typically at diploma level. With the growth of the accreditation of prior learning, some candidates may achieve degrees or Masters level studies in theology for ministry in their initial training. Other candidates may be able to top up their pre-ordination studies to degree or Masters level after ordination. In terms of formation or development for ministry, courses make use of the community of prayer and learning, especially during the residential elements (weekends and Summer or Easter schools), in conjunction with the candidate's continuing experience of work or home and his or her own parish and placements.

Ecumenical partnership

1.14   Much of college- and course-based training has an ecumenical aspect, although in a variety of different ways. Limitations of space preclude a full description of these partnerships, but the following examples illustrate the range. Among the colleges, the Queen's Foundation is ecumenical in foundation, staffing and operation, while, in Cambridge, the Federation shares teaching between eight institutes, representing five Christian churches. In both Oxford and Durham there is a common academic programme for ordinands from a range of churches. Trinity, Bristol shares staff and a programme with the Bristol Baptist College. Some of the regional courses are ecumenical in foundation, while others continue as Anglican institutions that the Methodist Church and the United Reformed Church use to train their candidates. At a national level, there is frequent contact between the Ministry Division and its equivalents in the two partner churches just named and with the much wider group of churches represented in the Ecumenical Strategy Group for Ministerial Training, under the umbrella of Churches Together in England. A map of Methodist districts and training locations is included on p.6, with further information on Methodist and URC training in Appendices 5 and 6. Throughout our work we have been aware of the ecumenical dimension of initial ministerial education and hope that our proposals will strengthen ecumenical partnership.

Ordained Local Ministry schemes

1.15   As outlined in the report *Stranger in the Wings* (1998), dioceses of the Church of England may develop Ordained Local Ministry schemes including the provision for the initial training of future OLMs. A diocesan OLM scheme may only train ordinands who are sponsored under the category of OLM, though the training is often shared with Readers and/or members of local ministry or training teams. Some dioceses train their OLMs wholly or partly through regional theological courses. As with the stipendiary and non-stipendiary categories, the purpose of the initial training is to prepare candidates to begin to exercise ordained ministry but, for these candidates, in a designated local context. At the time of writing 19 dioceses have OLM schemes approved by the House of Bishops, a number which has grown steadily over the last decade and continues to grow. In the past OLM schemes have generally not sought university validation. However, there is now a noticeable move to university validation at either certificate or diploma level. All OLM schemes emphasize two primary locations for the formation of candidates: the local ministry team or equivalent in the home parish and, secondly, the educational programme in its setting in the life of the scheme. The latter draws on the learning and worshipping community of staff, ordinands and others and includes placements and practical training.

Numbers of ordinands in training

1.16   The numbers of ordinands currently in each college, course and OLM scheme are set out in Appendix 3 with a 30-year overview in Appendix 4. Patterns of recruitment to the training institutions reflect a number of factors. These include the overall number of candidates, the rise in the number of older candidates, many of whom will be married and may have children, and the growth of OLM. This has resulted in a current pattern where there are roughly equal numbers in colleges and courses, with OLM candidates forming a smaller but growing group. The current numbers of ordinands, for the academic year 2002–03, are:

Colleges	554	40.7%
Courses	589	43.3%
OLM Schemes	217	16.0%
Total	1360	

However it should be noted that a significant number of candidates whose sponsorship includes stipendiary ministry now train on the regional courses. Of the 589 candidates training on courses in the current year, 293 are sponsored in the flexible category stipendiary/non-stipendiary. As a result the breakdown by category of sponsorship is as follows (2002–03):

Stipendiary/non-stipendiary	831	61.1%
Permanent non-stipendiary	310	21.8%
Ordained Local Ministry	217	22.8%
Accredited Lay Worker	2	0.1%

Some issues for colleges, courses and OLM schemes

1.17　Following the closures in the early to mid 1990s the twelve colleges benefited from the modest upturn in candidates in the second half of that decade. This in turn led to a greater confidence within the colleges and gave a platform for some controlled diversification. However, the fall in candidates in colleges which was apparent in 2002 has raised again the question of the viability of the colleges in their current form. Some of the colleges train ordinands for other provinces and all offer opportunities for clergy on sabbatical. Several of the colleges with evangelical foundations have always recruited additional, independent students who will offer themselves for Christian service in a variety of fields. Some of these colleges have now moved into the field of training Christian youth workers. Other colleges have developed Masters programmes suitable for clergy in service and other interested students. Where these programmes are successful they can help maintain or strengthen staffing levels. At the same time the colleges have to be careful not to be distracted from their main task of training ordinands and the demands on staff have to be carefully controlled. Where the proportion of ordinands and resident clergy in full-time training drops below 66 per cent of the student body, bishops' inspectors and the Church's validation service are asked to pay particular attention to this issue.

1.18　With regard to the regional courses, the Church's commitment is to a nation-wide provision of regional courses enabling all candidates, wherever they live, to train for ordained ministry while in their current employment or occupation. While the largest courses have grown to around 100 students and have up to five staff, inevitably some courses have remained small because of geographical and population factors. The Church has responded to this situation by encouraging co-operation with diocesan OLM schemes and Reader training schemes. In addition, many courses are either ecumenical in foundation or train ministers, sometimes in very small numbers, from other churches, particularly the Methodist Church and the United Reformed Church. This has financial, ecumenical and educational benefits, while also posing additional challenges (formation for ministries in different churches; the balance of community and liturgical life in a mixed community with a predominant majority and small numbers of students from other churches; staffing arrangements). Finally, the Church of England has developed a policy that courses should normally have a minimum of three full-time members of staff who are primarily at the disposal of the course. This is to ensure a good quality of preparation for ministry for all candidates wherever they live.

1.19　As a relatively new movement OLM schemes are in a stage of growth, initial review and consolidation. As they are intrinsically a diocesan initiative the numbers of staff and students in each scheme is very small. Many schemes that have been inspected have been given recommendations to increase their staffing levels. As with colleges and courses, OLM schemes are strongly encouraged to work in close partnership with other institutions providing theological education and ministerial training, at the diocesan level and at regional level. This strand of policy has to be attended to, however, with an equal care to ensure the coherence and appropriateness of OLM training.

Partnership between providers of ministerial and theological education

1.20　Throughout the 1990s, the Church of England, with its ecumenical partners in the initial training area, have encouraged the creation and development of partnership between the providers of ministerial and theological education.[3] These partnerships have been both with other providers of ministerial education and with universities or church colleges of higher education. With regard to the former, examples would include collaboration between two or more colleges, a college with a regional course, or between a course/OLM scheme and a diocesan Reader programme. The focus can be on a shared academic programme, sharing of staff, teaching of a range of students together or, more generally, sharing good practice or building fellowship.

Mixed-mode training

1.21   In 1995 the House of Bishops approved a report on mixed-mode training. Permission was given in outline for five schemes that combined long-term parochial experience, including lay ministry, with appropriate theological training and formation for ordained ministry. While the overall take-up by candidates has not been great, two schemes are in full operation and have received positive comment from candidates and in official reports. The St John's, Nottingham scheme combines paid lay ministry with blocks of study at college, before and after ordination. The Peterborough Project, mounted by the East Anglian Ministerial Training Course, is a specialist scheme for theology graduates in which long-term placements are the basis for training which includes an MA in Contextual Theology. These mixed-mode schemes were reviewed by the Ministry Division and we draw on the findings of this work below (paragraph 8.10).

The Church Army training college

1.22   This brief survey of ordination training within the Church of England would be incomplete without an acknowledgement of the Church Army's Wilson Carlile College, Sheffield which trains Church Army evangelists. At the Church Army's request the college has its curriculum approved by the Ministry Division and its training reviewed along the lines of a bishops' inspection. In this and many other ways, the college plays a full part in the theological education network.

University departments of theology

1.23   University departments of theology have played a significant role in ministerial training which we comment on further under the heading of partnership (1.27). The departments themselves offer a wide range of expertise in theology, religious studies, teacher training and numerous related fields. While it is difficult to generalize, most departments will see themselves as offering front-line arts and humanities programmes which are research-based and offer high-quality teaching. Important recent drivers of policy have been

- fluctuations in numbers in full-time study with a marked growth in part-time studies and MA programmes;
- a notable willingness to enter into partnership with institutions offering vocational training, for example, through the academic validation of diplomas, degrees and Masters programmes in theology for ministry;
- the Research Assessment Exercise (RAE), resulting in departments being graded according to the strength and depth of the research undertaken;
- Teaching Quality Assessment (TQA), through which departments have been given a score for their teaching quality;

- the government's general commitment to university education serving society and the economy directly;

- the need to serve an increasingly multi-faith society.

As a result of these changes, in general it is the case that some subjects which are important to the ministerial curriculum (such as patristics and liturgy) are much weaker than they were, with the Church needing to make its own provision. At the same time, as a result of the RAE and the TQA, theology and religious studies have become an extremely fit and highly esteemed subject grouping within humanities, with proven international scholarship, which attracts students from within various faith traditions and without.

Church colleges of higher education

1.24 There are presently 15 Church colleges and universities in England and Wales; of these, three are Roman Catholic, two are ecumenical and the majority are Anglican. They represent approximately 82,000 students with 3,000 studying a range of theology programmes. Present and future contribution to ministerial formation draws on the following. Church colleges have a theology and RE curriculum – from certificate, through undergraduate to Masters programme – whose strengths have been attested in a recent quality scrutiny. Scholarship and research underpin that curriculum. There are flexible routes through learning and teaching based on praxis. Theological reflection, through a work-based or Church-linked experience, is central to this approach. There are established and developing ecumenical and regional partnerships with schools; with dioceses and with other Church organizations. Presently, colleges contribute both to ordained and lay training through the regional courses and through readership schemes. Active involvement and experience for ministerial trainees with a wider higher education curriculum will be a particular strength in preparing future community leaders within the Church. Working with adult learners within a widening participation and lifelong learning framework is a particular characteristic, evidenced in terms of success against public benchmarks. Finally, Chapel is at the heart of campus life; and Christian values are integral to the mission of Church colleges and universities.

Theological educators for the future

1.25 Since 1990 the Church of England has had a policy of actively seeking to encourage the identification and training of potential theological educators, i.e. those who might, as part of their ordained ministry, teach in ministerial education or in comparable positions in the Church. This work continues to be focused in two main areas:

- a provision for additional funding for well-qualified candidates who are over 30 (for example, those with good first degrees in subjects other than theology) to train at a college for three years, rather than two, so that they can complete a degree in theology as part of their training;

- a provision for additional funding for suitably qualified candidates (for example, those with good degrees in theology) to take research degrees at Masters or doctoral level while training for ordination.

This work has continued and is beginning to attract additional and complementary funding from sources outside of central Church funds.

Diocesan training provision

1.26 The last few paragraphs have concentrated on the initial ministerial education of the clergy, the main focus of our work. However, it is vital to put this description of IME in the context of the provision for clergy CME and, secondly and equally importantly, of the wide range of training provision in the dioceses – for Reader ministry and other lay ministries and formal education for adult lay discipleship, a term defined below. Within the Church of England these are a diocesan, not a national, responsibility, though Reader training is nationally moderated. Thus each diocese has its own provision for clergy CME, initial Reader training and CME, training for lay ministries and the adult lay education work. This work includes:

i) programmes for clergy in the first four years of ministry;

ii) a wide range of consultative work with clergy and the provision of programmes on ministerial, developmental and theological issues, now often shared with Readers;

iii) courses to equip clergy for new roles, for example, first incumbency;

iv) initial training programmes for Readers, followed by opportunities for CME, now often shared with clergy;

v) a wide range of programmes and events at different levels to stimulate and equip Christians in their lay discipleship. Dioceses often collaborate with parishes and deaneries to develop a whole range of discipleship and leadership programmes. These often form the basis for the discernment of callings and act as a springboard for further study and leadership. In some dioceses these feed into more formal courses of theological and ministerial development. However, for our purposes it is vital to distinguish between the various levels of provision. Much Christian lay education is rightly the responsibility of parishes, with some resourcing from dioceses. In this report we do not address this area. We are concerned with the diocesan level of provision for lay education at a level that is, or could be, accredited, in higher education terms, at Level 1[4] or access levels. We refer to this as 'formal provision for lay theological education'.

Equipping Christians for lay discipleship is a very important part of the Church of England's training provision and any proposals for the training of the clergy will have to take it fully into account.

Partnership with UK higher education

1.27 Much of the Church's provision for ministerial education is now in a substantial and creative partnership with UK universities or church colleges of higher education. All the theological colleges and courses are related to one or more higher education (HE) institutions. In addition some OLM schemes and some diocesan Reader training and CME programmes have also gained university accreditation. The types of relationship between institutions of higher education and the training institutions include the following.

i) The most common arrangement is that an HE institution provides academic accreditation and validation for a programme designed and taught by a Church training institution. The programme could be for ordinands, Readers, for CME or formal lay theological education. A large number of ordination candidates take a qualification in 'theology for ministry' (DipTh, BTh, MTh) as an academic and ministerial component of their training. These awards are sometimes referred to as vocational awards.

ii) Some ordinands take academic theology degrees (BA), designed and taught by a university, as a component of their training. The specifically ministerial side of their training takes place in a college or course, which also oversees their training as a whole.

iii) As noted, the Church's training institutions relate both to a range of HE institutions, typically university departments (of theology, adult education or continuing learning) or the church colleges of HE and in a variety of ways. Some training institutions are within university structures or are affiliated institutions but the most common situation is one of a validation arrangement.

Growth through historic development and accretion

1.28 In summary, the current provision for training has grown up through historic processes of growth, decline and renewal. It reflects the history of the Church of England and its partner churches in the last century and a half. This has included the growth of diocesan colleges and of colleges representing particular traditions of churchmanship, the emergence of courses since 1960, an emphasis on adult education in the 1970s and 1980s, ecumenical initiatives in training and the local ministry movement, including OLM schemes, in recent decades. In many ways this organic and piecemeal development has served the Church well.

The achievements of our training establishment

1.29 We wish to set on record the strengths and achievements of staff and of the training institutions, both within IME and CME and in other forms of training and education. These would include:

i) the provision of good quality training for clergy and lay ministers in a rapidly changing educational and ministerial context;

ii) a genuine concern for the personal and spiritual, as well as theological, development of candidates;

iii) a developing expertise in dealing with the range of candidates coming forward today – in terms of age and of educational, church and ministerial background;

iv) the development by each institution training ordinands of a full theological and educational rationale through the ACCM 22 system, now revised in the Churches' Validation Framework. Institutions now not only know *what* they are doing, they also know *why* they are doing it;

v) university accreditation for all main programmes of ministerial education offered by all the theological colleges and courses, and now by some OLM schemes, Reader training schemes and programmes for CME 1–4. Gaining academic awards has encouraged learning among candidates and lays foundations for further learning. While being a significant call on staff time it has raised standards in the delivery of training and contributed to a sense of professionalism;

vi) the gradual growth of regional partnership between institutions and other providers of theological education, for example university departments and Church colleges of higher education. This has enabled a wider range of appropriate programmes to be offered to candidates;

vii) the growth of ecumenical partnership in some colleges and many courses, fostering ecumenical understanding;

viii) the significant development of local ministry schemes including 19 OLM schemes, contributing to new perspectives on ministry;

ix) the range of achievements on a tight budget, providing good value for the Church's investment in this field;

x) the development within dioceses of externally moderated Reader training schemes and of far higher expectations of continuing learning and ministerial development for all the Church's ministers, lay and ordained;

xi) the development by the Church of England of some of the components of a framework for IME and CME for its clergy in the publications *Beginning Public Ministry* (1998), *Mission and Ministry* (1999) and *Mind the Gap* (2001).

Our analysis and proposals have, therefore, been developed against the background of real and substantial achievement by those currently responsible for initial and continuing ministerial education.

1.30 We have noted above that our current training establishment has grown up through organic and piecemeal development. This has led to criticism of duplication of effort and a lack of co-ordination between the various parts of the system. We proceed now to the issues facing ministerial education in the current context.

Chapter 2

The issues that have driven our work

2.1   Our working party has developed its thinking in two main ways. Firstly, it has worked through wide-ranging conversations on ministry and training issues within its own large membership. We were set up with 16 members, two consultants and two secretaries. Whether we have been working in plenary or in groups, we have benefited from a wide range of views and of expertise, ministerial, educational and financial. We have especially valued having a Methodist representative from the outset and a URC representative from the interim report onwards on the group itself. (We regret that it was not possible for the Roman Catholic Church to be represented.) Additionally, we have consulted a wide range of churches in writing, thus building in a proper ecumenical perspective to our work. Secondly, we have learnt much from the three major consultation exercises we have conducted (see Appendix 2 for a list of those who contributed). We have sought to sift the many views put to the group from both within and without and offer the following analysis of the main issues.

A theological approach to Church and ministry

2.2   While it is beyond the task set us to produce a full theology of Church and ministry, it is clear that our work needs to develop a theological approach that can elicit widespread assent in a Church that contains a diversity of approaches. In this task we draw on our own reflections but within the parameters of our historic formularies, the ecumenical agreements which our Church has entered into and the recent statements of the House of Bishops, for example on presidency at the eucharist.[5] Thus, in Chapter 3 we have sought to make a brief statement of the theological principles that underlie the Church's ministry.

Formation for ministry

2.3   In its interim report, our working party tried to put forward an integrated view of preparation for ordained ministry, encompassing its formational, educational and training strands. However, it became clear through consultation on the interim report that we have been perceived as being more interested in academic attainment than in the formation of the person for ministry. One example of this type of criticism reads as follows:

'The report majors on educational criteria, whereas actually ministry is much more about skills and gifts. Chapter five of the report tries to lay out a new framework for ministerial education, but in the end capitulates to an understanding of priesthood that is more about educational attainment than about issues of holiness, prayer, calling, gifts in ministry, and apostolic charge.'

In this draft final report we have taken this point very seriously and have addressed the issue of formation directly (see 4.2–10 below) and in the report as a whole. By this means we have sought to present an integrated and balanced view of preparation for ordained ministry.

Expectations of IME and CME

2.4   All those who have worked in IME will know that there is great pressure on the curriculum. More than two decades ago Church History, Ethics and Liturgy were added to traditional courses in Bible and Doctrine. Pastoralia has become Pastoral Studies and now in some cases Practical Theology. In a similar way Spirituality has become not only the context for and accompaniment to the formal curriculum but an academic subject in its own right. In more recent times Mission, Communication and a whole range of important ministerial issues have made credible bids to be dealt with in training offered before ordination. These issues include child protection, ministry in urban or rural contexts and multi-cultural, inter-faith and minority ethnic matters. At times it feels that every review that is brought to Synod must make a bid to add something to the already crowded curriculum, which for many older candidates is being delivered in a shortened training. The most recent examples would include the report on Healing[6] and the Dearing review on Church Schools.[7]

2.5   Our initial training institutions have responded in a variety of ways. One tendency has been to pack more into the curriculum, producing the busyness often commented on by bishops' inspectors and, more worryingly, a temptation to reduce the depth of engagement with Scripture and the study of theology. Secondly, many creative attempts have been made to integrate the new topics into the curriculum. Thus, for example, inter-faith issues can be dealt with as a topic on its own or integrated into, for example, biblical studies and pastoral studies in different ways. ACCM 22 addressed the issue of pressure on the curriculum directly (paragraphs 16, 41–58), but the demand from the wider Church continues. However, there is a limit to how much can be credibly and successfully introduced within initial training. Our mentality appears to be to continue to 'frontload' training, seeking to achieve everything of importance before ordination.

2.6   Within the first four years of CME (CME 1–4), there has been real progress in terms of the publication of a nationally approved set of expectations, as set out in *Beginning Public Ministry*. Equally, many dioceses have invested more resources in developing this work, developing support and training that is appropriate to the needs of curates and to the contexts in which they minister. However, as CME 1–4 is a diocesan responsibility there is a wide variety of practice in the dioceses. Equally, the variety of approach to initial training means that CME has to be responsive to the range of knowledge and experience of candidates. Training incumbents have a key role in this part of the total training offered to the newly ordained but until recently they have worked in a vacuum in terms of national policy. Candidates themselves are being sent mixed messages about expectations of training and continuing learning. Most initial training will espouse the value of lifelong learning but ordination is such a major transition within the life of the Church that it is easy to think that training is now basically in the past. Further there is little visible connection between the training offered before and after ordination. We believe that there is too much pressure on IME to deliver everything in a frontloaded way combined with a lack of connection with, and coordination of, CME. Thus, as currently configured, there is a fault line between the pre-ordination training of the clergy and CME. This raises the question whether the Church could develop a framework within which ministerial education is clearly seen to begin in a substantial way in pre-ordination training and continues in a structured and related way after ordination.

The relationship of initial training for ordination to adult learning in the Church

2.7 In our review of the training provision of the Church of England we have been struck by a second fault line between pre-ordination training and other forms of adult learning in the Church – training for Reader and other lay ministries, and formal lay theological education. Initial training for ordination is nationally supervised, delivered and resourced through national or regional institutions. Thus, colleges take candidates from the Church as a whole, while courses receive candidates from a number of dioceses. Both are inspected and supervised by the Church through bishops' inspections, validation of their educational programmes and annual moderation, in addition to university quality control procedures where these apply. By contrast, Reader and other lay training and education for lay discipleship, along with clergy CME, are basically a diocesan responsibility. While Readers have a nationally supervised system of moderation, carried out in regional groupings, there is no national or regional system for the delivery of this learning, nor is there national inspection/validation of it, nor any national agreement about resourcing. (Initial training for OLM, though being based in dioceses, is nationally inspected and supervised as a form of training for ordination, but the training is locally delivered and resourced.) As with our comments on the relationship of the training of clergy before and after ordination, this provision is complicated and lacks coherence. It understandably leads to great local variation and quality of practice. Again there would appear to be a case for far greater coordination and sharing of resources across this second fault line, while recognizing that there are pitfalls to be avoided in moving to a greater sharing of programmes of learning.

2.8 While the Church of England has a national system to ensure a country-wide delivery of ordination training, by contrast its provision for the formal theological education of the laity is uneven. There are examples of good practice where formal programmes are laid on for a range of lay ministries, for deepening the theological understanding of the laity and for those considering offering themselves for ordination.

i) Many dioceses have made provision in terms of Bishop's certificate programmes. These have been of real value. At the same time the quality of the education has been varied and few have sought accreditation in further education or higher education terms, with the result that students have not gained credits enabling them to go on to further accredited studies.

ii) Some dioceses have worked with a local institution of higher education to gain accreditation for diocesan programmes. For example, Oxford diocese has worked with Oxford Brookes University to validate a programme of learning at certificate, diploma, degree and Master's level. This programme is designed for adult lay Christian learners, Readers and OLMs in training and for curates and other clergy, providing a route for accrediting prior learning and different learning tracks for different groupings of learners.

iii) A different type of example is a university programme such as the open access University of Exeter Certificate in Theology, which has been used by adult lay learners, potential ordinands and as a part of the programme offered by the South West Ministry Training Course. On this programme students can complete Level 1 in two years of part-time study. It can either be taken out of interest by attending the evening classes or students can do the accompanying written work and get the certificate, which in turn equips them to go on to diploma and degree level if that is appropriate.

It is worth reflecting on these examples, to which others could be added, because they show what can be achieved by creative partnerships between institutions of higher education, dioceses and ministerial training institutions. In terms of our task, they offer models in which basic theological study can be offered to ordinands, potential ordinands and a wide range of interested lay people. Their success raises the question whether our training establishments, in partnership with universities and Church colleges of higher education, can offer such opportunity for theological and ministerial education to a uniform level on a country-wide basis.

Expectations of candidates before they attend a selection conference

2.9   There is currently no nationally agreed statement of expectations for a level of attainment in theological education and ministerial exploration before a candidate goes to a selection conference. DDOs will of course work with individual candidates to prepare them to go to a conference, as they see fit. However, it may seem surprising that those who put themselves forward or are called to test their vocation are not formally asked to undertake some theological study or exploration of ministerial issues before they proceed to selection and training. As a result, training institutions have to deal with a wide range of prior knowledge and understanding, and candidates can make a slow start to their sponsored studies. They themselves may not know the range of possible ministries or forms of lay discipleship or whether they are suited to theological study. In the light of these considerations, we believe it is right to reconsider the Church's policy on this question. In addition, it is worth noting that any country-wide provision for basic lay theological education, as canvassed in the preceding paragraph, could also serve as a basic course of studies for potential ordinands.

The size of our training establishments

2.10   The Church of England currently has 1360 candidates in training for ordained ministry (paragraph 1.16 above) and 1192 in training for Reader ministry.[8] In addition there are many Church members in training for other forms of service and lay ministry. However, these candidates for nationally authorized ministries are spread between more than 80 training establishments or institutions.

i)   Thus, there are twelve theological colleges, twelve regional courses, 19 diocesan OLM schemes and 44 diocesan training establishments, which in turn provide Reader training, CME and formal lay theological education. However these figures are read or interpreted, the Church has a large number of, mainly, very small institutions or training units.

ii) In staffing terms, the English theological colleges average a teaching staff of 7.75 full-time equivalents, while the regional courses have an average of only 3.63. The numbers for OLM schemes would be much lower, probably an average around 1.5.[9] Particularly for courses and OLM schemes these are tiny staffs, when the required range of theological expertise and ministerial experience is considered, even if one takes into account the welcome contribution of clergy and of lay tutors on an occasional basis.

iii) While staffing levels expressed as average figures are one important indicator, the diversity within ministerial education means that averages can also hide the true situation, which in some instances is much stronger.[10] Two main points need to be made. Firstly, in some settings, colleges in particular[11] are able to benefit directly and substantially from arrangements to share teaching expertise in a federation or partnership. While a full review is not possible here, in terms of the substantial sharing of teaching, the Cambridge Federation is the strongest example in which two medium-sized theological colleges benefit from a far wider range of teaching resources and from a broad ecumenical partnership. Some shared teaching is also a feature of the Oxford Partnership for Theological Education and Training (OPTET), Trinity College, Bristol with the Bristol Baptist College, Cranmer Hall with the Wesley Study Centre and Mirfield with the Department of Theology and Religious Studies in Leeds. In addition to reconstituting itself as a single foundation to include the former college, course and research centre, Queen's College and the West Midlands Ministerial Training Course have recently gone over to a unitary staffing policy. Secondly, all training institutions make use of stipendiary clergy and other external theological educators to augment their teaching strength. This is particularly the case on regional courses and OLM schemes. In general, the value of substantial sharing of teaching and of teaching expertise within a partnership is an example of contemporary good practice that should be a building block for the future.

iv) The size of our institutions also raises issues about staff-student ratios. By conventional higher education standards the provision in ministerial education looks generous with a 1:10 ratio being the historic standard for theological colleges. However, it is crucial to note that this ratio is required by the nature of preparation for ordination. Thus, in addition to all the normal duties of teachers in higher education (preparation of and delivery of teaching, setting and marking of assignments, keeping up to date with teaching, research, working with the quality and accountability procedures), teachers in ministerial education are deeply involved in the ministerial formation of candidates. These duties include being a participant and role model in a Christian community of worship and learning, and the supervision and assessment of candidates' spiritual and ministerial development. These are extremely time-consuming but essential duties, working with candidates as individuals and in groups.

v) To return to the overall picture, the 23 English colleges and courses train a total of 1138 candidates, an average of 49 candidates per institution. Whether one compares this with higher education institutions or with schools, this is a low figure, with a range of consequences for staff and candidates alike. And of course, as an average figure it hides a range of student numbers from twelve to 88. The median is 56. The numbers are even lower for OLM schemes (average 13)[12] and Reader training (average 30), even if, as with colleges and courses, the low numbers are ameliorated by arrangements in some dioceses whereby OLM and Reader students have part of their training in common with other ministerial candidates.

2.11 Looked at in the round, the question has to be raised as to whether our current arrangements can provide the range of training needed at a good standard, for the candidates of today and tomorrow. Of course small institutions have some real strengths that we wish to preserve and build on:

i) they allow staff and students to know each other well as individuals;

ii) they enable a strong sense of community to be formed through worship, learning and residential elements;

iii) the principal can know every candidate, even if immediate supervision and pastoral care is delegated to staff members. This is valuable in dealing with reporting on candidates to bishops and in helping candidates find a first post.

These points make it clear that there will always be a need for personal encounter with, and pastoral care for, ordinands and, further, for training institutions which allow for a human scale of relating. A human scale is a strong feature of our current establishment that needs to be maintained and built into any future pattern of training.

2.12　However, we believe that small, unrelated institutions have serious weaknesses. It is important to say that the issues raised in the following list arise out of the structure and overall organization of our current provision, not the quality of individual institutions. However, looked at as a system as a whole, the smallness of most of our establishments and the lack of coordination between them raises serious organizational and educational issues. While these points will not apply to every current setting, they are issues that need to be addressed in many settings.

i) The size of many institutions reduces the range and variety of types of learner or student and therefore the potential quality of the student's training. The potential for learning through meeting and relating to other learners, with a range of backgrounds and experience, is reduced.

ii) The size of many staffs means there can necessarily only be a limited range of expertise and experience affecting a number of important areas (theological learning, ministerial experience, educational styles and expertise and managerial competence). A key example is that small training institutions cannot have expertise in the relevant range of types of learning – ministerial, formational and theological. This leads to staff teaching well beyond the range of their expertise and to too great a dependence on buying in part-time help with a range of consequent problems.

iii) Small institutions can develop in eccentric ways and change rapidly due to staff changes.

iv) It is difficult or impossible for small institutions to mount the range of programmes required by today's candidates to a consistently high standard, taking account of their prior academic and ministerial experience. Put in academic terms, the range required is from certificate level (i.e. first year undergraduate study) to Masters level and beyond. Similarly, small groups of students for any one of the range of programmes which are on offer can lead to educational problems.

v) The size of institutions means that the contribution of staff members to the life of the Church in terms of research, writing and publication and more general teaching is very limited.

vi) Similarly, there are few opportunities for those with the appropriate gifts to develop a longer-term career or ministry in ministerial education, which leads to short-term appointments, lack of staff development and rapid changeover of staff in many institutions.

vii) The smallness of institutions means that the burden of Church and university supervisory and quality control procedures is disproportionate to the size of the institutions. While the need for close supervision of very small institutions may be urgent, the resources to make creative use of external reviews is limited or not available.

While there is more to be said on the issue of partnerships (see 2.16 below), from this review we believe that that there is an urgent need for the Church of England to make much better use of its scattered training resources.

The place of research

2.13 Since 1990 the Church of England has had a policy of identifying 'potential theological educators' and funding them so that, with other sources of funding, they can equip themselves to teach in our training establishments. Equally, there is an expectation that staff in these institutions should undertake research or at least further study to equip themselves for their own teaching and, hopefully, to contribute to the wider life of the Church. However, in reality the pressure of day-to-day work and the small size of institutions means that study and research can often get squeezed out. If candidates are to be trained by those who are up-to-date in their fields of study and if staff are expected to contribute to the wider life of the Church through their broader teaching and publications, then the place of research needs a much firmer footing in our establishments.

2.14 However, it is important to state that our concern does not arise only out of a need to staff our institutions adequately, however important that is. Our terms of reference specifically asked us to look at the issue of research (see Appendix 1). By research we do not mean a narrow academic specialism but *enabling the Church to think deeply and clearly about specific issues, whether these are theological or whether they initially arise out of its mission to the world.* In defining research in this way, we also note the following:

i) the focus in some university faculties of theology has moved from Christian theology and practice as such, while the research agenda in universities will inevitably be driven by a wider range of concerns. In today's multi-cultural and multi-faith society, some faculties do not have the confessional basis they once had. Therefore the Church can no longer depend on the university faculties to provide the full range of Christian learning which it requires, however much it continues to value the contribution some faculties make.

ii) the Church has specific interests in Christian theology and practice related to its life and mission. Clearly the Church will have to sponsor such pieces of research.

iii) Finally, there have been isolated examples of good practice on which we should build. For example, a member of staff of a theological college was commissioned to carry out an important piece of theological writing which formed the basis of the House of Bishops' report on presidency at the eucharist.[13] However, this was a one-off commission that in itself points to a wider need. Other examples would include the contributions of staff members of training institutions on bodies such as the Faith and Order Advisory Group, the Liturgical Commission or representing the Church of England on bilateral ecumenical conversations.

Thus, a further issue for our agenda is an institutional basis for research that enables the Church to think deeply about its mission in and to the world.

Ecumenical partnership in IME

2.15 In the response to the interim report, many have commented that while the report acknowledged the place of ecumenical partnership in IME, it was deficient in recommending further ecumenical development. While there have been a few contrary voices in the consultation, the great majority have urged the importance of formation for ministry in an ecumenical context. As a working party we have strengthened our membership in this regard, have held a further meeting to discuss progress with our closest partners, the Methodist Church and the URC, and have been in touch with the Roman Catholic Church in England and Wales, which we learnt was also reviewing its provision in this area. In addition, in our further thinking we are keen to promote further ecumenical partnership at local, regional and national levels.

We take up this theme in Chapter 6.

Partnership with other providers of ministerial and theological education

2.16   Throughout the 1990s, the Church of England, with its ecumenical partners in the initial training area, have encouraged the creation and development of partnership between the providers of ministerial and theological education (see 1.20 above). As was noted, progress in this area has been real and hard won. Of the many problems to be overcome, one has been that the constituent units of a partnership or federation have brought with them ties with different universities or validating bodies. Secondly, where progress has been substantial, further development has been impeded by the fact that institutions are, by foundation, separate units with a particular purpose. As a result partnership with others can be seen as a secondary activity. Finally, some partnerships have not flourished or, having been started, have in fact been dismantled. Where this happens, despite the national policy of encouragement towards partnerships, the power of decision lies with the individual institutions. In summary, the policy of encouraging partnership has been successful but uneven in its impact. While we applaud those who have made real strides in this area, we note that the Church needs a more effective policy if it is to unlock the potential of partnerships in a uniformly effective way.

Partnership with UK higher education

2.17   We have also noted above that the Church's training institutions have entered a great number of individual partnership arrangements with UK universities and the Church colleges of higher education (1.24). There may be further issues here in terms of evaluating which sector or sectors of HE are the most useful partners for the Church. What weight should be put on research or teaching excellence, expertise in vocational training or on the Church affiliation of partner institutions? The current situation is a combination of long-term relationships and of more recent arrangements, mainly in the area of academic validation. This is a complex area but one issue that should be pursued is the potential for reducing the number of individual arrangements that currently have been (and, under the current system, have to be) negotiated between small training institutions and a range of institutions of higher education. In general terms two points can be made:

i) over the past decade the traditional universities have become more open to partnership with institutions of ministerial education than in the past. This has shown itself in a variety of ways, not least the willingness to validate ministerial and vocational programmes. There may well be potential here for more substantive, mutually beneficial, partnership or organic involvement;

ii) similarly in the last decade, the Church of England's Church colleges of higher education have continued to develop expertise in vocational training, to establish diocesan training links and to strengthen departments of theology, often signalled by professorial appointments. We also note that the Dearing review of Church Schools, endorsed by General Synod, encouraged a stronger role for the Church colleges in ministerial education.[14]

The issues that have driven our work

Thus, we wish to investigate if the Church can enter into further, mutually beneficial, partnership with the HE sector.

Issues arising from the framework for learning and the regulations for training

2.18   The Church of England's current framework for training is set out in the bishops' regulations for training, a set of rules which enables dioceses, trainers and candidates to know how much training, in terms of years of training, each category of candidate is required to undergo and how much training the Church will pay for. These regulations are, in the main, based on only three factors:

i) *the category of sponsorship*, with three categories of sponsorship: stipendiary/non-stipendiary; permanent non-stipendiary; ordained local ministry. If the candidate is sponsored for the first, 'flexible' category, the replacement of the former 'stipendiary' category, then there is a choice of college or, if the candidate is over 30, course. If the candidate is sponsored for permanent non-stipendiary ministry, training will normally be for three years on a regional course; if for OLM, then for three years on the diocesan OLM scheme. If the candidate is sponsored for the first, flexible category, then two further issues arise:

ii) *the candidate's age*, where the most common issue is whether a stipendiary/non-stipendiary candidate is over or under 30. If the candidate is under 30, then three years of college training are required and paid for; if over 30, then two years of college training or three years of training on a regional course is the rule;

iii) *whether or not the candidate is a theology graduate*. If the candidate is a theology *graduate*, then college training is reduced to two years.

Our earlier remarks about provision for training having grown up piecemeal over the years are pertinent here. These regulations have developed from a period when the most common issues were to do with whether stipendiary candidates were deemed to be young (under 30) or not, and whether they had substantial prior learning or not in theology. To this have been added considerations about candidates for non-stipendiary and latterly for OLM. Finally the simplicity of the scheme has been undermined by the introduction of the new flexible category, stipendiary/non-stipendiary.

2.19   These regulations are particularly vulnerable at four points:

i) the 30-year-old rule contains a somewhat arbitrary element: what about the gifted 31-year-old who would benefit from three years of college training?

ii) a cut-off at 30 is no longer a realistic marker between 'young' and 'old' candidates because of the overall rise in the age of candidates, rising life expectancy and changing attitudes to the potential of older people.

iii) the choice for candidates sponsored for stipendiary/non-stipendiary ministry over the age of 30 leads to a considerable grey area. On what criteria and by whom should the decision be made whether a candidate should train for two years in a college or three years on a course? Should most weight be given to the candidate's views, the needs of the family where this is an issue, the cost or to educational or formational issues? Should the diocese or the candidate decide?

iv) because of rapid changes in the curriculum of theology and religious studies degrees in recent decades in UK universities, it is not always appropriate for theology graduates' training to be automatically reduced to two years. Thus, for example, candidates may have a large religious studies or world religions component in their degrees and consequently not have undertaken sufficient basic studies in the Bible or Christian doctrine for the purposes of preparation for ordination.

2.20   Colleges and courses frequently comment that there are very few 'standard' candidates any more. The range of educational backgrounds, prior learning, candidates' experience of the Church of England or even knowledge of the basics of Christian faith is far greater than it used to be. In this situation the current regulations appear to be ill-suited to be the determining factor in coming to decisions about the length and mode of training. In the light of the last three paragraphs taken together, the current regulations appear to be a somewhat outdated framework. This view was strongly supported in the consultation exercise on our interim report. It raises the question whether a new framework, drawing on contemporary approaches to desired learning outcomes, may be able to address these issues in a more creative way.

A norm for the qualification for the clergy

2.21   One further feature of bishops' regulations for training deserves comment at this point. The ordained are primarily disciples of Jesus Christ and ministers of the Church. At the same time, however, there is a demand from congregations and from parishioners for ministry exercised to a professional standard. Most professions stipulate a minimum level of achievement, in academic or professional terms, as a condition of entry into the profession. Further, with rising standards in the professions and increased accreditation of vocational training, many groups in our society are becoming graduate professions. Obvious examples would be nurses and teachers. From these perspectives it appears anomalous that the clergy are not required to reach a common minimum standard in terms of their learning or to be graduates in the subject in which they will be practitioners. This issue is made more acute by the point that an increasing proportion of candidates for ordination train either for two years at college or for three years on a course, with the result that about 50 per cent of the newly ordained will not have achieved degree level studies in theology for ministry by the time of ordination. Of course the Church has an honourable tradition of emphasizing the special calling and the pastoral nature of the ministry. However, while there might rightly be room for exceptions, the question deserves proper consideration whether the norm should be that those sponsored for stipendiary and non-stipendiary ministry should be required to achieve graduate status in theology for ministry, either by the time of ordination or in the earliest years of ministry.

Financial issues

2.22   Much work was done on financial issues in the working party that led up to the publication and implementation of the financial framework contained in *Managing Planned Growth* and its supplementary report. We wish to consider the question of the proportion of financial resources that goes on the maintenance of candidates and their families, rather than directly on education and formation. It may be possible to redirect expenditure towards the latter or reduce costs, while still providing appropriate training. This question is raised by the observation that under our present arrangements, the Church of England spends about 45 per cent of its total expenditure on pre-ordination training on personal and family maintenance.[15] Secondly, at an institutional level we note that some of our institutions are already benefiting to some extent from public funding by being associated with universities and Church colleges. However, as part of our work, we wish to consider whether public funding might more generally be available to support the Church's training enterprise and if it would be right to seek such funding. We do this partly because of the many links we already have with higher education and because, aware of the increasing financial demands on the parishes arising from taking responsibility for clergy stipends and pensions, it would be irresponsible not to look into the possibilities for public funding for ministerial education.

The agenda for our work

2.23   Our analysis shows both that the Church can rightly be proud of its achievements in the area of training and that it is faced with a series of structural issues which need to be resolved if better training provision is to be established. The main issues we have identified are as follows. We have attempted to make a contribution in the following areas:

i)   outlining theological principles that underlie the Church of England's ministry;

ii) rethinking the initial ministerial education of the clergy so that it begins in a substantial way before ordination and continues in a structured and related way in the early years of ministry, as a contribution to stimulating lifelong learning;

iii) considering how to set ministerial education for the clergy within the context of a coordinated provision for adult learning and training in the Church – IME and CME for clergy and Readers, training for other lay ministries and formal theological education for lay discipleship;

iv) promoting a country-wide initiative for formal theological education for lay people and for a range of lay ministries, while enabling potential candidates for ordained ministry to embark on basic studies in Christian theology and issues about ministry before they enter training;

v)   addressing the issue of the smallness of many of our training institutions and the lack of coordination between them with a view to making better use of the Church's current resources in training;

vi) creating a structure that has potential to be developed with our ecumenical partners in other churches;

vii) maximizing the benefits of partnership:

   a)   between providers of ministerial education;

   b)   with UK higher education, including universities and the Church colleges of higher education;

viii) making proposals for a well structured, but appropriately flexible, framework for learning, within a continued financial discipline, for candidates for ordained ministry;

ix) establishing norms for the theological and ministerial qualification of the clergy;

x)   proposing a secure place for research for the benefit of the Church alongside the education and training functions of our institutions;

xi) reviewing the Church's financial investment in training, with a view to increasing the proportion which goes into education and training as opposed to personal and family maintenance;

xii) investigating the possibility of public funding for our training institutions.

These issues set a powerful agenda for the development of ministerial and lay theological education, even if this report cannot deal with all points in detail. As we turn to putting forward our proposals, we begin with the theological task.

Chapter 3

Some theological priorities

Introduction

3.1 This report is primarily about the initial ministerial education of the clergy in the wider context of a learning Church. It therefore concerns the knowledge and skills, and the habits of understanding, devotion and practice needed in the ordained clergy. This in turn presupposes some understanding of the meaning of ordination and of the nature and purpose of the ordained ministry of the Church.

3.2 Although it has not been the task of this working party to produce a comprehensive theology of the ordained ministry, we draw attention to the need for greater clarity within the Church of England on a number of these matters if any lasting rational solutions are to be found. The urgency of this task has been revealed on several occasions in recent decades when debates in General Synod on a variety of subjects have been complicated either by disagreements about the nature of ministry or by ignorance about the declared position of the Church of England on this matter. It is clear that a greater common understanding is essential if we are to resolve not only our internal but also our ecumenical dilemmas. In this chapter we are not so ambitious, but attempt to outline some of the theological and other principles that underlie our proposals.

Ordination training and theological education

3.3 As we noted in 1.5, the term 'theological education' is often used as a synonym for 'ordination training'. This usage may have both positive and negative implications. On the one hand, it suggests that theology is central to the preparation of ordinands for their ministry; on the other hand, it runs the risk of implying that theology may not be central to the life of other Christians. Much depends, of course, on what is meant by 'theology'. This word is often used in modern English to mean 'knowledge about God' (or even 'knowledge about what people think about God'), whereas in the greater tradition of Christian thought it has meant 'knowledge of God' or has at least included this as a central aspect of theology. In this report, we take it for granted that theology should be understood in this second sense, and that it is inseparable from faithful and believing discipleship. Theology as such is thus vital for every Christian, and that even though clergy might properly be expected to be 'theologians' this is not a 'professionalism' that belongs to them alone.

3.4 This is reflected in one of the most basic principles of our report, namely that the theological heart of ordination training should reinforce a sense that the clergy belong to the Church and are not apart from the rest of its members. The New Testament models of the Church are characteristically relational and imply mutual belonging: for example, spiritual stones in a living temple, the vine and the branches, the body of Christ. It follows from this that although candidates for ordination may reasonably be expected to possess a particular expertise in theology, the foundations of this expertise lie in the common faith of the people of God and should be developed as part of the whole Church's commitment to learning and being equipped for service. We are convinced that collaborative ministry is essential both in principle and practice. While improved catechesis and adult education in parishes are also necessary, the role of the clergy is central. As a result methods of training should be suitable to encourage a disposition towards collaboration and to equip candidates with the skills needed for it.

The Church as a school of theology

3.5   We consider therefore that as many of the Church's resources for ordination training as possible should be set within the context of the whole Church growing in faithful understanding of God. This theological principle lies behind our proposals that we deal with in the following chapters. Practical benefits to be derived from this may include increasing the level of understanding among the generality of Christians, which must surely be for the good of the Church in any case, and not least because it could raise the average standard among those embarking on formal periods of preparation for ordination. It is our hope that the new regional partnerships which we envisage as the basis of the provision for ordination training in the Church of England (see Chapter 6) will all be able to serve their constituent dioceses across a range of educational provision. Some of the institutions already offer some form of this service to the Church, but consistent and excellent provision throughout the country requires coordination of resources in every region.

3.6   Theology, as knowledge of God and of the things of God, is the possession of Christians because they are 'in Christ'; it is therefore essentially known not primarily by individuals but by people incorporated into the Body of Christ. Just as Jesus prepared the Twelve for their ministry by keeping them in close fellowship with him, so too discipleship today is typically learnt in a community environment by people committed to his fellowship and hence to fellowship with each other.

3.7   Our provision for theological communities should take account that these communities may be of more than one kind: colleges, courses and schemes, religious communities, congregations, parishes or cells within parishes, workplaces or institutes of further or higher education could all have the capacity to be this kind of community. The essential principle is that communities of faith, devotion and shared learning are the normal context for theological education and thus for ordination training. (The word 'normal', here and elsewhere in this report, is significant. Paul as well as the Twelve is among the apostolic foundations of the Church. Nevertheless, making allowances for the exception is not a justification for making the exception the norm!)

3.8   A further principle is also important. Just as the Church, although not of the world, is inescapably in the world, the theological community cannot live in isolation. As a community of learning and understanding it must share with the academy; as a community of service it must be deeply engaged with the life and needs of society; and as a community of mission it must know and understand the world in which it has to reveal the world to come.

3.9   This points to the need to achieve a proper balance between detachment and engagement in the process of theological education and indicates the need for a more thoroughgoing integration of the distinctive strengths of different methods of training. Rather too often in recent years in the Church of England this has been seen as a competition between 'college' and 'course'. In practice, of course, every ordained person has learnt in a number of different contexts and a variety of styles of training has been the reality. The fact that this has not been explicit has meant that its benefits have not been fully realized. This is one factor that has led to the difficulty experienced in many quarters in welcoming the principles of accredited prior experience and learning (APEL). Our working party hopes that its proposals will help the Church create a more integrated approach which will discriminate more clearly between what kinds of learning are best acquired in which environment. This principle underlies several of our proposals, particularly those concerning the use of residence and those concerning the reconfiguring of initial ministerial education (i.e. pre-ordination training and CME 1–4; see Chapter 4 below). We see this development as an important element in creating a sense of Church and an ordained ministry that is always entering more deeply into the meaning of faithful discipleship, witness and service.

Theological education and formation

3.10 This concern is echoed in the preference felt by some people and some traditions for using the term 'formation' rather than either 'education' or 'training' for ministry. This has the advantage of implying a process that shapes the whole person, has resonances with ideas of growth and change and fits in well with theology as a spiritual discipline. A further advantage of the use of the term 'formation' is that it encourages the concept of lifelong growth and learning. It is central to the thinking of this working party that the purpose of the early stages of ministerial education should not be to provide the knowledge and skills which will be necessary throughout ministry, but to establish the patterns of learning, piety and competence which will sustain an appetite for continued growth. This seems to us to be required by our belief in the living God who is constantly drawing us deeper into the mystery of Christ. It is also demanded by the exigencies of a rapidly changing world. The ability of the Church to serve the mission of God does not depend on the clergy alone, of course, but their role is crucial and we believe that the work of Christian apologetics as well as of social engagement requires ministers who are versatile and equipped to 'read the signs of the times'.

3.11 It is important not to see formation merely as a process of moulding. Formation for ministry, like Christian formation as a whole, must take its tone from Paul's expression in Galatians 4.19 where he describes himself as being 'in travail until Christ be formed in you'. It is rather a matter of being conformed to the pattern of Christ and his ministry. As such it is a creative process initiated and sustained by God and is inseparable from the call to sacrifice and the cross that are implied in Christ's call to 'Follow me'. While we are rightly concerned with the knowledge, skills and competences needed for the exercise of ministry, these alone can feed a kind of triumphalism which belies the heart of the gospel and discourages collaboration. It is also important not to understand formation as being concerned solely with questions of spirituality and discipleship which is then added as a third element alongside 'education' (= academic study) and training (= learning skills for ministry). Rather 'formation' should be seen as the overarching concept that integrates the person, understanding and competence.

God's mission, the Church and the ministry

3.12 We have already indicated some of the priorities that have driven our thinking and the way in which they have shaped our proposals. Central to this thinking is a theological understanding of the place of the Church and its ministry in God's mission. Although this report has been commissioned to make recommendations concerning the preparation and equipment of those members of the Church who are entrusted with the Word and Sacraments which lie at the heart of the Church's life and task, and the bulk of the report is about that, no talk about the ministry can be authentic unless it is set first in the context of the Church of which the ordained ministry is a part and second in the much more fundamental context of God's purposes for creation. As John Robinson wrote in a famous essay, 'the New Testament bids us have as high a doctrine of the Ministry as we like, providing always our doctrine of the Church is higher. But it does not stop there. For as the Ministry is a function of the Church, so the Church is a function of the Kingdom, of the universal Lordship of God in Christ'.[16] In a much more recent statement, the Kanuga report rightly sets theological education in the context of mission:

> Theological education is fundamental to the renewal of Anglicanism today. It is the means by which wisdom – the learning of Christ by the power of the Holy Spirit – is developed in the Church, and directly serves the practices by which the Church sustains itself in its mission in the world.[17]

3.13 A biblically rooted ecclesiology has to take account of the Church both as 'the fullness of him who fills all in all' (Ephesians 1:23) and as an historical institution, and may ignore neither its eschatological nature and vocation nor the contingent and changing contexts of its earthly existence. Furthermore, the ordained ministry exists within and not apart from the common royal priesthood of the people of God, who themselves derive their primary responsibility from their call to participate in Christ's ministry serving God's purposes in the world – itself a world without meaning except as God's creation, oriented towards the fulfilment of God's reign.

3.14 Initial ministerial education for the clergy, together with all other aspects of the Church's provision for education, should reflect this perspective. Since the publication and adoption of ACCM 22, institutions offering training for ordination in the Church of England have been asked to explain their understanding of their task by answering the question, 'What ordained ministry does the Church of England require?'[18] Some people criticized the form of this question, first because the ministry of the Church is a gift of God and not the choice of the Church or any perception of what it (or any part of it) may 'require', and, second, because it could tend to isolate the ordained ministry from the life of the Church as a whole. Both these criticisms were heeded when the validation questions were revised in 1999: 'What is the training institution's understanding of the mission to which the Church of God is called and of the pattern of Church life and order through which the Church of England responds to that calling?'[19]

3.15 This revised form of the question makes it explicit that the Church is called to mission and that questions of Church life and order (and by implication ordained ministry) are matters of responsiveness to this calling. Whatever freedom the Church possesses in changing circumstances to give particular forms to the way in which Christ's ministry is exercised, this cannot touch ministry ('*diakonia*') as such, as this is a synonym for the overall task of the Church which does not depend on changing fashions or needs, but upon the gift and choice of God. In all this the Church of England claims its ministry to be part of the ministry of the universal Church, and not the officialdom of a 'denomination' or a 'national' church. Hence the basic categories for the Church's understanding of ministry and its equipping are those of Scripture and the ways in which under the Spirit's guidance these have taken particular forms in history.

All ministry is Christ's ministry

3.16 It is a basic theological principle that all ministry, in and through the Church, is Christ's ministry. In the same essay to which we have already referred, J. A. T. Robinson wrote, 'the Christian ministry is no other than the ministry, the liturgy, of Christ himself as He channels through preaching and sacrament, through forgiveness and healing, the continuous creation of the New World wrought on Easter Day' (p.13). Ecclesiology flows out of the biblical understanding of humanity created in God's image, transformed and perfected in

Christ. God equips the faithful with a rich diversity of gifts that they might participate in this work of re-creation.

3.17   Any discussion of ministry must ask the question of the Church whether its ministry is for the sake of the world, and not simply or even primarily an office within a religious community. The Bible testifies to a God who throughout history has called a particular people to be God's own and to be the focus of God's purposes for the whole of creation. When St Paul wrote that because 'one [Christ] has died for all; therefore all have died' (2 Corinthians 5:14), he proclaimed the heart of the Christian gospel, namely that in Christ God has done all that is necessary for the salvation of the world, even though human beings have to respond to it.

3.18   There can therefore be, in principle, no limits to the scope of the gospel or of the missionary obligation of the Church. As Jesus himself said in Matthew, 'Go therefore and make disciples of all nations...' (28:19). The Bible suggests both terrestrial and eschatological dimensions to this task. We are told that the end will not come until the gospel has been proclaimed to every creature, and we look forward to the time when God will gather all the nations to Jerusalem. At the same time, we believe that the resurrection is not merely resuscitation but 'new creation' (2 Corinthians 5:17), and thus we expect 'a new heaven and a new earth' (Revelation 21:1; Isaiah 65:17) whose signs, though not perfection, can be discerned even while we live this mortal life.

3.19   Within the gifted community God calls all into discipleship and all Christians are called to represent Jesus Christ by virtue of their baptism into his death and resurrection. 'I live, yet not I, but Christ lives in me' (Galatians 2:20). Similarly there is a sense in which all Christians participate intimately and intrinsically in the royal priesthood of the Church (1 Peter 2:4-5, 9-10).

3.20   Nevertheless, the Church from New Testament times onwards has recognized a distinctive ministry as among the constitutive elements of the Church. Notwithstanding the God-given character of *diakonia* as such, it is also clear that from the earliest days the forms of this ministry have known some diversity of practice and understanding. Anglicans, however, together with most other Christians, acknowledge the authority of early developments where these are compatible with Scripture and embody their understanding in their practice and in public historic statements of the Christian faith concerning ministry. Among these developments are included the threefold ministry to which the Thirty-nine Articles, the Book of Common Prayer and the Ordinal testify. In more recent times our Church has approved a number of ecumenical agreements that, having been endorsed by the General Synod on the advice of the House of Bishops, are also authoritative statements of the position of the Church of England.

Models of the Church and ministry

3.21   The New Testament offers several models of the Church. We have already (3.4 above) commented on the dynamic and relational character of these models. It is this character which has led some to see *koinonia* ('communion' or 'fellowship') as a unifying concept lying at the heart of them all. For the same reason the model of the Church as the Body of Christ may be taken as typical. It is important in using this model to bear in mind first, that the body can only be spoken of in conjunction with its crucified, risen and exalted head, present through his Spirit; second, that properly understood, this model is a guarantee of a diversity of functions; and third, that it is ultimately an eschatological image, 'the body of him who fills all in all' (Ephesians 1:23).[20]

3.22 The Church is organized, and must adapt its own organization itself, on the model of an organic body, formed by the Holy Spirit, which is understood as Christ himself in his present historical reality. Central to this approach is the principle that all parts of the body relate to each other and to the whole. They can only properly understand themselves in that inter-relationship. Individual members of the body are distinguished both by their different functions and by the symbolic and representational role they play. The body as a whole only functions effectively when all contribute in a vital way to its totality and completeness.

3.23 Bodies have a number of organizing principles that give coherence and structure and sustain the life and energy of the whole. Most fundamental among these, and different in kind from any other, is the mystery of life itself – in traditional terms, the soul – but there are also more definable features of the body which give it structure and order, such as the blood circulation, the nervous system and the skeleton. In the Body of Christ it is Christ himself, through the Holy Spirit, who provides the fundamental vivification, but other agencies, with a limited, created dimension, are also vital if the life of the Body is to flourish. Ministry that tries to claim an independent existence, such as that which promotes clericalism over and against lay discipleship, is always in danger of denying the fundamental character of Christ's ministry.

3.24 There is however a particular and distinctive way in which the ordained ministry is called to give order to the body of the Church of which Christ is the life and the head. This has been recognized from the early centuries of the Church, and is vividly expressed in our rites of ordination which are always celebrated in the eucharist, where, within the people of God as a whole, the distinctiveness of the ministry as such and its three orders are illustrated. The word 'ministry' is a translation of the New Testament term *diakonia*, which has resonances of proclamation, service and authoritative commissioning, links the work of Christ with the vocation of the Church and finds a particular focus in the ordained ministry. The diaconate, as part of the threefold ministry, points to enduring characteristics of the calling of bishops, priests and deacons. It was partly because of a close association with the eucharist as the central and symbolic rite of the Church's existence, seen as the 'showing forth of the death of the Lord until he comes' (1 Corinthians 11:26) – understood as showing forth the sacrificial death of the Lord – that images of priesthood came to be specially linked with the ordained ministry. Although the New Testament complexity of the relationship between bishop and presbyter has left its mark on subsequent developments and is still a matter of controversy today,[21] a dominant strand of early tradition linked the language of priesthood first with the bishop, and then by extension with presbyters as they came to share the bishop's presidency of the eucharist, and thus also his oversight of the Church.

Ministry should be marked by the holiness that Christ gives to the Church

3.25 Within the gifted community God calls some to the distinctive ministries of bishop, priest or deacon. The Church of England acknowledges this three-fold ministry as 'from the Apostles' time'.[22] The ordained have special responsibilities that contain functional, representative and symbolic aspects. Ordination training is concerned both with personal formation and with the knowledge and skills needed for ministry. Thus it is the work of Christ that is exercised in ministry. The biblical motif of the Church as the 'Body of Christ' presupposes that different elements will work harmoniously together, confidently and collaboratively, in order to manifest that ministry to the world. In order to strengthen both the organic life and order of the body ordained ministers are designated by God and their training must take account of the focus of their calling in Christ, the wider ecclesial context of ministry and the distinctiveness of their ordination.

3.26 These theological themes lead us to believe that a key pursuit for ministerial training should be a holiness that seeks to maintain the integrity and effectiveness of the Church. If we seek to participate in and embody a ministry that belongs to Christ himself we can only pursue the highest standards of faithfulness of discipleship, spiritual wisdom, commitment to common life and deep wells of motivation. As we seek to equip the ordained to fulfil their responsibilities within the Body we will guard against incompetencies and complacencies which undermine the creativity and harmony of the whole people of God. Thus, a key theological theme that should inform training is that *the ordained ministry should be marked by the holiness that Christ gives to his Church.*

Ministry seeks to express and fulfil the vocation of the Church

3.27 The ordained ministry stands in intimate relation to the ordered nature of the Church and is one of the instruments for pointing the Christian community to its foundation 'on the apostles and prophets'. In the Church of England this is acknowledged when clergy (and some others) affirm in the Declaration of Assent that 'the Ordering of Bishops, Priests and Deacons' is part of the Church's faithful witness to the faith 'uniquely revealed in the Holy Scriptures and set forth in the catholic creeds'.[23]

3.28 The ordained ministry has a distinctive role in guarding and promoting the vocation of the Church, for instance in guarding and promoting the four marks of the Church as one, holy, catholic and apostolic:

i) a single ministry in three orders serves as a symbol and instrument of *unity*, with the bishop having a special responsibility in this regard;

ii) the *sanctifying* work of the Church is especially seen in the celebration of the eucharist and the absolution of sins, functions of the episcopal and presbyteral ministry. The diaconal call to proclamation and pastoral care, focused in the diaconate, yet present in all ordained ministry, is also for the purposes of sanctification, so that throughout the preaching of the gospel and the care of those in need the holiness of God's people can shine forth;

iii) and iv) the distinctive role given to the ordained ministry in teaching the faith expressed in the creeds serves to promote and secure the *apostolicity* and the *catholicity* of the Church. The 'faith uniquely revealed in the Holy Scriptures and set forth in the catholic creeds' has to be proclaimed 'afresh in each generation'. The unity of the Church in every generation and across the generations is, *inter alia*, a unity in faith. The episcopate, and by extension the other orders of ministry, have a particular responsibility to oversee this ministry of teaching and mission.

3.29 In the New Testament the marks of the Church were secured by the personal ministry of the apostles, sustained by the communities gathered by their preaching, and the charismatic ministries listed in the New Testament epistles. As the apostles, and apostolic assistants, died out, and challenges to the gospel continued, the need for various instruments to safeguard the apostolic witness came to prominence. These echoed those that we now know as the Lambeth Quadrilateral:

i) *The Scriptures*, representing the foundation of Church upon the prophets and apostles.

ii) *The sacraments*, representing the ordered life of the Church, conformed to the death and resurrection of Jesus Christ and empowered by the Holy Spirit, most characteristically expressed in worship.

iii) *The catholic creeds*, representing the teaching ministry of the Church.

iv) *The historic episcopate*, representing the ordered ministry of the Church. (This was augmented later by reference to a common ministry universally recognized as possessing the authority of Christ and the inward call of the Spirit.)

In this overall scheme, it came to be seen as important to be able to point to those authoritative teachers whose message could be demonstrated as one with that of the apostles. Both bishops and churches could be acknowledged on the basis of this inheritance. As heads of apostolic churches, bishops were seen as successors to the apostles. This has been maintained in Orthodox and Catholic theology, including classic Anglicanism, for example in Richard Hooker's writing.[24]

3.30 The ordained ministry as we have known it was thus developing especially rapidly under the same pressures and at the same time as the New Testament was finding canonical recognition. Its shape was drawn partly from the examples of ministry recognized or established by the Apostles (cf. Romans 12, 1 Corinthians 12, Ephesians 4 and the Pastoral Epistles), but more fundamentally from the apostolic ministry itself.

3.31 If we seek to set the context and objectives of training within these perspectives, then we are provided with a set of criteria based on the vocation of the Church. What structures of ministerial training, education and formation will strengthen the foundational purpose of unity, sanctification, apostolicity and catholicity of the Church afresh for this generation and the next? Training needs to maintain a breadth of reference which keeps in focus the vocational scope which we see acknowledged in the New Testament, where many different images of the Church remind us of its ambitious calling, and which has been handed down to us within an apostolic faith. A second theological theme that should inform training is that *ordained ministry should enable the vocation of the Church as a whole, which it receives from Christ, to be fulfilled.*

The mission of God shapes the Church and its ministry

3.32 The Church is a sign, instrument and foretaste of the Kingdom of God.[25] In its very nature it is missiological, expending itself in the redemptive work of God in the world. The purpose of ministry is to participate in the transforming grace of God, not merely running external aspects of the Church conceived primarily as an earthly institution.

3.33 It has become increasingly clear in recent years that some of the inherited structures of the Church, as of society as a whole, no longer serve their original purposes as effectively as they should. It is important therefore to consider afresh what fundamental values those structures were designed to serve. Although neither the New Testament, nor apostolic practice, prescribes every aspect of ministry for all time, the Church of England has consistently maintained the historic episcopate and the three-fold ministry. This has been reaffirmed in a number of recent texts and ecumenical agreements. The Church has the duty in every generation to seek to fit this inherited pattern of ministry to the needs of the changing world.

3.34 One particular priority today must be to reconsider patterns of ministry which were well-suited to serve the pastoral needs of essentially static, largely rural and geographically based communities in which Christian faith could be taken for granted. In the changing social and intellectual climate of today, these patterns will not always be flexible enough for the particular demands of the apostolic, mission-focused, ministry required. Therefore, we believe that in its understanding of ministry and in patterns of training for it, there needs to be close attention to the Church as it is, valuing and building on the patterns of ministry that currently exist, and to the Church as it is called to become as it responds to the mission of God in the world. This requires the ordained to be both stewards of traditions that are entrusted to the Church, and watchers who by discernment and engagement in critical conversation help the Church to re-form its life and ministry in order to be more faithful to the call of God.

3.35 The underlying motive for all training should be to equip the people of God to witness more effectively in this age to the reality of the age to come. The emphasis therefore should be on learning to serve the world for God's sake rather than merely the institutional task of running the Church. We need to develop systems of both initial and lifelong training that encourage confidence and produce flexible responses such that the Church can most effectively participate in the mission of God in the world. A third theological theme that should inform training is that *the ordained ministry should embody and reflect the Church's missionary endeavour in the name of Christ.*

Chapter 4

Lifelong learning: a better trained clergy

A learning Church

4.1   By its very calling the Church is invited ever deeper into the worship of God, service to the world and renewal of itself through worship and learning. If it is to flourish it will have to become more fully a learning Church[26] – a body that promotes a dynamic and reflective discipleship for all its members. This is well expressed in the recent report of the working party on theological education, sponsored by the Anglican Primates, with its focus on people, practices and mission. To quote:

> Since people are the most basic and mobile resource of church life, and the most direct embodiment of God's life in Christ, theological education is committed to bring each person to full stature or wholeness in the mind of Christ by continuously developing in them the dynamic of Christian wisdom.[27]

This learning is a task and gift for the whole people of God and will no doubt take many forms. Much of the learning will be broadly informal in nature, a regular part of the life of parishes and congregations. Other parts will be through diocesan and ecumenical initiatives or through formal programmes offered by educational and training institutions. It is within this broad context of learning that the very specific tasks of training for particular ministries, lay and ordained, should be set.

The education of the whole people of God and the formation of the clergy

4.2   From the late nineteenth century onwards the Church of England regarded the formation of the clergy as a highly distinctive task that required a community of formation, separated from the everyday life of the Church. Theologically, educationally and organizationally, the last decades have seen this pattern under question from several perspectives:

i)   the theme of the education of the whole people of God has raised the question about whether the initial training of the clergy should take place, at least in part, alongside the education offered to lay people;

ii)   the theme of lifelong learning has meant that an earlier emphasis on pre-ordination training, plus practical training in a parish, has been superseded by the importance of continuing learning and development throughout ministry;

iii) theological colleges and courses have been encouraged to work with other providers of theological education and to diversify into other related fields. Examples include offering programmes to independent students and to Christian youth workers;

iv)   within dioceses the recent emphasis has been on integrated training for Readers, OLMs (where dioceses have gone down this road), other lay ministries and formal lay education for Christian discipleship;

v) the themes of shared or collaborative ministry have also raised questions about traditional patterns of training. As the ordained are being trained for a collaborative ministry, their training should be collaborative in style. While the ordained will need parts of their training which enable them to prepare for a distinctive ministry, other parts are better shared with those with whom they will minister in the future so that mutual understanding and trust can be built up.

As a result of all these developments, the older model of formation in a community solely devoted to priestly or presbyteral formation has, in practice, been giving way to a model that emphasizes the education of the whole people of God. Within this latter model ordinands both share in learning with other learners and also have parts of their training devoted solely to them.

Formation for ordained ministry

4.3 The term 'formation' is widely used in ministerial education, but often without explanation. As there is a diversity of views about the nature of priestly or presbyteral ministry in the Church of England, there is a corresponding range of views about formation for that ministry. To what extent should one emphasize a ministry of Word or one of sacrament? Should one stress the functions or the being of the minister? Thus, any view of the nature of formation for ministry will be dependent on prior assumptions about the nature of ministry. In the light of our reflections on ministry in Chapter 3, we regard ministerial formation as development towards the role of particular responsibility for enabling and ordering the Church's life, under God. Thus, it is formation *in the holiness which Christ gives to the Church, in enabling the vocation of the Church as a whole which it receives from Christ and in enabling the missionary endeavour in the name of Christ.*

4.4 The debate then turns to how this formation is to be encouraged and structured. At one level this is an impertinent question as formation is not the product of any human institution but is the outworking of God's grace, the activity of the Spirit. At the same time there is a tradition within which the Church has lived and it is important to revisit former and contemporary views on formation. The Bunsen report of 1968 appears to be the last discussion of this subject in Church of England reports, starting from the statement, in the language of that decade, that 'community formation' is 'the deepening of a man's prayer and commitment and self-knowledge, in a way that is integrated with his growing knowledge of theology'.[28] This is a sophisticated statement, attempting to draw together the deepening life of prayer and the Christian life lived, with deepening self-knowledge and developing theological knowledge and understanding.

4.5 The Bunsen report continues on the subject of how this formation is deemed to take place. Within its view, two strands can be identified:

i) The traditional view is that ministerial formation comes about primarily *through the relation between a holy and wise priest, the principal, and the ordinands*, gathered around him, or today, her. The priest acts as a role model and (flawed) exemplar of the life of prayer, within the regular and disciplined round of the Church's worship, study and the practice of ministry.

ii) A more contemporary view is that 'community formation' comes about *through the formative power of the community of staff and ordinands, gathered for the particular purpose of preparation for ordination.* It is through this intentional community that the deepening in prayer, Christian commitment, self-knowledge and theological knowledge and understanding take place, integrated in the person of the ordinand.

4.6 In today's context, it would be necessary to be much more clear and explicit about the ministerial or 'representative' role for which candidates are being prepared. While personal development may well be a welcome, indeed, necessary part of ministerial formation, it is not the goal in itself. The term 'formation' is at the best a convenient short hand. It alludes to elements of *transformation*, the Spirit of God at work in fallible human beings, *forming* Christ in them. At the same time, candidates put themselves at the service of the Church, and participate in a process of being *conformed* to the public role of:

- prayer, within the Church's life of worship;
- acting as a spokesperson on behalf of and to the Church;
- continued theological and ministerial learning, not least to support a ministry of teaching, preaching and interpretation;
- leadership of the Christian community in its calling and in its service to the wider life of the community.

At this point the Church's demands on ordinands are strongly counter-cultural. Ministerial formation is preparation for the role clergy are given in ordering, enabling and leading the life of the Church in the light of the gospel for the sake of the world.

4.7 The discussion of ministerial formation also has to take into account the developments in ministerial education since the late 1960s. In particular, we might list:

i) the experience of 'residence' in theological colleges has changed significantly for most candidates through a variety of factors – the rising age of candidates, marriage, more flexibility in educational and formational patterns, placements of various sorts, and greater personal freedom for candidates;

ii) regional courses now train half of candidates for stipendiary and non-stipendiary ministry, offering programmes of part-time study in the context of formation for ministry;

iii) OLM schemes have pioneered formation for ministry that emphasizes the importance of ministry being grown collaboratively and in the local context;

iv) the considerable growth in the importance of theological reflection, understood as a semi-technical term, which refers to the dynamic process of reflecting on the contexts of communal and Church life and the candidate's own experience, in the light of the gospel and the faith of the Church;[29]

v) the development of a formal framework for continuing ministerial formation in the early years of ministry itself, in publications such as *Beginning Public Ministry* and *Mind the Gap*, building on older traditions of formation through shared daily prayer and ministry with colleagues.

These developments should move the debate about formation decisively away from an assumption about a mysterious process that 'happens in theological colleges' or even what happens through 'residence'.

4.8 To sum up, in contrast to a former generation, there is no one model of ministerial formation. The following common themes are being developed in a variety of ways:

i) a common dedication to a deepening discipleship of Jesus Christ;

ii) a commitment to and practice of a regular pattern of corporate prayer within the cycle of the Church's life of prayer and worship;

iii) a growth in qualities associated with the office of the ordained: trustworthiness, holiness or closeness to God, the ability to offer guidance in the life of faith;

iv) the value of ordained role models, whether these are parochial clergy, principals, bishops or other senior clergy;

v) the importance of experience of, and learning about, shared or collaborative ministry, across a range of ministries, lay and ordained;

vi) a deepening understanding of self and of others, including understanding how others see us and experience our actions;

vii) theological reflection on the candidate's experience of life, of context and of ministry;

viii) the making of connections at a deep level between a person's evolving understanding of faith, the life of prayer and Christian practice, through a range of stimuli including the faithful reading and study of Scripture, the Christian theological tradition and the experience of Christian life and witness;

ix) learning to act corporately, with and on behalf of the Church, rather than just as an individual Christian;

x) all the above in the light of a deepening understanding of, and growing towards, the role of the intended ordained ministry.

4.9 In the light of this review, we would argue that *ministerial formation is a dynamic and continuing process that draws on a range of contexts, in which the candidate moves between gathered and dispersed settings of the Church's life, and, under supervision, is helped to grow towards the role of the ordained, defined above in terms of service, holiness, vocation and mission.* We comment briefly on the key elements of this understanding of formation:

i) Formation is a dynamic and continuing process. It is dynamic in that it is a creative process initiated and sustained by God, to which the candidate, and later, minister is invited to respond. It is continuing, in that it cannot be confined to the period of formal training, having roots in the candidate's earlier and continuing discipleship and goes on in ministry.

ii) Formation takes places in a range of settings, and not just in the intentional communities of training institutions, however vital the latter are for this purpose. Ministerial formation takes place:

- in Christian life in the world;
- in the parish or church setting;
- in college, course or scheme, both in their gathered and dispersed modes;
- not least, in ordained ministry itself.

There are of course particular moments or phases which focus and give shape to the process:

- the exploration of vocation at parish and diocesan level and through a national selection conference;
- belonging to a community of learning that lives with the call to ministry and all that that entails;
- the event of ordination itself;
- significant experiences or events in ordained ministry.

The Church's provision for IME needs to be able to set a framework for these stages and to respond to the candidates who are in the process of testing their vocations in the midst of complex contemporary lives.

iii) The themes of gathering and dispersal are important because in them the candidate is shaped by the constant movement between the Church gathered for worship, learning and fellowship and the Church in its multi-faceted engagement with the world.

iv) Formation is not a process that happens in isolation or one that is directed according to the agenda of the candidate, even though the candidate has of course to be a full and central part in it. The models of the Church's corporate life that are held up to the candidate, the role model of significant figures in ministry with which he or she comes into contact, and learning to put the life of the Church before self are all important factors. The Church is represented to the candidate by the DDO and bishop, the principal of the training institute, the placement supervisor, the training incumbent and CME officer, all of whom are vital figures who give direction and who supervise the process.

4.10   In the light of these reflections on ministerial formation and of the great diversity of candidates being called to the ordained ministry, the Church needs to provide a *diversity* of pathways towards ordination and beyond, and should be *flexible* in its use of full-time and part-time modes of training. However, in order to handle diversity, it will be necessary to have a Church-wide framework for ministerial education, which we offer in Chapter 5. This movement between communities and settings puts renewed emphasis on the supervision offered by key personnel and the quality of communication between them. In Chapter 5 we make proposals about training arrangements that will bring dioceses and training institutes into partnerships that should facilitate supervision and communication, while in Chapter 8 we return to the use of 'residence' and the question of pathways to ordination.

Lifelong learning

4.11   We have just seen that formation for ordained ministry is a dynamic and continuing process. This is in line with recent reports on ministerial training where the emphasis is on lifelong learning – as is the case with secular and Church statements on adult education and learning. Thus, *Mission and Ministry* (1999), addressing the initial training of the clergy, sees the aim to be to prepare candidates *to begin* ordained public ministry. Part of their learning should precisely be an increasing ability 'to evaluate their strengths and weaknesses, evaluating their own needs for future and continuing development and growth'.[30] Similarly, *Reader Ministry and Training, 2000 and Beyond* states:

> 'The day on which a Reader is admitted and licensed should be looked upon, therefore, not as the end of training but as the first day of a lifelong experience of further development and spiritual growth.'[31]

The same is of course true for the clergy at ordination, whether this is viewed from the perspective of the learning and development which will be needed to sustain them in their ministries or of the particular needs they will have as they move from one task or appointment to another, or to more senior positions. This is in no way to underestimate the significance of the act of ordination or of the change in the relationship between the candidate and the Church that it signals. However, as clergy in holy orders, ministers are called to continue to grow theologically, spiritually and professionally. As a result of this approach, any proposals for the initial training of the clergy must be set within a framework for their lifelong learning and ministerial development.

Rising expectations of the clergy

4.12   A further relevant factor is the continuing rising expectation of ministerial and professional competence in the clergy, an expectation coming both from the Church and from society. This is partly a matter of rising expectations of professionals and of authority figures in general. At the same time an increasingly educated and skilled laity will rightly ask for corresponding competence in the clergy. For stipendiary clergy, this expectation is further fuelled by the realization that they are a scarce and valuable resource who will increasingly have to exercise an episcopal, as well as priestly and diaconal, ministry. All these factors mean that both IME and CME are crucial in resourcing the clergy.

4.13   One of these expectations is that clergy will be equipped to minister in the changing ecclesial and social context within which they will serve, as noted in 3.34 above. These changes in the nature and style of ministry have been well documented elsewhere and we will not repeat that analysis here.[32] As a result both initial and continuing ministerial education must enable the clergy to develop and be equipped to face these new challenges.

A guiding principle for ministerial education

4.14   Our initial consultation exercise has left us in no doubt about the *range* of priorities for the training of the clergy. These include:

- a deep grounding in the Scriptures and Christian theology;

- the ability to reflect theologically and to make connections between the tradition, an understanding of the world and society, and contemporary experience;

- a disciplined life of prayer and worship, and an ability to communicate with others in these areas;

- a collaborative approach to ministry and mission;

- leadership, communication and other practical skills.

These areas are important and it would be easy to produce a much longer list. However, we have also seen that ministerial education needs a guiding principle to inform choices that have to be made. Without this there will be little sense of coherence and the curriculum will continue to grow through accretion. Several correspondents noted the contribution of ACCM 22 to this debate and Professor Daniel Hardy, who chaired that working party, offered this approach to our first consultation:

> Theological education needs a clear conception of its distinctive thrust – its goal ... The *goal*, I think, is an inhabited Wisdom (immersed in Scripture, the continuity of the Church's life in God, and in a Spirit-informed reason) in the Church, one that is active in responding to the issues of present day life.

This makes it clear that the aim of preparation for ordination is not merely the acquisition of knowledge about the Bible, theology and pastoral studies or even the practice of prayer and worship. Rather all these are in the service of this 'inhabited Wisdom', a goal and a standard for all types of training. This helpful definition brings together the theological, formational and practical dimensions of training commented on above. We believe that it is only those deeply immersed in the habit of this wisdom who will have the creativity and imagination to respond to the challenges of the future. Professor Hardy concludes his letter by asserting strongly that:

> 'the Church needs *more intensive, better focused, higher quality* and *more extended* theological education of the sort outlined above – if it is to serve the Church's mission adequately'.

It is to this task that we can now turn.

From pre-ordination training to CME 1–4

4.15   If we bring together the imperative of lifelong learning (4.11) and the need for a deeper and more extended ministerial education, the focus properly falls on the transition from training undertaken up to ordination and the training offered within the first few years of ministry. It is in these years that the priorities of the recently ordained are likely to be set – and therefore whether continued learning and development will be seen to be central to the ministerial life.

4.16   However, before we can make a proposal we should review this transition as it is currently structured. With very few exceptions, candidates are expected to complete their initial training before ordination. Typically they will receive an academic award at this point. Apprenticeship training, with the candidate's training incumbent, and CME 1–4, the old post-ordination training, then follows and complements the pre-ordination phase of training. As a result of this pattern, the pre-ordination period is cast as 'academic', even though it is strongly formational and pastoral in character, and the post-ordination period as 'practical'. In addition, CME 1–4 can easily be seen as of marginal importance, in contrast to the 'real' training. The latter is seen to take place either in the pre-ordination period or in the parish, according to whether the commentator is predisposed to the theological or practical dimension of training. This situation is made worse by the point that we do not have a Church-wide agreement on the place of continuing theological study and ministerial education in the first years of ministry. In some dioceses the emphasis is on a complete immersion in the practice of ministry, in others there is encouragement for continuing study and education in a broader sense.

4.17   In a few dioceses there are certificated forms of study through which the newly ordained can work towards an MA in ministerial studies, drawing together practical learning, reflection on practice and continued theological study. For example in his review[33] of the initiative of the Diocese of Rochester in partnership with the Diocese of Canterbury, Canon Gordon Oliver identifies four main obstacles to the success of such a scheme:

i)   the initial resistance of candidates to the scheme, on the assumption that training is something they have now left behind at ordination, or put more widely, that 'ordination is a rite of passage into a self-directed freelance ministry without any real authority structures';

ii) the clear deficit in theological knowledge and skills in curates. In particular Oliver specifies:

- poor levels of biblical literacy;

- a lack of awareness of the implications of particular modes of interpretation;

- poor levels of historical perspective in relation to Church traditions, worship and doctrine;

- poor levels of understanding of different models of ecclesiology;

- a lack of confidence in the ability to reflect theologically about ministry as it is experienced;

iii) initial resistance from training incumbents, gradually overcome as the programme became a part of the culture of CME;

iv) In addition the study notes that, while bishops were supportive of the scheme, they had some difficulty working with the need for a more disciplined approach to making appointments from curacy to a post of responsibility.

This study shows that there is a real need to continue the ministerial education of the clergy after ordination – a point made strongly by the diocesan CME responses in our initial consultation. Secondly, it demonstrates that, even when a diocese makes a significant initiative to promote sustained learning in the first years of ministry, there are structural impediments to the success of the scheme because of the current arrangements for ministerial education.

4.18   We note also that the provision for continued learning in the earliest years of ministry is uneven across the dioceses and that as a result the Church is sending mixed messages about the importance of continued learning and ministerial development. On the one hand there is the developing good practice of recent decades that has given priority to the training agenda in the first post. This has resulted in improved selection of training parishes, better training for training incumbents and a good balance of parish-based and diocesan-based learning for the newly ordained. However, on the other hand, the picture is not uniformly good and the pressures are real. The second curacy has almost disappeared with the result that the whole training agenda that used to stretch between two posts is now thrown on to the title parish. There has also been some diversity of practice with regard to the length of the first curacy. The House of Bishops has agreed that four years is the norm, though arrangements for appointments can be made in the course of the fourth year, but not before the end of the third year.[34] However, more generally, with the current pressures on the Church, it is all too easy to see the newly ordained as an extra pair of hands, rather than someone in training. The pressure is increased if the incumbent has been given the curate because of having additional responsibilities. Candidates themselves have picked up this ambivalence in the Church's attitude to continuing learning after ordination, which contributes to them seeking posts of responsibility from the earliest years. Again it is hardly surprising that the impetus to continue to learn and to develop is difficult to sustain.

4.19   As we noted earlier, as a result of all these factors, *there is little or no visible connection between learning before and learning after ordination* (2.6 above). The impetus for lifelong learning is left primarily with the individual, with the result that some take up the challenge and some do not.

4.20   In this review of the relationship of IME to CME 1–4 our main concerns have been:

- the candidate's sense that the various aspects of training are part of a coherent package;
- the possibilities for sustaining learning in the theological, formational and practical dimensions of training throughout this period;
- relieving the pressure to 'frontload' training in the belief that all that is important in training must be included in the pre-ordination phase;
- the sharing and integrating of the experience and educational expertise of dioceses and ministerial training institutions.

It is against this background, that we make our first main proposal. We believe that the initial ministerial education of the clergy should be regarded as the whole period from entry into training to the end of the first curacy.[35] IME could then be treated as a coherent whole. Within this, the pre- and post-ordination phases may have different emphases with regard to the balance of theological learning, formation and contextual and practical training, but this could be taken into account in planning from the outset. This proposal will of course have significant organizational implications, to which we will return, but it is important to state the issue in principle first.

Proposal 1

We recommend that initial ministerial education be reconfigured as the period from entry into training to the end of the first training post.

4.21   We note, firstly, that at one level this proposal merely formalizes the current convention that the initial training offered to our candidates is a combination of training before ordination, apprenticeship with a training incumbent and CME 1–4. However, this proposal provides an agreement to make this a reality that is visible to and acknowledged by all involved. It provides a principle and a structure around which the desired outcomes, specified in recent publications for clergy training for IME and CME 1–4, can be delivered in a more coherent and consistent way. Secondly, our proposal does not alter the point that a fundamental change takes place at ordination in terms of the relationship between the Church and the candidate. In ordination the Church has acted and made a public and solemn declaration concerning the newly ordained and his or her place in the Church, and the candidate has accepted a call to a particular place in the Church and its life. However, the candidate has only just started in this new life and ministry and it is entirely appropriate that he or she is regarded as a minister who is continuing in a formal phase of training and development.

4.22   If the above proposals are to succeed they will have to be supported by a wide range of parties including sponsoring and ordaining bishops, those responsible for pre- and post-ordination training, training incumbents and candidates. With regard to the title parish, the key figures are the bishop who ordains and licenses, the training incumbents who supervise the newly ordained on a day-to-day basis, the CME officer who is responsible for the diocesan part of CME 1–4 and the newly ordained themselves. This proposal will have significant implications for:

i) *candidates' understanding of their training*: the initial training agreement between the candidate and the Church will extend past ordination and into the early years of ministry, as a stimulus to lifelong learning;

ii) *the work of training institutions responsible for IME and of CME officers*, i.e. those who under our proposals would be primarily responsible for the pre- and post-ordination phases of this newly defined IME, and its organizational basis. We address the implications of this proposal at the institutional level in paragraph 6.34;

iii) *training incumbents*[36] and their understanding of the training agenda in the first years of ministry. It will be vital that training incumbents are seen as key figures and partners in the continuing ministerial development of the newly ordained, and that the current best practice in their training and development is identified and becomes the standard for all. Proposals for the development of post-ordination programmes for the newly ordained will need to make full use of their contribution as mentors and they will have to oversee a delicate balance between the continuing IME programme mounted by training institutions and the important practical and ministerial learning on the ground in these vital first years of ministry. Training incumbents will also have a role in supporting the recently ordained in their continuing learning and development, and, further, in explaining the training agreement to parishes;

iv) on one specific point, we would envisage that the working agreement for the recently ordained must include *the provision for an agreed allocation of time for the minister for continuing studies and reflection*. This general principle would normally hold good for all but the allocation itself would vary according to the particular situation of the minister. Thus, we would expect that a stipendiary curate would devote a day in each working week, or its equivalent (for example, to allow for blocks of study and reflection), while others would need to come to an agreement over the proportion of the time given to the Church which could be allocated to continued learning. In practice this will entail a reduction in the extent of other ministerial duties during the title post. To sum up: for all the newly ordained, our proposal will mean that formally supervised study and reflection will be a part of ministry in these earlier years, just as we would hope that continued learning will always remain an integral part of ministry;

v) CME officers: they will have a role in communicating the Church's policy on training in the post-ordination phase to training incumbents, incorporating it into diocesan policies for CME and offering suitable training to training incumbents. Many of them might also be involved in the shaping of IME programmes themselves in their new role in the proposed training arrangements (see below, Chapter 6);

vi) *bishops and senior staff* responsible for placing clergy in second posts: the requirements of completing initial training in the title post would require discipline over the timing of second appointments. Our proposal about the extent of initial training fits well with the current agreement of the House of Bishops about the timing of appointment to a second post (see 4.18 above). The same discipline would need to be exercised before a recently ordained OLM is given wider responsibility within the home parish or benefice;

vii) while most candidates will need the three to four years after ordination to complete the envisaged level of training, some will be able to show evidence that they have completed that level in a slightly shorter period. As with every stage of training, the framework for ministerial education, proposed below, allows for *a proper flexibility with regard to individual candidates*.

4.23   In the round of consultation on the interim report, there was a very high level of agreement and approval for this first proposal. There were some concerns addressed, for example, that the post-ordination phase of the proposed IME should be properly contextual, which the working party would only wish to endorse. This will mean that the local, in this case the diocese and the parish, will need an effective voice in the debate about the curriculum in IME as it is redesigned for the pre- and post-ordination phase which will be available for it. Another concern was that lifelong learning should be just that, life long. Our proposals should not be construed to create another fault line in learning and development at the end of the reconfigured IME; rather learning needs to continue, to accompany and to give life to every phase of ministry. Here we would commend the dynamic approach taken in the recent review *Mind the Gap*, with its use of the metaphor of mapping and its CME framework.[37] However, the general response to this proposal concerning the reconfiguring of IME was very positive.

4.24   In this chapter we have tried to set our main proposal for the reconfiguration of initial ministerial education within the context of the necessity for lifelong learning for clergy, lay ministers and for all the people of God. Having done this, we now turn to the need for a new framework for learning.

Chapter 5

A new framework for ministerial education

5.1 We have argued that a learning Church is one that promotes a dynamic and reflective discipleship for all members of the Church community (4.1 above). Accordingly, the future ordained minister will be one whose developing vocation is to nurture and lead communities – either through the parish system or through new sets of relationships that engage individuals and communities – in ways that locate matters of spirituality and faith at the heart of contemporary culture. The expectations of those who enter ministry will be complex; they will arise both from the Church itself and from diverse communities and they may, on occasions, appear contradictory. Importantly, our ministers will be expected to respond to contemporary demands for professional competence within ministry – while representing the discipleship of one who walks with Jesus Christ.

What do we mean by a framework for ministerial education?

5.2 Essentially, the framework is a means for underpinning the character and identity of ordained ministers. It maps out a formational journey. It is *not* an end in itself. The framework proposes and outlines the maximum opportunities for candidates to serve the Church and to engage in forms of education, formation and training that exploit the rich resource of a learning Church. We propose a framework to meet the future needs of the Church to respond to the differing circumstances of those candidates who seek to develop their vocation. In other words, we seek to foster what has been described as 'inhabited Wisdom' and prepare students for lifelong engagement with it.

5.3 The proposed framework for ministerial education has two main components:

a) *agreed phases of development in a formational journey*, which are marked by specified levels of achievement in ministerial education, from initial exploration of vocation, via entry into training, ordination itself, title post and on into ministry;

b) a *statement of expectations for ministerial education* that would indicate *the qualities and learning expected of candidates* at the important 'thresholds' of entry into training, ordination and further phases of ministry or appointment to a post of responsibility.

The former sets out the pathway for the candidate, while the latter indicates the expectations or standards for crossing important thresholds, such as entry into training or ordination itself. The former is set out in chart form immediately below, while the latter will be explained and set out later in this chapter.

Agreed phases of development in a formational journey

5.4   We start our consideration of this area by setting out two worked examples in chart form. The charts are then explained in the following pages.

5.5   The diagrams are illustrations of just two of many possible pathways for different types of candidate. As illustrations they can easily mislead but they are intended to give the general picture.[38] Having entered this qualification, *the main point of the diagrams is that each phase of development is marked by attention to and attainment in the three ministerial, vocational and educational strands, in preparation for a movement into the next phase.* In the educational strand, most phases are marked by learning that can be recognized by a publicly acknowledged level of attainment. However, this is subservient to the general growth towards the role and practice of ordained ministry. An important point is that candidates may well be at different stages of development in relation to the three strands. To give two examples, one candidate may have a great deal of experience of lay ministry, a thought through sense of vocation but little study of theology, while another might be a theology graduate with little experience of the Church's ministry. Their needs in training will be very different. For this reason the Church cannot have a single academic or vocational award for all candidates but it could stipulate minimum levels of attainment as norms which can be applied across all three strands (see 5.30 below).

5.6   Our focus on phases of development can be related to the development of the credit accumulation and transfer system (CATS) in the higher education system, widely, but not universally, adopted in higher education in the UK (and beyond).[39] We note that this approach works for the professions of law and medicine as well as the newer professions of nursing, teaching and social work. While CATS is still being developed, and is not utilized by all HE institutions, it can still be a helpful indicator of the level and extent of learning undertaken. Thus, the Church can make use of this system, as many of its training institutions already do, without having to be driven by it. For example, where a university's qualifications are not credit-rated, the Church, through the Ministry Division's Educational Validation Panel, could give such qualifications a nominal credit rating as a guide so that the qualifications can be used within the proposed framework. While we think a system of credit rating has value as an indication of levels and amounts of learning and development, at no point would we wish it to be determinative.

5.7   In developing this framework, we have made use of the terminology currently employed in further and higher education and in vocational training. This terminology will of course change and develop, just as the framework for ministerial education as a whole will need updating from time to time. We have provided a short glossary of contemporary educational terms on p.54.

5.8   Within the CATS system, typically, students will work through levels one to three to achieve graduate status, accumulating 120 education credit points at each level – which, in turn, will be equivalent to a year's work for a student in full-time study. Importantly, part-time students may work through the levels at a different pace; moreover, entry and exit points can be managed flexibly, depending on the circumstances of the individual student. Thus, in this system, attainment is expressed in terms of the *number* of credit points achieved at a certain *level*, rather than in terms of the length of the period of study. For example, the first full-time year of undergraduate study is replaced by the gaining of 120 credits at Level 1, irrespective of whether this is achieved by full-time or part-time study, or how long or short a time it takes. Thus, CATS allows for flexibility in patterns of learning, for students to pick up and temporarily

A framework for ministerial education: example 1

Phases of development for ordinands and stipendiary/non-stipendiary clergy who will exercise a ministry in a post of responsibility

Ministerial	Vocational	Educational
Education for Discipleship, where appropriate, to include exploration of ministries	Exploration of vocation	For example, introductory modules up to Certificate (or higher levels if candidate has prior learning)

Selection conference for training for ordained ministry

Ministerial	Vocational	Educational
Supervised ministerial tasks	Preparation for beginning ordained ministry	For example, Diploma, Foundation Degree,[40] Honours Degree Or Masters, as appropriate to the individual

Ordination and appointment to title parish

Ministerial	Vocational	Educational
Exercise of ministry under supervision	Completion of IME as preparation for a post of responsibility	Further level of study, for example, Diploma converted to Honours Degree, as appropriate to the individual

Appointment to post of responsibility

Ministerial	Vocational	Educational
Experience of ministry in a post of responsibility (parish or sector)	Continuing CME for ministerial development	Specific pieces of study or reflection on ministry, as appropriate

Further phases of ministry and development; some including further roles such as a training incumbent or rural dean

A framework for ministerial education: example 2

Phases of development for ordinands and permanent non-stipendiary clergy or ordained local ministers who will exercise an assistant ministry

Differences from Example 1 are marked in italics

Ministerial	Vocational	Educational
Education for Discipleship, where appropriate, to include exploration of ministries	Exploration of vocation	For example, introductory modules up to Certificate (or higher levels if candidate has prior learning)

Selection conference for training for ordained ministry

Ministerial	Vocational	Educational
Supervised ministerial tasks	Preparation for beginning ordained ministry	*For example, Diploma,* *Or* *Foundation Degree (or higher if candidate has prior learning)*

Ordination and appointment to title parish

Ministerial	Vocational	Educational
Exercise of ministry under supervision	Completion of IME as preparation for post of responsibility	Further level of study, for example, Diploma converted to Honours Degree, as appropriate to the individual

Development of, or appointment to, new area of ministry

Ministerial	Vocational	Educational
Experience of ministry with a defined area of responsibility, with continuing supervision	Continuing CME for ministerial development	Specific pieces of study or reflection on ministry, as appropriate

Further phases of ministry and development; some including further defined areas of responsibility cease formal learning as their availability allows. Further, there is potential in a CATS approach for learning undertaken in one educational institution to be recognized by another, thus allowing for mobility among students.

5.9 The framework proposed, therefore, enables theological education and training to be designed as an integrated process, enabling the fault lines identified in this report – between IME and CME, or between ordination training and other forms of theological education – to be overcome. Instead of viewing theological education and training for different forms of ministry as self-contained, independent programmes, the framework offers a means by which progression, continuity and development can be properly recognized. This means that the framework also offers flexibility for students and candidates, allowing proper recognition of prior learning and development and movement between different modes of study. Flexibility is further enhanced since students may 'trade' credit (through recognition agreements) between different educational settings. And beyond graduate level, Masters level credits can be accumulated to ensure continuing formation – towards post-graduate certificate, diploma and Masters awards.

5.10 Within the Church's development of such a framework, it could pay particular attention to pathways for lay ministers and other learners who now are proceeding to other forms of lay ministry or to ordination. Similarly, if lay ministry or discipleship schemes become credit-rated, then it will be easier to give credit for such prior learning. This is a complex area,[41] given the need for the three strands of ministerial, vocational and educational development to be intertwined in preparation for ordination, but, nonetheless, a system of credit rating would be helpful.

The rationale for the framework for ministerial education

5.11 The rationale for this framework is as follows.

i) The framework promotes *integration* of theological education and training, allowing continuity of learning, progression and recognition of prior learning in ways that value the formational journeys of people. In addition, it gives clarity to the expectations appropriate for different types of ministry.

ii) The framework can *harmonize intellectual and formational elements* of education and training. By holding together the three strands of the ministerial, vocational and educational, it can promote and enable growth into 'inhabited Wisdom'.

iii) The framework promotes *flexibility* and *transferability* of learning for new kinds of learners, developing their vocation within an integrated system. It will enable common understanding between dioceses and training organizations and this in turn will permit movement of individuals. It will do this by taking their general and specific credit from one location to another as circumstances change, enabling exit and re-entry, thus ensuring the appropriate kind of course for a diverse set of entrants.

iv) The framework offers *transparency* to different participants and agencies, clarifying what is required/offered by all parties to the learning contract: the training provider; any central agency responsible for quality and/or funding; and the individual student. This also assures equity of treatment and promotes effective monitoring and evaluation.

v) The framework promotes *alignment with other parts of higher education* and thereby facilitates shared learning with students from other programmes; for example, nonvocational theology students or professional community workers such as teachers or social workers. This will be important to underpin learning in both the pre-ordination and post-ordination phases.

vi) The framework operates as a *negotiated contract* between:

- bishops who have responsibility for enabling a new generation of ministers to serve the Church and for securing the continuing development of ordained ministers;
- the Ministry Division, with responsibility for proposing policy, and specifying and monitoring quality and standards;
- training providers, responsible for designing and developing programmes of study that meet those standards;
- the key constituency of aspiring ministers.

vii) The framework offers *clarity and consistency* both of process and outcomes. In other words it demonstrates clearly the graduate status and professional standing of the ordained minister with respect to both his or her journey in discipleship *and* the critical intellectual practice that has enabled achievement to a specified level of achievement in theological understanding and ministerial practice.

viii) At the same time, the framework *could be extended* to embrace all voluntary and professional workers within Church communities who engage in education and training. By this means their learning and development can be properly recognized in their formational journey. For example, it could include initial Reader training, with the possibility of setting a goal of accreditation at an appropriate level. (Diploma level might be thought to be the appropriate norm.) Whatever the details of the framework, this would be a big step towards a full recognition of the prior learning of recently trained Readers who then receive a call to the ordained ministry, while at the same time clarifying the further formational and educational goals appropriate for preparation for ordination. The framework also extends to CME, both for the initial years and beyond into lifelong ministry.

ix) Within this new approach to learning in the Church it will be vital that there is *clarity about pathways for different types of learner*. Learning together is important, offering great benefits in terms of learning to respect other forms of ministry, modelling shared ministry and an efficient use of scarce resources in teaching and learning. However, neither a collaborative style of working, nor formation for particular ministries is served by merely bringing different types of learner together indiscriminately. For all concerned there needs to be clarity about which parts of any programme can be shared and why this is appropriate. Parts of the programme should be dedicated to the formation of particular groups, whether these are for Readers in training, for other lay ministries or for ordinands. Our proposal is not that all training should be shared between the various ministries and types of discipleship, but that some should be shared, while at other points various groups of learners should proceed on their own tracks.

5.12 One of our terms of reference refers to a review of sponsorship category. We have discussed this issue several times, with some members proposing a significant move away from the use of different categories to a single category, while a majority continue to see value in a range of categories, though not necessarily the three that we currently have (see 1.10 above). We are glad to note that work is currently being done on this issue in the Ministry Division and we await their findings with interest. Our contribution to this discussion is in part to offer the proposed framework for ministerial education (5.17) and the illustrative charts of the pathways through the discernment of vocation, training and the early years of ministry (5.4). Further, in the proposed criteria for allocating training (8.32), we have put consideration of category of sponsorship as the last item in the list, after other important factors. We consider that our framework with its benchmarks provides a flexible route for all ministers to grow and develop and for proper assessment of the possibility for their deployment to be made.

Articulating the Church's expectations: the qualities and learning expected of candidates

5.13   The second key feature of this framework for ministerial education is the points of transition from one phase to another. These points of transition ('thresholds') are marked by levels of appropriate attainment in ministerial education – which includes vocational development, theological education and the requisite skills. At this point our working party can build on a number of recent reports on selection, IME and CME that have explicitly or implicitly used the language and ideas of a common learning framework. If we put together the work of recent years and follow a candidate's progress towards ordination and ministry, the following sets of expectations and desired outcomes have been articulated:

- the selection criteria used by bishops' selectors;[42]

- the 'agreed expectations of ordinands', an expression of the qualities that training programmes should enable candidates to achieve in the pre-ordination phase of their training;[43]

- a list of qualities that should be gained by clergy in the first three years of CME;[44]

- a wider CME framework, which uses the metaphor of mapping in order to relate and integrate different dimensions of learning and training throughout ministry.[45]

All these reports gained broad acceptance by the wider Church and by the specific constituencies. The more detailed outcomes specified in this report seek to build on this work and develop it further.

Glossary of educational terms

Credit points	A way of reckoning by means of which learning can be quantified; typically 120 credit points equates to one year's full-time study.
	General credit: learning that counts in general towards a qualification
	Specific credit: learning which matches the required knowledge/ skills/ aptitudes closely
CATS	Credit Accumulation and Transfer System: the system by which learning can be quantified, counted towards an award (certificate, diploma, etc.) and recognized by other institutions of higher education, employers or agencies.
Level	Commonly recognized stages of achievement in higher education. Completion of Level 1 leads to a certificate in HE (equivalent to year 1 of an undergraduate course), Level 2 to a diploma in HE (equivalent to year 2), Level 3 to an Honours degree (equivalent to year 3); Level 4 or M to a Masters qualification.
Learning outcomes	The specification of the desired and measurable qualities or knowledge in the learner in a unit of learning (for example: by the end of the module, the learner should be able to: i) outline the history of the development of eucharistic prayers in the Church of England; ii) set the major developments in historical context; iii) show an appreciation of the pastoral and liturgical principles which might contribute to the choice of eucharistic prayer in a variety of settings).
Module	A unit of learning and of assessment. Modules can be of various 'sizes', for example 10 credits or 20 credits.
Entry and exit points	The points at which learners can enter or leave a programme of learning.
APL	Accreditation of prior learning: giving credit for prior learning which has been formally assessed by a recognized institution of higher education (also called 'certificated learning'), allowing a learner to proceed directly to a higher level module or programme.
APEL	Accreditation of prior experiential learning: giving credit for prior learning from informal learning settings (e.g. the workplace) and which has not been formally assessed as with APL, usually carried out by asking the learner to reflect on the experience in a piece of written work or by showing other evidence of the learning.
Benchmarking	The statement of qualities or learning deemed to represent a particular standard, for example for the qualities and learning required of a graduate in a particular discipline.
Threshold	The level of qualification to allow a learner to pass from one stage to another, including in practical competence, hence the phrase 'fitness to practise'.

5.14 Any attempt to articulate what is required of a candidate for ordination in terms of learning, formation or skills must contain either implicit or explicit criteria. If criteria are to be used in forming a judgement, rather than merely resorting to personal insight or judgement, it is better for all concerned that the criteria are publicly stated and open to scrutiny and revision. Thus, there is a connection between the Church's use of criteria, for example in the selection of candidates, and the attempts in HE and secular vocational training to specify the knowledge, understanding and skills that learning aims to bring. At the same time, there is a clearly marked difference between areas of the Church's practice and the wider use of benchmarking statements, specifically in the area of the value and admissibility of what can broadly be called the measurable and immeasurable. All those involved in IME know that it is much easier to assign a mark to a written piece of work than to come to a view on whether a candidate's character or interaction with others is such that the candidate can be recommended to a bishop for ordination. However difficult this is, the Church requires it of the principals and staff of training institutions and indeed has developed good practice in this area. Out of this good practice, it has generated broad statements of the areas to be covered.[46] Thus, the creation of a statement of expectations for ministerial education builds on the Church's own traditions of discernment of character, as well as the measuring of intellectual growth or of skills.

5.15 Within preparation for ordained ministry, there will always be a place for wise judgement about a person and for the conviction about the grace of God at work in a person's weaknesses, as well as their strengths. Thus, recommending a candidate to a bishop will be far more than assessing the measurable and will continue to depend on discernment of calling, tested in relationships within communities of worship. At the same time something can be said that can be publicly owned. To give an example: while it would be inappropriate and impossible to measure a candidate's prayer life, it is possible to describe how a candidate is maintaining a life of prayer through attendance at corporate worship and a pattern of personal devotion. While we deal more fully with training issues about individual candidates in Chapter 8, we can anticipate the point here by saying that the statement of expectations for ministerial education will need to be applied with flexibility and discrimination by bishops and others who bear particular responsibilities for selection, training and deployment. The following tables are offered as a flexible guide in an attempt to set out how the aims of ministerial education might be construed.

5.16 We acknowledge that there has also been work done in the HE sector to develop a framework for the study of theology, using the language of benchmarking standards and levels.[47] While this work has informed our thinking it cannot be used directly for the purposes of ministerial formation. The needs of the Church in its preparation of public ministers overlap to some extent with the interests of higher education study of theology, a fact that is unsurprising given the extensive sharing of resources that currently exists, but the priority we give to the formational journey, and the need to provide a framework for this, requires us to develop a substantially different framework. In particular, where the higher education sector expresses its desired outcomes and methods in terms that can appear relativistic, value-free or uncommitted, the Church needs to express the outcomes and framework for its ministers in terms of godly wisdom, passionate engagement, discipleship and holiness. It is this task we now attempt. We do so with the explicit intention of creating a framework, not a curriculum; a tool not a template. Thus, a framework seeks to make a general statement for ministerial education in the Church of England and sets out qualities sought in candidates. It is a guide for the purposes of assessment, not a curriculum. Our concern has been to draw up a statement that is clear enough to be useful for the task of making decisions about the training needs of individual candidates but without the statement becoming unduly prescriptive for those who will draw up curricula in the light of the statement. Within these limits, the framework seeks to provide the following:

i) an account of how three areas or domains of learning, that are already widely agreed, can be described. These domains are: 'Knowledge and Understanding', 'Spiritual and Ministerial Formation' and 'Ministerial Skills'. The three domains are described separately *only* in order to ensure that the importance of each domain is clearly recognized. In terms of the development of an individual or the design of a syllabus their integration is of primary importance.

ii) An indication about the balance of time or weight given to each domain, expressed in the language of credits. Therefore, at an introductory level in a formational journey we believe that more weight should be given to the engagement with Scripture and the Christian tradition in various contexts, than with the development of ministerial skills. This coheres with our conviction that level 1 work needs to be focused on the fostering of an educated laity, rather than revolving around the specific interests of particular ministries.

iii) An account of how each of these domains can be described at different levels. Thus, for example, the desired outcome at level 2 in each domain represents a threshold for practice as an ordained minister, someone who can demonstrate sufficient understanding, skill and ministerial integrity that the Church with confidence can ordain them to positions in which they continue to be supervised, and in which they continue to learn and develop.

iv) An account of how this framework relates to the expectations of higher education and professional bodies. Our aim is to show that the Church's language of levels and thresholds is congruent with the language and expectations of these sectors, with whom the churches will be cooperating.

Some might expect a more specific and detailed account of syllabus content, but we continue to commend the method and approach begun by ACCM 22 and continued in *Mission and Ministry*. In this system, responsibility for the development of syllabus and curriculum is vested with the training institutes, subject to the agreement of the Ministry Division through the Educational Validation Panel. We believe that the institutes envisaged in this report will be better placed to do this work, and to offer more creative ways of providing integrated yet flexible pathways in the formational journey involved in IME and beyond. It will be necessary, and we believe helpful to training institutions, to develop policy and guidelines for the curriculum in order to enable transfer between training institutions. Thus, many candidates will take the pre-ordination phase of training in a college and then move to another part of the country for first years of ministry. It is vital that these candidates experience their training as a co-ordinated whole across the pre- and post-ordination phases. We take up this aspect of policy, which was never fully developed after ACCM 22 but which our proposals make more urgent, in paragraph 8.21.

5.17 In the following pages we present our proposed statement of expectations for ministerial education. It is made up of a short summary statement that is followed by a more detailed account of the expectations distributed between the three, interconnected, domains of being, knowing and doing.

A Statement of Expectations for Ministerial Education

Summary statement

The Church seeks that all God's people grow in faith, deepen their discipleship, and learn more deeply to 'inhabit godly wisdom'. As part of God's people, and in order to enable such growth in others, the Church seeks ministers who:

- Are firmly rooted in their love of God, discipleship of Jesus Christ, and dedicated to a deepening pilgrimage of faith in the Holy Spirit;

- Are passionate about the transformation of the whole created order into one that reflects the redemptive love of God;

- Are deeply committed to loving service in the Church as a sign and instrument of God's love for the world;

- Immerse themselves, with faithful obedience, in the Church's life of prayer and worship, and its critical engagement with Scripture and the Christian tradition;

- Are dedicated to bringing their gifts of leadership, pastoral care, worship and mission to the service of the Church through their calling to ordination.

A Statement of Expectations for Ministerial Education – Detailed Statement

	Being – growing in faith, discipleship, prayer and vocation	Knowing and understanding	Doing – developing skills in and for ministry	Key words from the world of Higher Education and other professional bodies
		Level 1		
120 credits	30 credits	60 credits	30 credits	Balance of credits across the 3 areas to indicate relative weight
	Christians who are growing in their discipleship, and those seeking to be ministers, will be able to describe: how they are maintaining a life of prayer; how they are becoming more aware of themselves and others; how their learning is helping them to shape their calling as disciples and (where appropriate) their calling to ordained ministry, and leadership of the people of God.	Christians who are growing in their discipleship, and those seeking to be ministers, will be able to show: a basic knowledge of the Bible and the Christian tradition; a basic understanding of how the Church's beliefs and practices have been understood and used in different contexts; a basic understanding of the current contexts in which Christian witness is to be lived and how the Church's beliefs and practices engage with them.	Christians who are growing in their discipleship, and those seeking to be ministers, will be able to show basic skills in: communicating their beliefs and understanding; working with others collaboratively and respectfully; developing as reflective practitioners; (where appropriate) pastoral care, leading worship and preaching.	Sound knowledge and key concepts, and accurate communication skills. Practice within a professional framework with personal responsibility. Observing and exercising.
		Level 2		
120 credits	40 credits	50 credits	30 credits	Balance of credits across the 3 areas to indicate relative weight
	Ministers will be able to: evaluate their prayer life and spiritual development in the light of the wide tradition of prayer of the Church; evaluate how their growing awareness of self and others impacts on their ministry; evaluate how their learning in areas of knowledge and skill is helping them to shape their calling and lifestyle as ordained people.	Ministers will be: able to show that they can use a variety of interpretative methods to study the Bible and a wider range of basic Christian texts from different historical periods and cultures; able to evaluate contemporary cultural trends in relation to the beliefs and practices of the Church; developing an Anglican theological framework which will sustain further study.	Ministers will be able to: demonstrate competence in areas of mission, pastoral care, leading of worship and preaching in supervised and limited contexts; evaluate their gifts (strengths and weaknesses) in areas of mission, pastoral care, leading of worship and preaching as skilled reflective practitioners; evaluate and demonstrate their ability to work in teams and with other people.	Sound understanding in their field of study and apply these more widely. Practice within a professional framework with personal responsibility and decision making.

	Being – growing in faith, discipleship, prayer and vocation	Knowing and understanding	Doing – developing skills in and for ministry	Key words from the world of Higher Education and other professional bodies
		Level 3		
120 credits	30 credits minimum	30 credits minimum	30 credits minimum	Balance of credits across the 3 areas to indicate relative weight Minimum, allowing 30 elective credits to specialize
	Ministers will be able to show: how they can reflect critically on the practice of prayer, and both the joys and struggles of their spiritual journey; how their life of prayer and learning is being integrated into a sustainable life of public ministry; how their experience of public ministry and its varied roles is set in the wider mission and life of the Church.	Ministers will be able to: demonstrate an educated ability as interpreters of the Bible and a wider range of basic Christian texts from different historical periods and cultures; critically evaluate contemporary cultural trends in relation to the Church's mission and life; explain the faith of the Church and how it will sustain further study.	Ministers will be able to: demonstrate competence in pastoral care, leading worship and preaching and mission, collaborative leadership in supervised and unsupervised and varied contexts; demonstrate skill as critically reflective practitioners; show how they have taken responsibility for their further learning; show how they are developing one of these areas as a special area of professional development.	Understanding of complex body of knowledge, some of it at the current boundaries of academic discipline. Powers of analysis and problem solving. Ability to evaluate arguments and come to sound judgements. Practice within a professional framework with personal responsibility, decision making in complex and unpredictable contexts.
		Level M		
180 credits	20 credits Minimum shown here to allow specialization.	20 credits Minimum shown here to allow specialization.	20 credits Minimum shown here to allow specialization.	(Most MA modules are 20 credits, and expect 60 credits for dissertation.)
	Ministers will be able to show how their practice of prayer has sustained them in the varied phases of their ministry. They will be able to make an honest assessment of their gifts and areas of need as a licensed minister as a framework for guiding others. They will be able to make and justify plans for their possible development in this area.	Ministers will be able to choose an area of special research in one of the academic or professional disciplines of theology or ministry and expect to be able to teach and lead others in this subject up to graduate level.	Ministers will have specialized in a chosen area of leadership, mission, pastoral care, liturgy, supervision, etc. Through a critical study of the literature on the subject and critical reflection on their own practice, they will be expected to be able to teach and lead others in this area.	Study at and informed by forefront of academic or professional discipline. Originality in application of knowledge, and able to deal with complex issues both systematically and creatively. Originality in dealing with problems. Practice within a professional framework with personal responsibility and initiative in complex and unpredictable professional environments.

5.18 This statement of expectations for ministerial education will need further refinement and development, particularly in the area of the practical skills and knowledge that should be expected in the ordained in the early years of ministry. However, in principle such a statement, as part of the framework for ministerial education, could enable the Church to come to decisions about the training needs of candidates, rather than relying on the current rules based on age and category of sponsorship. One of the advantages of our proposal is that it would allow greater flexibility in terms of pathways to ordination. The intention would be to use the framework in order to plan each candidate's pathway in the light of his or her training needs. While the candidate's own preference will be a component of this discussion, it should be the Church that decides on the appropriate pathway, following discussion with all relevant parties.

5.19 We now summarize this part of our thinking in our second proposal.

Proposal 2

We recommend that the current bishops' regulations for training be replaced by a framework for ministerial education, based on:

i) agreed phases of development in a formational journey, and

ii) statements indicating the qualities and learning expected of candidates at key points in that journey.

5.20 We turn now to review the response to this proposal in the consultation on the interim report.

i) There was widespread agreement that the current set of rules known as bishops' regulations for training is no longer a useful approach and needed replacement.

ii) The proposal for a framework for ministerial education with its focus on phases of development and levels of attainment was in general well received.

iii) By contrast there was sharp criticism of the first version of our statement of expectations that was seen as being too dependent on the controversial benchmarking statement for Theology and Religious Studies in UK universities, and reflecting what was seen as its relativistic stance. In response to this we have completely revised the statement itself and have tried to demonstrate how our statement is related to the Church's own traditions of discernment.

iv) Some respondents criticized the use of any approach related to benchmarking. However, this criticism was not accompanied by any suggestions for an alternative approach that would allow the Church to make decisions about training that can command general confidence.

v) Finally, there has been criticism from some quarters that do not use the CATS approach that the Church is buying into an approach that some see as utilitarian and inappropriate. In reply, we note the continued growth in the use of the CATS approach over the past decade, as well as the continuing debate about its value. As a result in this report we have made only limited use of CATS. However, we remain convinced about the underlying issues concerning the need to develop *flexible pathways* for candidates and to *value and give credit for prior learning*, where this is rigorously assessed. We would encourage universities of all types to work on systems that promote these values, whether they are developed through a CATS-type approach or some other approach, e.g. giving exemptions for prior learning. Lastly, as we have stated above, a system of credit rating can be a useful tool but does not need to be determinative.

5.21 In the light of the proposed framework for ministerial education, we now address issues related to the pathway through training and into ministry. In turn we will deal Education for Discipleship (see below), entry into training and standards of attainment.

Education for Discipleship

5.22 To start with we need to step back from the needs of ordinands and consider the wider picture. If our goal more generally is to contribute to the education of the people of God (4.1 above), a Church-wide provision of programmes of learning under the title of Education for Discipleship could be of great benefit. This initiative would build on the great range of work currently done in dioceses and parishes, most of which is appropriately not accredited at HE level. Some dioceses do have what we have called a provision for the formal theological education of the laity, i.e. programmes that are academically accredited, and our proposal would build on these initiatives. In other words our proposal is to offer programmes to lay Christians that would be a further step than most dioceses currently offer, making use of the resources we have in institutions of ministerial education for the benefit of the Church as a whole. As its name indicates, the focus would be on deepening the knowledge and understanding of the Christian faith in order to inform discipleship, ministry and mission.[48] We envisage that these programmes would be of interest to lay people who wish to serve God in their ordinary lives. At the same time, they could also contribute to the initial training of Readers, other lay ministers and prospective ordinands. Thus, our proposal for the provision of Education for Discipleship could be a practical contribution to a Church-wide initiative in theological education benefiting lay and ordained alike.

5.23 It is widely recognized that candidates for ordained ministry beginning initial training today do so from a huge range of starting points in terms of the level of their experience of the Church and its ministry and in terms of theological knowledge and understanding. Some may well have a relevant background, for example, they have been lay ministers or Readers or have undertaken theological study of other sorts. However, the majority are, in general, less securely grounded in a knowledge of the Scriptures and the Church's tradition than previous generations. Some are relatively recent converts, others have not had a secure or substantial Christian formation or education. As a result basic studies in the Christian faith – for example, a Bishop's certificate – are of value. However, we think that it would be very helpful if more candidates had already embarked on preliminary, where possible accredited, theological and ministerial studies before they have been formally selected. Candidates who are considering a call to ordained ministry could be encouraged to undertake a range of types of learning:

- modules such as 'Knowledge and understanding of the Bible', 'Introducing Christian theology', 'Introduction to Christian vocation' and 'Christianity in contemporary society';

- producing a portfolio of evidence in the area of reflection on their own spiritual journey and life of discipleship;

- going on a placement to give them a wider appreciation of the contexts of the life of the Church or the variety of its ministry, lay and ordained;

As will be seen from this list, the envisaged learning is not confined to one type of theological or ministerial learning. Further, as the focus will be on education for discipleship, the learning should be of real, continuing value, even if the learner does not proceed to any form of accredited ministry. The amount and level of study could be tailored to the needs of the candidate. Thus, for those who are reasonably academically able and have no formal prior learning in theology for ministry, the level of these studies could be between 60 and 120 credits at Level 1, though even one or two modules would be of benefit. For other candidates the amount and level could be adjusted according to their needs and personal circumstances. The key aspects of the proposal are that they would be *offered on a Church-wide basis* and that there would be *encouragement* to engage in them.

5.24 For potential candidates and the Church, we believe that this encouragement to learn would have a number of important benefits.

i) As candidates go to a selection conference there could be a body of evidence that could be helpful to the selectors in their task. This would not be primarily about judging a candidate's ability but about the way they have responded to their new learning in the light of their sense of call to ministry.

ii) If candidates have undergone some theological and ministerial studies before selection, they should have a much better sense of whether they are in fact well suited to the course of education and to the envisaged ministry.

iii) Candidates in training would start their period of training on the basis of recent studies and learning, rather than starting from scratch.

v) Candidates who attend a selection conference may be recommended for training but subject to the condition that they undertake some learning or preparation before they proceed. This area of work, known as 'pre-theological education',[49] is the successor to the Aston Training Scheme. The provision of programmes under the Education for Discipleship initiative could be complementary to pre-theological education. It could provide a range of modules of general interest that also might be useful for the particular needs of individual candidates undertaking pre-theological education.

vi) In the financial area, it is prudent to expect candidates to have undertaken reasonable preparation before being finally accepted into ordination training. Putting a candidate through IME costs money and it is only responsible to take reasonable measures to check that the candidate will benefit from a course of study and preparation, and further, to ensure that the candidate gets the most out of it by good preparation.

vii) This proposal would complement the current practice within the Methodist Church and its programme of Foundation Studies.[50] At the same time, it is important to clarify that our proposal is not the same as Methodist practice. In particular our proposal is not envisaged as studies that are intended to lead to some form of authorized ministry.

Using credits gained in Education for Discipleship in ordination training

5.25 It will be asked why the learning in Education for Discipleship should receive a credit rating. While all relevant learning is to be valued, if a credit rating can be given this has great advantages in terms of the candidate being able to put it towards an award or to get credit for it, if it is necessary to move to another institution of higher education. With the growth of the accrediting of prior learning, these studies could be used in a variety of ways if a candidate proceeds to training for ordination. These would include enabling candidates to reach a higher academic level within training; to shorten training; or to give a candidate longer in training to achieve a basic level of attainment. All these uses are valuable, and fit with our emphasis on flexibility. As at all stages in IME, we would encourage the rigorous application of the accreditation of prior learning. Thus, where students can present appropriate prior learning or experience, this should be fully recognized and accredited. We would not wish Education for Discipleship to be another compulsory phase for all potential ordinands.

5.26　In the consultation on our interim report, the original form of our proposal had a mixed response.

i)　In the interim report, we gave this proposal the name of Foundational Studies, which did not indicate its focus clearly enough. As a result we have renamed it 'Education for Discipleship'.

ii)　Overall there was a general welcome for the idea of candidates having had the benefit of some theological study and exploration of ministerial issues before entering training. The wider concern for formal theological education available to lay people also met with approval.

iii)　Many have expressed concern about the effects of such a policy on some groups of candidates and on the level of study we had suggested. Thus, there was concern for younger candidates who might have demanding jobs and family commitments that precluded part-time study.

iv)　Some believed that our original proposal would unduly lengthen training.

In responding to points iii) and iv, we would wish to reassert the value of preliminary studies for most candidates but are no longer recommending that they become mandatory, nor are we now suggesting a fixed level of attainment in terms of completing half of Level 1 for OLM candidates or the whole of Level 1 for other categories of sponsored candidates, by the time of entry into training. Thus, while reasserting the principle of preliminary studies, as part of a Church-wide initiative in theological education available to all, we have built in an appropriate flexibility for individual candidates.

5.27　With regard to the financing of Education for Discipleship, we envisage a similarly varied pattern. At one level the Church should take the main responsibility for them in that they are a service to the Church as a whole. As a result we have included them within our proposals for new institutional arrangements for training set out in Chapter 6 below. Thus, the majority of the cost should be borne by the Church, with the corollary that the fees for individual modules should be modest. In terms of individual learners, there are a variety of possibilities. Some learners will be willing to pay the fees themselves, some may be supported by parishes. Where a student is working with a diocese in exploring a vocation, a diocese could offer full or partial funding for such potential candidates, where this is necessary.

5.28　We sum up this discussion in our next main proposal.

Proposal 3

We recommend that

i) **opportunities for learning, under the general title of Education for Discipleship, are offered on a Church-wide basis for a range of students, which might include lay people seeking to deepen their Christian discipleship, trainee Readers and other lay ministers and potential candidates for ordination;**

ii) **prospective ordinands are encouraged to engage in such preliminary studies before they enter training;**

iii) **for prospective ordinands the amount and level of such studies should be decided in the light of the candidate's abilities, needs and circumstances, with the guideline that candidates with no prior formal learning in theology for ministry are encouraged to attain 60–120 credit points at Level 1, or its equivalent.**

5.29   After selection, candidates for ordained ministry would continue their studies and preparation in a part-time or full-time mode, or in a combination of the two. We take up further issues in the area in Chapter 8. We turn now to the question of norms for attainment.

Standards of attainment: thresholds for ordination and for posts of responsibility

5.30   In our setting out of issues to be addressed, we raised the question of whether the clergy should, as a norm, be required to achieve graduate status in theology for ministry, either by the time of ordination or in the earliest years of ministry (2.21 above). As set out above, the *prima facie* case is strong, given the rising expectations of ministers in Church and society. In today's world it is imperative for men and women who lead and serve in God's name to be properly prepared, which for most will mean theologically and ministerially prepared to a level which the higher education sector would call graduate level. Thus, we believe that at a time of transition in which the Church faces major challenges those who are entrusted with responsibility for its life and mission require *both the depth of engagement with the theological tradition that graduate study involves and the level of creative, analytic, reflective skills that are appropriately described as graduate-level qualities of mind and character*. We note further that the qualities of mind and the skills described for degree-level study correlate with the qualities and skills expected in clergy – qualities that include higher-level skills of critical analysis and understanding, as well as developed skills in team working, communication, awareness of self and others, and collaboration. We propose that, as a norm, anyone who has pastoral charge and responsibility for the life of a parish or in sector ministry should complete Level 3, graduate study, in ministerial theology and practice.[51]

5.31   However, ordination may also properly be to an assistant role. In this assistant role, where responsibility is more limited and where a person is more closely supervised, the qualities and skills required are correspondingly less developed. We propose, therefore, that as a norm the threshold for ordination to an assistant role should be set at the completion of Level 2 or Diploma study, though many will be able to achieve Level 3, and some beyond, by ordination. This part of the proposal merely formalizes the current position for stipendiary and non-stipendiary candidates; we discuss the position of OLM candidates further in paragraph 5.35 v) below.

5.32   These suggestions do not arise from a narrow concern for gaining academic awards but because the clergy should be properly prepared for their work and that preparation should be accredited in a publicly accountable way. Further, we need to clarify that any norm should be set in terms of ministerial education as a whole, not simply the academic study of theology, even though the latter is an important component of the former. Finally, while many candidates will achieve this norm before ordination, if the Church regards the first curacy as an integral part of IME this will allow other candidates to complete this level of study in this latter stage of initial training. Thus, some candidates in colleges and many candidates on courses will achieve diploma level in their pre-ordination studies and can then complete a degree in two or more part-time years after ordination.

5.33   We turn now to the response to the proposals about standards of attainment in the consultation on our interim report.

i)   There was a broad agreement, firstly, about the desire to raise standards and, secondly, that degree-level attainment in ministerial theology and practice was the correct level, as a norm, for those who will exercise ministry in a post of responsibility.

ii) There was some misunderstanding that our proposal was that all should be theology graduates, in the traditional academic sense, rather than in the vocational and applied sense that we had proposed.

iii) There was fairly widespread comment that the report was overly concerned with the gaining of academic awards and that our proposal would prevent those whose gifts are primarily pastoral from becoming incumbents. Others commented that the qualities required in an incumbent are not those that are encapsulated in degree-level work.

iv) There was criticism from some that the interim report set a different and lower standard for OLM candidates, thereby opening up a hierarchy among the ordained.

In response to these points, we have re-emphasized that our concern is with the continuity of learning, contributing to establishing patterns of lifelong learning. While academic awards create motivation and are useful markers of achievement, our proposals are designed to continue patterns of learning in the ordained as an integral part of the ministerial life. Secondly, whatever the situation in the past, the great majority of those now entering training and who will hold posts of responsibility in the future should have no difficulty in reaching degree level. Good support, formal encouragement to learn and additional time available to reach this goal should enable even those whose strength is primarily in the pastoral area to complete these courses and benefit from them – particularly as the post-ordination phase could include much learning that is directly related to the practice of ministry. With regard to whether degree-level study is the appropriate yardstick for incumbency, we would agree that not all the qualities required will be directly tested by degree-level work. However, alongside the necessary qualities of leadership and vision, we would want a good level of theological knowledge and understanding, ability to interpret the social context and present the faith in a way that is both faithful to the tradition and takes account of contemporary culture. All these values are characteristic of the proposed degree-level qualification in ministerial theology and practice. Finally, we have reconsidered the standard of attainment at the point of ordination and now propose that this norm is the same for all ordinands. We hope in these ways to have built on the points of general agreement and to have met the specific criticisms.

5.34   We comment further on this proposal in the paragraphs that follow.

Proposal 4

We recommend, as a series of norms, that

i)   candidates for ordained ministry should have successfully achieved a minimum of diploma level in ministerial theology and practice before ordination;

ii) they continue with further learning at an agreed level according to their ability in the post-ordination phase of IME;

iii) typically, those who are to hold posts of responsibility (for example, team vicars, some chaplains or incumbents) achieve a minimum of degree level in ministerial theology and practice, or its equivalent, by the time of appointment to a post of responsibility.

5.35   In order to clarify these proposals we wish to underline the following points:

i)   Our primary concern is the *continued learning and ministerial development* of the candidate and minister. While we have used the currency of diplomas and degrees to express and make concrete our thinking, the qualifications themselves are secondary.

ii) These are a set of norms. They are intended to set a general standard, not to constrain or straightjacket either the Church or the candidate. Thus, there will continue to be times when it is right to make decisions in the light of the particular gifts of candidates, even when they do not comply with these norms. At the same time they are intended to set a challenge to candidates and to encourage an ethos of learning.

iii) The language of norms intends a proper flexibility to respond to candidates' actual gifts and abilities. For example, while all clergy should continue their learning and study after ordination, not all will be able to do this at Level 3. Therefore, some clergy may continue their study at Level 2. Further study at Level 3 does not of course assume that the person will exercise ministry in a position of greater responsibility, but Level 3 constitutes a target for those who will.

iv) Candidates who have already achieved degree-level study in the pre-ordination years should of course have an appropriately rigorous programme to enable them to continue learning in the early years of ministry, a programme that could be at postgraduate certificate, diploma or MA level. Thus, we do not wish these norms to be used to reduce standards of attainment for able candidates who in the academic side of training should rightly be expected and encouraged to achieve higher standards than those set out in these norms. In this respect these norms are minimum general standards.

v)   We note the current debate within OLM schemes about the value of academic accreditation and the level at which schemes are validated, ranging from no accreditation at all, via certificate level to diploma level. For those schemes that have academic accreditation, the majority have opted for diploma level. Thus, in principle we do not believe our proposal should present a problem to OLM schemes. We repeat that we are seeking to establish a norm and that it may well be appropriate for individual candidates properly to be exempt from that norm. Nor does our proposal require all OLM schemes to have full academic accreditation – the Church, via the Ministry Division's Educational Validation Panel, can use the diploma level as a benchmark in its work. Thus, this norm should not be applied to constrain the proper concerns of OLM schemes for candidates from weaker educational backgrounds or for a strongly contextual form of training.

5.36 Within our current systems of appointment and patronage, bishops, advised by their staff, will continue to have a vital role in the question of whether and when a curate should be offered a post of responsibility. However, our development of a statement of expectations for ministerial education and the close working of training institution and diocesan staff that we envisage could be of help here. The statement of expectations sets out the qualities that are required to begin the exercise of ordained ministry and then for those who might minister in a post of responsibility. Thus, part of the evidence that the bishop requires could come from the diocesan officer and training institution, in addition to a view from the curate's training incumbent. Thus, the statement of expectations can help in making a publicly defensible judgement, based on criteria, as to whether the candidate has the qualities for the envisaged ministry.

5.37 In this chapter we have outlined our proposals for a new framework for ministerial education, pointed to some of the possible implications of such an approach and dealt with some related issues. We now need to turn to the question of the type of training establishment that the Church needs in order to deliver the flexible, high-quality, integrated training that we envisage.

Chapter 6

Reconfiguring the Church's training resources: proposals concerning training institutions

6.1   As we saw in Chapter 1, the Church of England has an impressive range of training resources in the area of theological and ministerial education – theological colleges, regional courses, OLM schemes, diocesan provision for Reader training, CME, lay training and formal lay theological education, much of which is in partnership with UK universities and church colleges of higher education. The Church of England as an institution does not directly own all these resources – the colleges and courses are governed by their own councils, which as voluntary bodies choose to work with the Church. Some of these resources are shared with partner churches, bringing a valuable ecumenical dimension, which we hope will be strengthened in the future.

6.2   As a Church, we have usually looked at these resources in their constituent parts and emphasized their particular tasks. Thus, historically, the sole purpose of theological colleges was to prepare stipendiary clergy for ordained ministry. However, recent trends in theology, Church policy and organizational practice have begun to shift the emphasis towards trying to make connections between the various parts of the Church's training and educational establishment. To give just two examples, colleges and courses have been encouraged to share resources with each other and to diversify into related fields, while some dioceses have been integrating their Reader training into their other training provision. Given the history of focusing on particular and distinctive purposes, it has not been surprising that progress has been both hard work and slow, if real. While applauding the efforts and achievements in this area, we believe that the time has come to view our training resources as a whole and see if the best examples of partnerships and collaboration offer a model which could be developed, in relation to local circumstances, on a Church-wide basis.

A role for cathedrals?

6.3   Before we pursue this line of thought, we first need to cast our net wider in terms of the possibilities for learning that currently fall outside our provision. We have debated the question whether cathedrals and their chapters should have a primary role in the delivery of clergy training. Some individual members of cathedral chapters are of course already involved. For example, some dioceses site their CME officer on the staff of its cathedral and many members of chapters will contribute to CME programmes and other forms of training. However, in general we do not think that cathedrals and their chapters should have a primary role in the training of the clergy. A move towards training through cathedrals would necessarily lead to 44 institutions, which again would be too small to be effective. Finally, such a move would go against our view that training ought to be set in the context of higher education and vocational training. Thus, we welcome the contribution of cathedrals and their staffs to the training of the clergy and of lay people, but do not believe that ministerial education should be reorganized to focus primarily on these resources.

The place of ICT

6.4   ICT (information and communication technology) is playing an increasing part in the life of the Church and in education and training. It will therefore be asked whether it can be a significant, or even primary, provider for the ministerial education of the future. While it is doubtful that ICT can be the main deliverer of programmes of ministerial education, we think that there will increasingly be a place for ICT as a resource for learning. Thus, we note that communal learning and worship and, secondly, the face-to-face relationship between teachers and learners are central features of ministerial education. Secondly, the set-up costs for going fully down the ICT route would be massive – both in terms of hardware that needs to be maintained and updated, and in the creation of high-quality programmes for teaching and learning. However, there will be real opportunity to complement and improve our current provision by the judicious use of ICT, including making use of the much greater ICT resources of partner institutions in higher education. The full use of the developing role of ICT should be an integral part of any future provision of ministerial and wider theological education.

Towards new institutional arrangements for training

6.5   In this chapter, we wish to challenge the Church to:

i)   view our training resources *as a whole*, including our existing institutions and the potential of UK higher education;

ii)   consider ways of harnessing these resources in a coherent and interconnected way for the mission and ministry of the Church, where possible in partnership with other churches.

This is a very considerable challenge and will require all concerned to rethink cherished ways of working and to change habitual ways of acting. Not least, it will require the existing theological colleges, regional courses, OLM schemes and a range of diocesan training arrangements to develop or change habitual ways of working and to move towards a new pattern of provision. However, we believe that this is demanded of us if we are to make the appropriate provision for the education of the people of God, and within that for the distinctive ministry of the ordained, as well as for Readers, other lay ministers and for formal adult Christian learning.

6.6   Our current system for the ministerial education of the clergy is not intended to provide a form of training that encompasses the pre- and post-ordination phases as an integrated whole. Rather, the baton is passed from theological college, course or OLM scheme to training incumbent and CME officer at ordination – and there is a danger that the baton can be fumbled or even dropped in the process. A proposal for new institutional arrangements could ensure those who are currently responsible for the pre- and post-ordination phases of training work together to deliver and supervise the training. Such arrangements could tackle the structural problem, identified above, that there is currently little or no visible connection between IME and CME (2.6, 4.15–23). They could give candidates a much more coherent sense of their training for ministry, while relieving the pressure on the curriculum in the pre-ordination phase.

Revitalizing the relationship between the Church and the training institutions

6.7   As we have noted, the Church of England has a stake in 40 training institutions providing IME, while the provision for CME 1–4 and beyond is a diocesan responsibility in the 44 dioceses. The two types of establishment are accountable in quite different ways to the Church. Thus, a theological college or course is responsible to its own governing body, while also requiring recognition by the House of Bishops. By contrast, the CME component is responsible to individual diocesan bishops. This organizational division in itself can lead to a lack of confidence between the providers of pre-ordination training and the wider Church.

6.8   While we believe that individual training institutions and the training establishment as a whole has much of which it is rightly proud, it is also the case that there is something of a climate of suspicion within the wider Church with regard to our training institutions. (Similarly, questions are raised about the quality and consistency of CME and diocesan training provision.) This is shown from time to time in questions to General Synod and in other settings. Although, because of its nature, this is a difficult area about which to be precise, these feelings can sometimes underline a range of questions raised in public discussion. These questions would include:

- whether colleges, perceived negatively by some as narrowly academic or quasi-monastic institutions, are an appropriate place to train for the realities of parochial ministry;
- whether courses and OLM schemes provide sufficiently rigorous and extensive theological training, or, on another front, adequate ministerial formation.

These questions, while entirely legitimate in themselves, may show both a lack of knowledge in the wider Church about ministerial education and something of a climate of suspicion between the wider Church and initial training in its current form. *In terms of structures, this situation is related to the lack of sense of ownership of pre-ordination training by the dioceses.* This is felt especially, though not exclusively, of the colleges. Secondly, there are no formal, structured channels of communication between dioceses (as dioceses) and the colleges. More generally, there are few formal points of meeting between, on the one hand, staff of colleges and courses and, on the other, diocesan training staff. For our present purposes, a reconsideration of the institutional arrangements for our training provision could be a very creative opportunity *to revitalize the connections between our institutions and the wider life of the Church.* This last point has both strategic implications in terms of the Church's thinking about ministry and educational implications.

6.9   To this must be added the continuing debate over the place and value of theological colleges founded in a particular tradition of the Church, whether this is evangelical, catholic, radical, liberal or some other form. For some, preparation for ministry in, for example, an evangelical or catholic college is central to their understanding of preparation for ministry; to others, it is a narrowing of what it means to be Anglican. The Church of England at every level has to live with the tension between, on the one hand, allegiance to a particular form of Christian life and understanding and, on the other, allegiance to the Church of England as such, and indeed to the universal, world-wide Church. In our context, one general principle can be articulated: *training for ordination must, in principle, be training for ordained ministry in the Church of England as a whole, and not just part of it.*

6.10   At the same time, the Church of England rightly values its various traditions. Many parishes, clergy, other ministers and lay people are deeply embedded within the particular traditions of the Church and value the opportunity for ordinands and others to learn within them. The advantages of places of formation that are based on individual traditions are:

i) they can offer a theological environment which is coherent and secure;

ii) they are valuable as places where the particular tradition can be explored and be subject to critique without disdain;

iii) they maintain and reinforce the comprehensiveness of an Anglican way of being Church.

If these are the main advantages, our task is to address and minimize the perceived disadvantages of training institutions based on individual traditions:

i) they can restrict engagement with and learning from other traditions;

ii) they can become a locus for party activity, the legitimate tradition narrowing itself or hardening itself to a point where it ceases to be healthy;

iii) where the institution is a college, there is the further possibility of training being removed from the local context of the Church's life, or being limited to the tradition's own expression of the local form of the Church. An example of this would be where a candidate from a party college only undertakes placements in the same tradition as the college.

In response to these points, we would want to affirm the value of training within the individual traditions of the Church but insist on the importance of making those traditions available to the Church as a whole. This is a two-way process. The individual traditions need to continue to engage with the wider Church, including making themselves and their sometimes considerable resources available to the wider Church. Similarly, the wider Church needs to be willing to engage with and learn from the particular traditions. These considerations point to the desirability of a better coordinated use of the Church's training resources.

6.11 With regard to strategic thinking about ministry, dioceses and training institutions have, in different ways, done work in recent years on their understandings of the mission to which the Church is called and the patterns of ministry which will further that mission.[52] While this work is highly commendable, it is remarkable that, with the exception of OLM schemes that are embedded in dioceses, the work has been done in isolation. Thus, the dioceses and the training institutions have both been reflecting in some depth on the mission of the Church of England, but without reference to each other. (There are of course connections between dioceses and training institutions, but not formally at the level of policy about ministry or reflection on a theology of ministry.) New institutional training arrangements, in which the dioceses and our training institutions both had a stake, could release and channel a great deal of creative energy to assist the Church's thinking about its mission. Secondly, if dioceses worked closely with training institutions together they could offer training to current and future clergy in the light of a shared understanding of that mission.

6.12 On the educational front, we have already noted that the area of the coordination of education for clergy, Readers, other lay ministers and some forms of education for Christian lay discipleship would benefit from review (2.7). Each diocese currently draws up its own approach to and curriculum for Reader training (within national guidelines) and for lay ministry schemes. There could be real benefits in sharing good practice and developing curricula together. Additionally, vocations to the ordained ministry often arise out of training undertaken for other forms of ministry and discipleship, and yet there is little coordination of these forms of training. Similarly, there is no widely accepted way of giving credit for studies undertaken for one form of service when a candidate goes on to another. Thus, there is a strong reason in the educational area to consider establishing new types of institutional partnership.

Types of research

6.13   We noted above the value of research as *enabling the Church to think deeply and clearly about specific issues, whether these are theological or whether they initially arise out its mission to the world.* We envisage at least four ways in which the agenda for research might be formed, the last three of which are pertinent to our current theme:

i)   the continuing work of theological and related research in higher education, mainly funded by research scholarships and government postgraduate funding. The Church already plays a small but valuable role here through funding potential theological educators to take research degrees (see 1.23 above).

ii) research that could be closely related to the specialisms that we hope our training institutions might develop in the future (see 6.27 ii). This type of research might well be supported by partnership with a local university or through the raising of endowments and capital for a particular purpose.

iii) research which is commissioned by the Church itself, by a number of bodies – by the House of Bishops, the General Synod, Church house departments, dioceses and others. Thus, there could be a fruitful partnership between a training institution and particular Church bodies that have research needs.

iv) research that is directly related to the practice of ministry, for example, using an action-research model. Thus, the research itself does not need to be carried out directly by the staff of the regional training partnership (RTP), though it should be related to it.

These last points would make a further contribution to our general theme of revitalizing the relationship between the Church and our training institutions.

Addressing the smallness of institutions

6.14   As we have seen, the Church of England's total training resources in the area of ministerial education are currently divided between a large number of mainly small diocesan training establishments, theological colleges, courses and schemes (2.10–12 above). The proposed new institutional arrangements could be of direct benefit here with institutions helping each other in terms of sharing staff expertise. This could include teaching, subject and ministerial expertise, as well as the more technical areas of curriculum design and development, and university and Church accreditation. This proposal has at least two aspects: sharing of teaching resources can enrich the experience of learning for the learner, while, at the same time, it makes much better use of scarce and valuable resources. While this sort of sharing happens already in some locations, it could be much more systematically developed between diocesan training establishments, colleges and courses.

6.15   Similarly, in terms of the training of ordinands and other students, there could be real benefits in new or renewed partnerships. In addition to the bigger pool of staff available, there is the possibility of greater interaction among candidates and learners of different types. Learning about the range of service from continuing lay discipleship to various forms of ministry could be much enhanced by learning together in parts of programmes.

6.16   Thus, new or renewed partnerships could provide high-quality training and education for clergy and lay, on the basis of a greater pool of staff expertise and experience. The quality of the training could in turn be enhanced, and a contribution made to the life of the Church more generally, by ensuring that the institutions include a research dimension. Larger training partnerships would of course need greater management expertise but at least this work would be done to support a range of educational and formational work. Finally, the weight of Church and university quality control processes could be borne much more appropriately by larger training partnerships.

The ecumenical potential

6.17   A reconfiguration of institutional training arrangements would also be a major opportunity to reconsider, build on and develop ecumenical partnership in the training area. It is difficult to be specific here because much will depend on exploration and negotiation of the issues with ecumenical partners. Nonetheless, there is a range of possibilities. Firstly, the potential for ecumenical partnership will vary in different places because the pattern of training resources is very different in the various churches. Secondly, the nature of ecumenical partnership varies significantly from region to region. Sometimes it is at the level of shared academic programmes, sometimes at an institutional level of various sorts. Thirdly, the history of ecumenical partnership varies strongly from area to area. Where there is already good ecumenical practice, this history of collaboration could encourage the formation of the new types of partnerships that we envisage. Where ecumenical partnership is currently not strong, our proposals give an excellent opportunity to revisit the possibilities in a new context. But in principle, new or renewed partnerships offer the opportunity to advance the ecumenical agenda and we strongly recommend that the Church of England take up this opportunity. In addition, we would respectfully invite other churches to review the possibility of new and renewed ecumenical working in the light of this review.

The potential for partnership with UK higher education (HE)

6.18   Our proposals for new institutional training arrangements could also have a significant gain in terms of the Church's partnership with institutions of higher education in the United Kingdom.

i) At the moment it is the task of each individual unit (whether a theological college, course, OLM scheme or diocesan CME or Reader training unit), or groups of units, to negotiate with universities or Church colleges of higher education for the appropriate academic arrangements. This is a time- consuming process for a very small number of students in each case. New institutional training arrangements would clearly be an advantage here, allowing for this specialist task to be undertaken for larger groups of students.

ii) Were they more substantial, the Church's training institutions or partnerships would have more weight in the negotiations, and, therefore, could enter into partnerships on more equal terms. This could lead to mature and mutually beneficial arrangements.

iii) Departments of theology in the universities, with their commitment to intellectual enquiry and research in theology and related fields, continue to be a valued partner for ministerial education. The Church, however, could make a much clearer contribution to the study of Christian theology if its own resources for training were deployed in larger units. Recruitment to the study of Christian theology in universities has ebbed and flowed in recent years and at times some departments are dependent on ministerial students for their health. Thus, our proposal could have the additional advantage that the Church would be making an important contribution to the study of Christian theology in our universities. This in itself should be seen as part of the Church's witness to the Christian faith, held in an intellectually credible way.[53]

iv) The Anglican colleges of higher education have a particular remit to serve the nation by offering a distinctive and Christian character for higher education. They are increasingly seeking to confirm and renew this relationship in the context of ministerial training and in their partnership with dioceses. There is potential here for new and renewed partnership with training institutions, particularly in locations where they have strong theology departments and where they represent the main resource in terms of the study of theology in an HE setting.

The rationale for new or renewed partnerships

6.19   In summary, the Church of England has a good track record in the creation of a variety of types of ministerial and of lay theological education but this has led to a pattern in which resources have been dispersed thinly and lack coordination. While this has come about through complex historical development, it has resulted in a training provision that does not now fully reflect the changes in the Church's models of ministry or of training. Nor do our current structures, which impose a divide between the various forms of training, enable the aspirations of many training institutions to work co-operatively in substantial ways with other training institutions. We believe that there is a case for significant change, building on the current best practice, to bring about the necessary partnership and co-ordination. In order to support the mission and ministry of the Church in the coming decades, there is a need to:

i) reconfigure the Church's training provision to enable it to:

- deliver initial training for the clergy in a coherent way from initial exploration of vocation to the end of the first training post, and beyond;
- set this training provision within a wider framework for other forms of training for ministries and some forms of education for lay discipleship;
- provide opportunity for formal, where possible accredited, theological education for lay people and for those considering a call to ordination, which we have called Education for Discipleship;

ii) reconfigure the substantial training resources used by the Church to:

- create new or renewed partnerships, addressing the issues of the small scale of most of our institutions;
- create partnerships within which a range of types of training would command parity of respect with each other and, collectively, with other institutions of higher education;
- enable equality of access to a range of possibilities for training, including full-time and part-time modes;

iii) serve the Church by incorporating a research element in these new institutions, both to support the teaching programme by developing specialisms (for example in urban[54] or rural ministries) and, more widely, to resource the Church's mission.

6.20   In the light of these points we make our next main proposal.

Proposal 5

We recommend the creation of new institutional arrangements for training through structured and effective partnerships, drawing on diocesan training establishments (including OLM schemes), theological colleges and courses, in collaboration both with other churches and with UK higher education. The purposes of the new training partnerships should be:

i) **to provide initial ministerial education for the clergy from entry into training to the end of the first training post;**

ii) **to develop expertise in particular areas of mission and ministry to enhance training for ordination and other ministries and types of service;**

iii) **to contribute to the initial training of Readers and other lay ministers and to continuing ministerial education for all ministries;**

iv) **to contribute to the formal theological education of the laity through the provision of programmes of Education for Discipleship;**

v) **to provide capacity to do research for the benefit of the Church.**

6.21   We envisage that the new training partnerships would:

i) incorporate the strengths of small groups and units within larger partnerships. There will always be a central place in ministerial education for *personal encounter, worship and learning in small groups and sustained pastoral relationships between principal, staff and candidates*;

ii) include communities of *learning with a particular theological tradition*. All contemporary education needs to engage with a range of views and experience but candidates also benefit from studying in a context that has a particular tradition or traditions;

iii) promote the value of *ecumenical partnership*, broadening the horizons of ordinands, increasing their understanding of other Christian churches and helping them to reflect on and deepen their own ecclesial identity and tradition;

iv) incorporate the value of *diversity*, for example, the benefits of :

- students and candidates for different forms of service to the Church sharing part of their training together;
- students and candidates being introduced to a range of views, ways of Christian life, worship and service, through staff teams and communities of learning with a range of expertise and experience;
- a range of types of residential experience for candidates and a variety of pathways towards ordination and beyond;
- opportunities for shared learning and worship with students on other HE programmes.

6.22   As a church, our starting point is the existing provision for ministerial education and other forms of training. We have set on record some of its main achievements (1.27 above).

Any successful plan for the future will need to harness the considerable financial, staffing and training resources of our whole training establishment – diocesan, college, course and OLM schemes, with their potential for creative partnership both with other churches and with higher education in the United Kingdom.

6.23   Within the current polity of the Church of England, the theological colleges and regional courses are independent bodies, governed by their own councils, rather than by the Church of England directly. If new partnerships are to be formed, the dioceses, other interested churches, colleges and courses will need to become partners in new or renewed partnerships. While we have some experience within ministerial education of creating new institutions[55] or new partnerships with a number of stakeholders, this is a large and sensitive task, which needs to be done well if it is to succeed. Such an undertaking would no doubt require additional, transitional, funding.

Models for the new provision for theological education

6.24   If it is proposed that the Church of England seeks to establish new institutional arrangements for training, the question is immediately raised as to what these arrangements might look like. While in one sense the status quo, as spelt out earlier in this report, is a continuing option for the Church, in the light of the case put forward in this report, it is not one that the working party can commend. The following models all start from the viewpoint of the Church's training resources as a whole and go on to address the underlying issue of the relation of the local, regional and national.

6.25   In its interim report, the working party put forward three broad models for the provision of ministerial and theological education within the Church of England. In summary the models were (1) a distributed model, based on a regional approach, with local delivery, (2) a centralized model, resulting in one national or two provincial staff colleges, complemented by regional and local delivery, (3) a hybrid model, leading to a small number of large institutions, with some regional and local delivery. All three models combined, in varying ways, elements of national, regional and local provision, along with the potential of distance learning and ICT.

6.26   In the consultation on the interim report, there was a range of responses to the three models:

i)   A fair number of respondents stated that the models were not sufficiently developed to engage with and expressed no preference.

ii) In the interim report we wrote of 'new institutions' drawing on the resources of our current training establishment. In the light of the consultation we have clarified that to mean *new or renewed partnerships, resulting in new institutional arrangements for training*.

iii) There has been little support for the centralized model, one national or two provincial institutions, though some pointed to the value of Church-wide standards being located in a central training institution and noted the potential of this model for research and for higher-level CME, along the lines of a staff college.

iv) There has been quite a lot of support for a regional approach, the distributed model, but with the caveat of the importance of mobility for candidates within the Church as a whole and value of some or all centres developing specialisms.

v) Quite a few respondents had read the interim report to mean 'closing all the colleges and starting again', in other words offering a revolutionary, rather than an evolutionary, approach. In this report we have sought to make it clear that we would encourage the Church to build on existing strengths, while creating a structure that would promote effective partnership.

6.27 In the working party's own further reflection on the options we have come to regard the regional approach (option 1) as the preferred and recommended option.

i) Perhaps the strongest reason in its favour is the importance of subsidiarity, giving responsibility to and working at, in structural terms, the lowest level that remains effective. As we wrote in the interim report, *the regional option maintains a strong sense of local connection*. A very clear sense of partnership between the dioceses, other churches in the region, the training institutions and institutions of higher education in the region could be developed. In time, with a significant redirection of the Church's own training resources, their quality and richness could be made much more evenly available across the country. Further, both the Church and the government have been attempting to work in a regional way. However much it is the case that there is no one regional map suitable for all purposes, there is a real sense that regions are becoming a key part of English life.

ii) The regions could develop specialisms because of the particular resources available to them and because of the particular regional context. These specialisms could, for example, include ministry in particular contexts (the city, the countryside and so on) or aspects of theological learning.

iii) Many (though by no means all) students and candidates for ministry would be training within their own region and with others from either their own diocese or a nearby diocese. This would have both practical advantages and in time would build up a sense of a regional identity.

iv) Finally, this option builds on the work of the last ten years since the Lincoln and Hereford reports.[56] As a matter of policy the Church has encouraged regional and institutional partnership and this option would be a development of this policy and would honour the work done by training institutions to implement it.

6.28 These points lead us to make our next main proposal.

Proposal 6

We recommend

i) **the creation of regional theological training partnerships, with each partnership offering the range of training and education listed in Proposal 5;**

ii) **that the House of Bishops grants its recognition for ordination training to these regional training partnerships.**

6.29 As was seen above, one of the main issues to be addressed is the relatively small size of most of our institutions. Correspondingly, the aim should be to increase the size of staff teams and the numbers of students and candidates. This will be one of a range of issues that need to be considered in the decisions to be made about the regions to be established.

As an illustration, if the decision was made to establish eight regions, this would result in partnerships of varying sizes but each partnership would be made up of at least four to six dioceses, the contributions of ecumenical partners, at least one theological college,[57] plus the provision for course-type training and the relevant OLM schemes. This would result in a staffing situation where even the smallest staff would be at least 22,[58] while several would be more than 30. These figures would be the Church of England's contribution and they would be increased where it is possible to benefit from partnership with other churches. Thus, while there would be a range of tasks for the partnerships to carry out, the creation of regional theological training partnerships can powerfully address the issue of the smallness of many of our institutions.

6.30   An important benefit of this approach is that the particular expertise of the partners in an RTP could be made available to the new partnership as a whole. The expertise would include styles of learning and of training and the range of theological and ministerial experience. Thus, there could be a creative interaction between diocesan-related staff and those whose background or expertise is in full-time or part-time modes of training. There would also be scope for regional co-operation between those dioceses offering training for OLM.

6.31   If full-time and part-time modes of training are to be made available across the country as a whole, this model would require either the relocation of some of the existing colleges or the setting-up of new full-time units where these do not exist. For example while our partner churches have resources in the region, there is currently no Anglican theological college in the north-west. Given the historic ties of colleges to the contexts in which they are now set, most will wish to stay in their current locations. However, there have been very positive examples of colleges relocating themselves, for example, the move which saw St John's move to its current site in Nottingham. Thus, there could be relocation or it may be that new full-time units can be founded within the RTPs. With our emphasis on encouraging new patterns of training and on flexibility, these would not need to be full-scale theological colleges but could be developed in the light of local resources, but must be within an RTP.

6.32   This model could be of significant benefit in terms of the recruitment of stipendiary clergy to regions where there is currently no Anglican theological college. The experience of a diocese such as Lincoln, much of which is remote from centres of population and feels cut off from the main centres of national life, is that it is much more difficult to attract stipendiary clergy to work in the diocese since the closure of the Lincoln Theological College. In the past candidates were prepared to move to Lincoln to train, got experience of rural ministry while in training and then some of them either stayed in the diocese or were prepared to move back to it at a later date. Other dioceses would echo this experience – for example, in the north-west where there are both large urban and remote rural contexts but no theological college to attract (younger) stipendiary ordinands. Having a powerful training presence in the regions could help with these important recruitment issues.

6.33   While there are many advantages of a regional approach, for the benefit of the Church of England as a whole and for some candidates, it is vital that there continues to be mobility in training, especially in its full-time mode. Thus, we envisage that as today a significant number of candidates will move from their own diocese to another region to train, for example, to train in a theological college in another region. However, this needs to be regulated so as not to undermine the new regional partnerships and to have a financial discipline. One way of tackling this would be to adapt the Bishops' Agreed Maximum (see 1.12 above), which currently applies only to theological colleges, for this purpose.

Implications for our current training establishment

6.34 As we noted in the interim report, any of the models proposed, while offering substantial benefits in terms of the quality and coherence of training, would have required significant changes for all involved. For the recommended regional option, the main points can be summarized:

i) Dioceses will bring to the partnerships their training and ministry experience (programmes for OLMs, Reader training, and clergy and Reader CME, training for other lay ministries and, where it exists, accredited or formal lay theological education). Rather than being in sole charge in these areas, as equal partners they will vest their control and authority in a new way in the proposed partnerships, alongside other parties. At the same time they will gain a more active voice in matters relating to the training of ordinands and others – through decisions about the overall priorities of the partnership, reconsidering the curriculum in the light of opportunities of a coordinated pre- and post-ordination phase and so on. Like other parties they would have opportunities to contribute to, and benefit from, the whole range of the partnership's activities – training in full-time and various part-time modes, CME 1–4 and beyond, Education for Discipleship, the specialisms that the partnership will evolve and areas of research.

ii) The theological colleges will bring their educational and formational expertise in full-time training. Rather than being in sole charge in the area of training for ordination, as equal partners they would work in the new context of a regional partnership that together will deliver a range of types of training. This will mean combining a Church-wide role in the training of ordinands on full-time routes with a contribution to, and active voice in, regional training of various sorts. They could contribute to the full range of activities listed in i) above.

iii) The regional courses would bring their educational and formational expertise in part-time training. The extent of change for them would depend firstly on the outcome of consultation and decisions about the extent of regions. We take this up below. Secondly, like other parties, rather than being in sole charge over the programmes that they have offered, as equal partners they would work with other partners to offer the full range of training through the regional partnership. However, the provision for training in a part-time mode would no longer be through separate, small institutions but would be part of a bigger, better-resourced, multi-faceted RTP. Those responsible for ordination training in a part-time mode could contribute to the full range of activities listed in i) above.

iv) OLM schemes would bring the educational and formational expertise in a part-time mode with particular emphases on training in the local context and on collaborative approaches. Like other parties, they would no longer be in sole charge of OLM training but, as equal partners, would work to deliver the full range of training. They would both relate to their own diocese and be a part of a larger, well-resourced RTP. Those responsible for OLM training would have an active voice in, opportunities to contribute to, and benefit from the whole range of the partnership's activities listed in i) above.

v) In addition there would of course be implications for the work of the national Church institutions in the area of ministerial and theological education. Issues about the funding framework and inspections and validation are taken up further below in Chapters 7 and 8.

At the same time we believe that the proposed changes would offer many substantial overall benefits – a much better use of the Church's human, training and financial resources, a much more coherent training provision and better-resourced, multi-faceted, larger training partnerships. We set out the gains in more detail in paragraph 9.4 below.

Structures and constitutions

6.35   Under our proposals each RTP would be charged with the responsibility for agreeing a constitutional framework whereby the dioceses, other churches and other stakeholders (for example, theological colleges) establish both the legal entities (e.g. a trust or charitable company) and a Memorandum of Agreement necessary for the smooth operating of the partnership. The model of co-operation chosen by the RTP could vary from region to region. The models could include:

- A covenant between separate and distinct entities, with protocols for co-operation;
- One legal entity providing ordination training, with a covenant relationship with dioceses and other denominations relating to Reader and lay theological education;
- One legal entity where all resources are organizationally subsumed under one legal framework.

We envisage that the creation of RTPs will often involve a process of growing together and that an individual partnership may initially come into being as a covenant and then move forward over a period of years to become one legal entity.   Appendix 7 sets out an illustration of the way in which a RTP may be created and operate. The shape and structure of the individual RTPs should be decided by the dioceses and churches in negotiation with their future partners in each region. If at the end of a stated period an RTP has failed to achieve a negotiated partnership through the refusal of one or more bodies to co-operate, the appropriate Church authorities should consider exercising their powers to withdraw future candidates. With respect to the Church of England, this will mean that the House of Bishops should be invited to recognize the RTPs, not the individual institutions as at present. The form of recognition would mirror the type of partnership that is set up. For example, where a covenant relationship is entered into a constituent institution would be recognized as such within a recognized partnership. Where institutions choose to enter a unitary arrangement, it would be the partnership which would be recognized.

Defining the regions

6.36   The defining of the regions for a Church-wide system of regional theological training partnerships is in itself an important and sensitive task that should not be undertaken without further consultation. In any case, before this detailed piece of work is done, there needs to be a decision in principle that the regional option is confirmed as the preferred and approved option. In process terms, we propose that if the final report of the working party is accepted by the Archbishops' Council, the House of Bishops and the General Synod, then an appropriate body could be asked to do this further piece of work in consultation with dioceses, other churches and training institutions. At the same time it is difficult to make a decision in principle about an option without a clear understanding of how it might work and what it might look like. As a result we have set out some principles and given some illustrative examples to help with this process.

6.37   A major issue is whether or not the boundaries between regions must run along diocesan boundaries or not. Our strong conviction is that it is vital for the regions to be made up of dioceses as a whole *because the intended partnership between the diocese and the training institutions in the proposed regional theological partnerships is central to our vision.* This is partly an ecclesiological matter, because the diocese is a fundamental unit in the life of the Church of England, but it is also a practical one. Thus, if a diocese is going to site resources for CME 1–4, formal adult theological education and OLM training, and potentially for later CME and Reader training, in a regional partnership, they need to do so in one partnership, and not more than one. Equally, if our aim of an IME for clergy that encompasses in a coherent way the pre- and post ordination phases is to be realized, it will be helpful that at least those candidates who have trained within the region will continue to be supervised by the same partnership. Thus, we propose that, in terms of structure, each diocese must relate primarily to one regional theological training partnership. At the same time, we also note that the needs of participating ecumenical partners must be taken into account in the work of defining the regions.

6.38 It is important to state again that this does not mean that candidates or students will only be able to train or study in the region of their sponsoring diocese. The principle we have just articulated should apply to the structural relationships between dioceses and RTPs, and not across the board in terms of candidates or students. With regard to learners, our earlier statements on the importance of *mobility* and *flexibility* in training pathways, and on the value of interchange across the country, are relevant here. There will rightly be movement because of the particular characteristics of some settings – training in a particular tradition of the Church, in the setting of the religious life or in a particular ecumenical setting, or training that includes study at a particular university. We also hope that regional partnerships will develop specialisms, such as ministry in urban or rural contexts, which will attract candidates from outside the region. While OLM and permanent non-stipendiary ministry (PNSM) candidates will continue normally to train locally, it may well be right for many stipendiary candidates to move to train. Equally, as now, because of complex patterns of living and working, some candidates training basically in a part-time mode may well train at a place in relation to their work to facilitate travelling.

6.39 In the light of our proposal that, at a structural level, each diocese relates to one regional partnership, the definition of regions is, unfortunately, not an area in which our proposals can build directly on existing patterns of training. The current regional course boundaries were created to ensure country-wide coverage but without reference to other training establishments or, indeed, in some cases, to diocesan boundaries. They are another example of our training establishment having grown up in an *ad hoc* way and in 'separate boxes', without reference to other forms of training. Thus, some dioceses relate primarily to one course while others regularly send candidates to two or three. To give examples of the latter, the Diocese of Bath and Wells sends candidates to the Southern Theological Education and Training Scheme, the West of England Ministerial Training Course and the South West Ministerial Training Course, while the Diocese of York sends candidates to both the North East Oecumenical Course and the Northern Ordination Course. The corollary of this history is that there will need at the least to be changes in the catchment areas of 'course-type' training or indeed a reconstitution of the courses.

General factors in relation to regions

6.40 The shape of the RTPs should be determined firstly by principled criteria and then by local and historical factors. We are also mindful of some important considerations that arise out of recent experience and reflection on what contributes to effective training.

i) A region needs to be of sufficiently large scale to provide a critical mass of theological, ministerial and educational resources sufficient to their task and to allow for the establishment of a significant training community. Thus the region is likely to be larger than the area covered by any single existing course and to involve a staffing core at least as large as a present course and college combined, plus diocesan staff and those of other churches.

ii) The region also needs to be small enough for the dioceses to have a realistic chance to co-operate as they seek to influence the training on offer. We believe that for this plan for training to succeed, the dioceses and the relevant organizational units of other churches need to become significant stakeholders, clear about the quality, scheme and outcomes of training offered to their candidates and committed to shape the nature of the training partnerships in their region. If that is to happen effectively, then regional boundaries will need to include not less than three dioceses and not more than seven.

iii) The extent of the region also needs to make sense in terms of the actual lives of potential students. Transport routes, patterns of social relationship and diocesan loyalties all play a part in how candidates will perceive themselves in relationship to the training on offer.

Criteria for regional partnerships

6.41 Bearing these factors in mind, we have identified principled criteria that we believe should underlie any regional theological partnership:

i) That every regional partnership should be able to offer *a balanced provision of existing or potential resources*. These should include:

- a residential centre or centres offering facilities necessary for both short- and longer-term residence;

- an existing theological college or colleges, which will bring expertise in full-time modes of training;

- the regional course or courses,[59] which will bring expertise in training in this mode of training;

- the relevant OLM schemes which will bring expertise in this local and contextual form of training;

- diocesan training provision for work-based supervision and learning, CME 1–4 and Reader training and the potential for later CME;

- higher education establishments with theology departments with a proven record in both quality of teaching and research and expertise in vocational and dispersed forms of training;

- a validating body (or, if necessary, bodies) that will enhance the education and training to be offered. This is a complex issue, in which the criteria for choosing can be in conflict. We would value arrangements with higher education institutions that bring, at reasonable cost, additional a) theological and other relevant expertise; b) vocational and training expertise; c) practical regional commitment.

ii) That the partnerships work out and implement a plan to share teaching, learning events, staffing and other resources.

iii) *The capacity to offer programmes under the Education for Discipleship initiative.* We have argued that such studies would strengthen and widen the base of lay education for the churches as well as providing a stepping-stone for candidates training for formal ministries.

iv) That every RTP should be able to provide *the scope for and develop a strategy for future ecumenical development.* This means ensuring that students from different churches but who live in the same locality find themselves relating to the same region. It also assumes that within the partnership there may be a significant contribution of non-Anglican resources.

v) That the partnerships *should have the capacity to develop expertise in particular areas of mission and ministry* and *a research base*, related to their existing and potential theological resources and particular contexts in which they are set.

Once having agreed such criteria, the question of how we draw the regional boundaries becomes a matter for consultation and negotiation. There will be aspects of regional identity and working that only the dioceses, other churches and participating bodies in the locality can know or resolve. However, we offer four possible regional maps for illustrative purposes and in order to highlight some of the issues that will need to be faced.

6.42   Illustrative regional map 1 (p. 85) draws the boundaries as close as possible to those of the existing regional courses while enabling the dioceses to relate to one region. It has the value of causing least disruption to the present regional courses, but beyond that has little to commend it. The boundaries of our existing courses have grown up and evolved because of many – sometimes haphazard – factors and, rather than formalizing that history, we now have the opportunity to re-think the scope for co-operation. More concretely, four of the twelve regions do not include a theological college (south-west, south central, south-east, north-west), and therefore do not meet our first criterion. Equally some of the regions have very small populations and would not have the necessary critical mass (south-west, north-west), thereby not complying with our first general factor.

6.43   Illustrative regional maps 2, 3 and 4 (pp. 86–88) offer eight new regions. Three maps are given in order to illustrate differing options, but they all reflect three assumptions:

i) That we aim for as few regions as possible, without the travelling distances involved becoming unsustainable. The temptation is always to want more, smaller units, but it is our belief that if we multiply beyond eight regions or thereabouts we return to the problem of small-scale partnerships.

ii) That we should build on policy of the Hereford report that set up our current system of eight centres for college training (Durham, Leeds-Mirfield, Nottingham, Birmingham, Oxford, Cambridge, Bristol, London). However, this point needs to be modified by the further issue of the need to provide training in a full-time mode in all the regional partnerships (see 6.31 above).

iii) That there are some demographic characteristics and some diocesan boundaries where there is no ideal solution available. For example, in what way should we divide the north of England with its north-south and east-west lines of communication? Should we treat London as a metropolitan unit or encourage the outer suburbs to relate to outlying dioceses? Should the Northern province contain several regions or should it be one large region? Whichever way we configure some regions, there will always be anomalies. The task then becomes discerning which anomalies are least disruptive to the process of education and training.

We offer these reflections to stimulate thinking on the issue of regional identity and boundaries and to indicate what the regional option might look like in practice. The maps provided attempt to convey some broad options. They are by no means exhaustive in terms of the information they include because they are basically concerned with possible regions based on Church of England dioceses. At the same time in drawing up these illustrative maps we have taken into account the training resources of the Methodist Church and the United Reformed Church that are listed in Appendices 5 and 6. However, we need to repeat that the maps are merely illustrative, and that the defining of regions is a further piece of work to be done once the Church has decided to adopt the idea of regional partnership in principle.

How would regional training partnerships work in practice?

6.44 We have also done some illustrative work on possible management structures for the RTPs. In doing this, it is vital to bear in mind that we envisage there may well be different arrangements in the different RTPs. In 6.35 above we noted the range between a covenant type arrangement and a unitary body. We have given the example of an RTP that initially has a covenant-type arrangement and then later moves to a closer organizational arrangement. There may well be other types of arrangement in addition to these. The purpose of the illustration, set out in Appendix 7, is to show an outline organizational structure, not to be prescriptive about particular outcomes with regard to institutions. In Appendix 8 we then set out three charts which illustrate three organizational possibilities.

6.45 Much work will need to be done creating the proposed new regional theological training partnerships, including thinking through their ways of working. One immediate issue will be the distinction between the programmes which the partnership will itself *deliver* and those programmes and activities which it will *supervise and coordinate.* An example of the former would be IME for the clergy, while examples of the latter might include training for training incumbents or diocesan adult education programmes. Thus, we do not envisage all training and education being directly delivered by the proposed new partnerships. There will be activities where it is entirely appropriate for individual dioceses to offer different programmes, as well as those where (either early on or in time) they will want to share a common approach. Where a diocese wishes to offer its own programme, it will still benefit from being able to draw on the collective expertise and resources of the larger training partnership for its own programme. In addition, there will be the opportunity for learning undertaken to be a given a credit rating, as an incentive to further learning. On the other hand, there are some activities that are currently a diocesan responsibility, notably Reader training, where it could well be right to move to a shared approach, because of the importance of a common standard for Readers across the dioceses.

6.46 In this chapter we have made proposals for the reconfiguring of our training resources through the creation of regional theological training partnerships, thus building on the developments proposed in the Lincoln and Hereford reports. We now turn to the financial dimension of ministerial and theological education.

Illustrative regional map 1 showing the current position adapted to diocesan boundaries

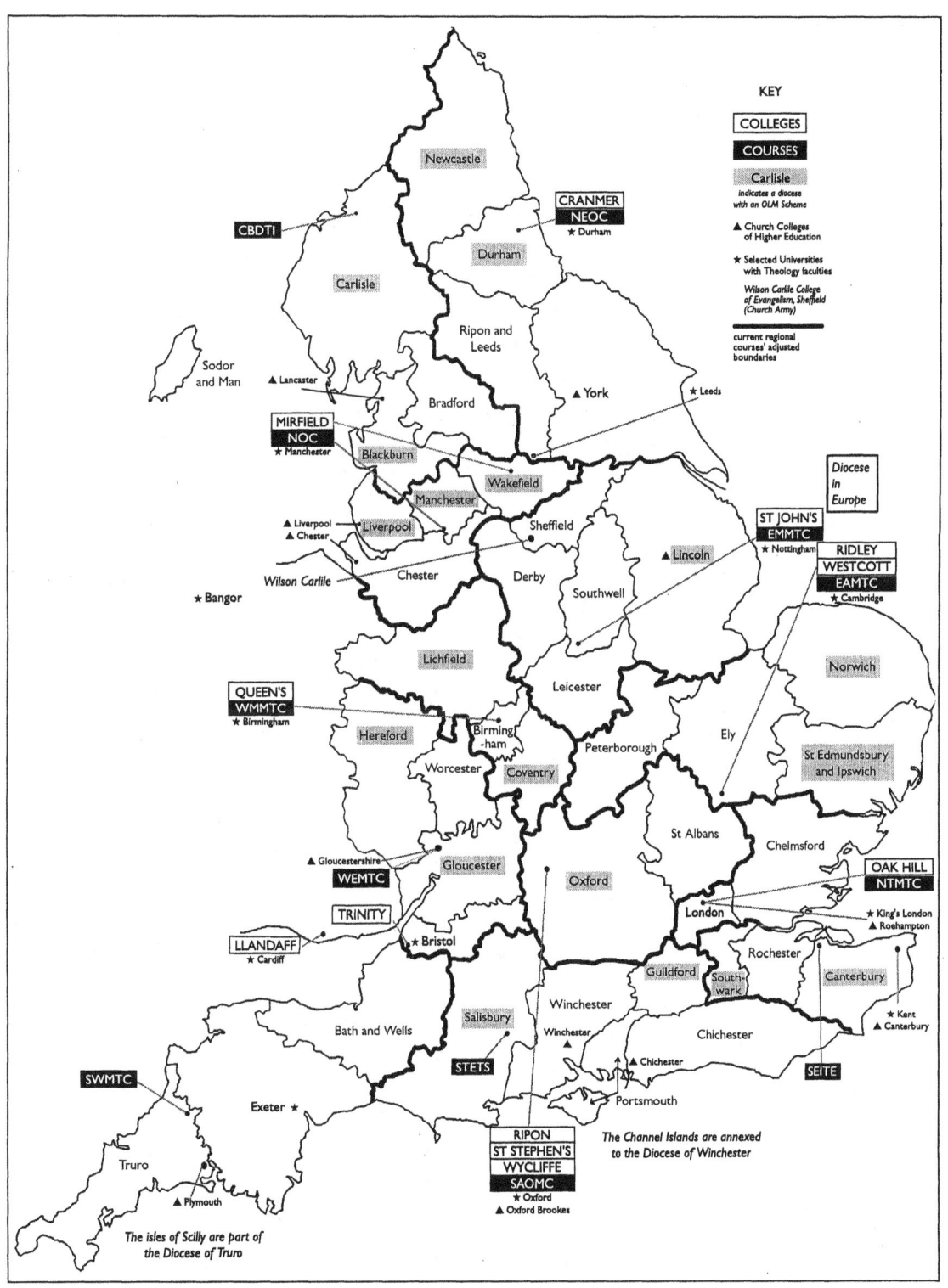

Illustrative regional map 2
showing eight possible regional training partnerships
(example 1)

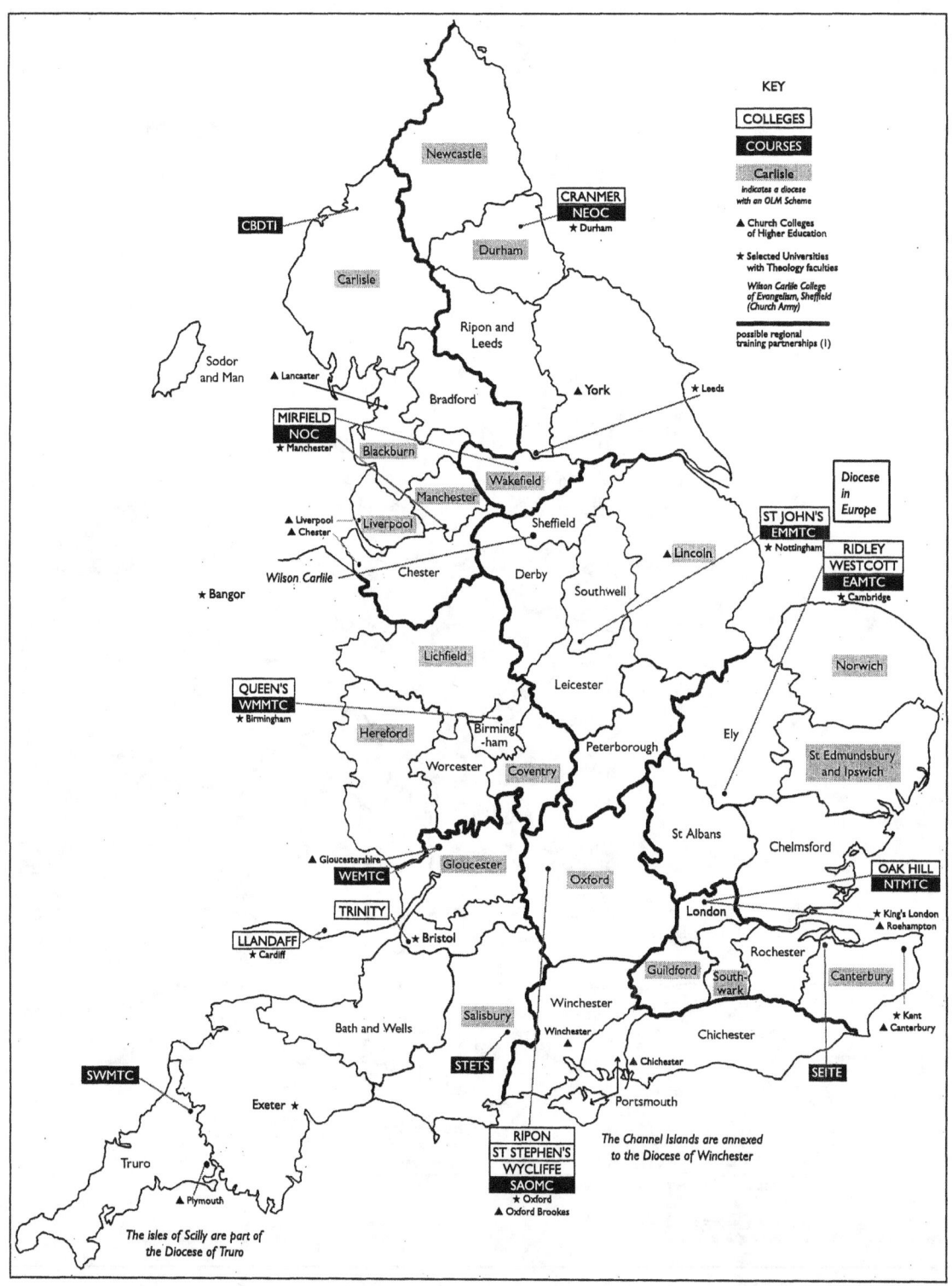

Illustrative regional map 3
showing eight possible regional training partnerships
(example 2)

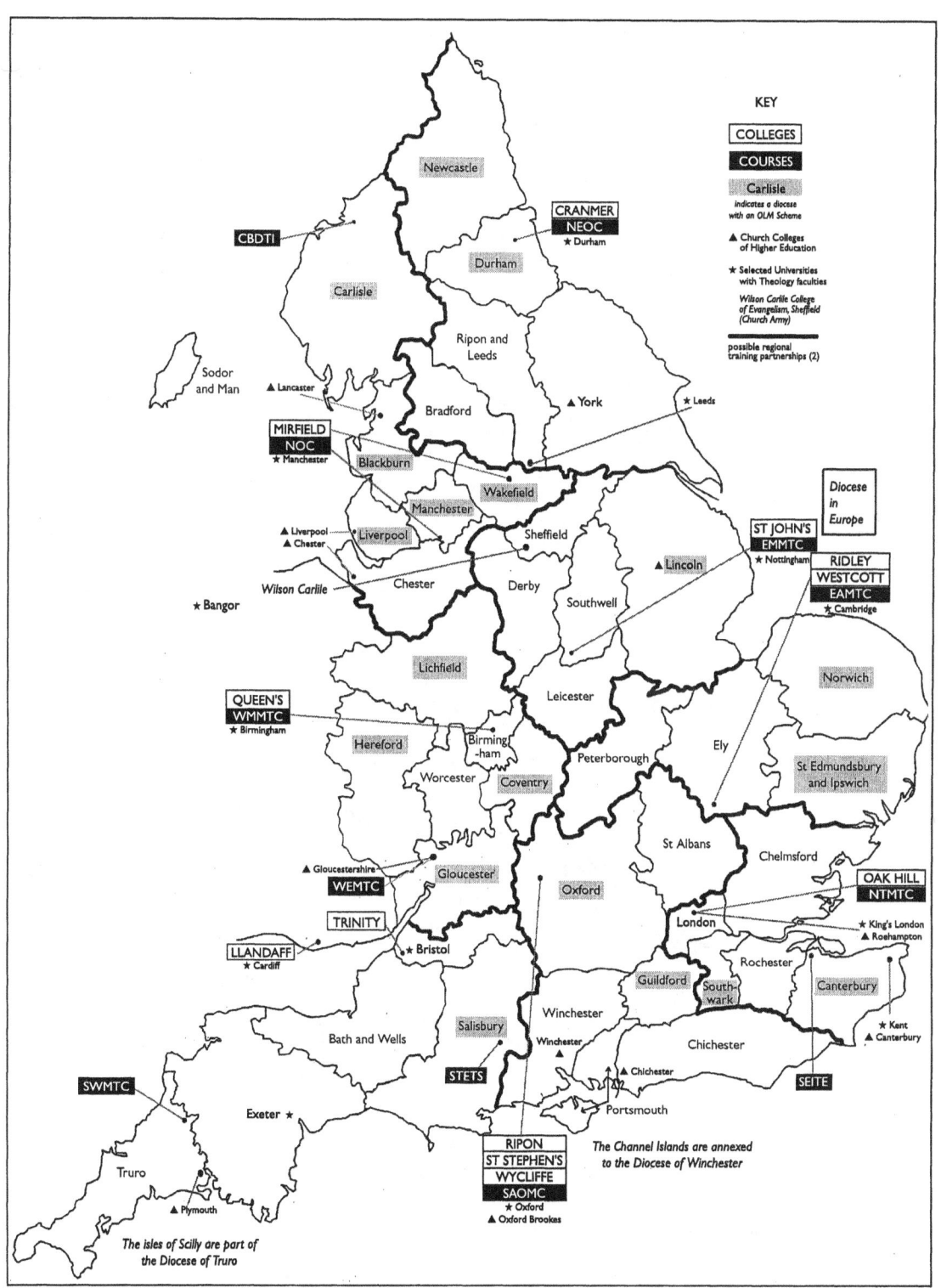

Illustrative regional map 4
showing eight possible regional training partnerships
(example 3)

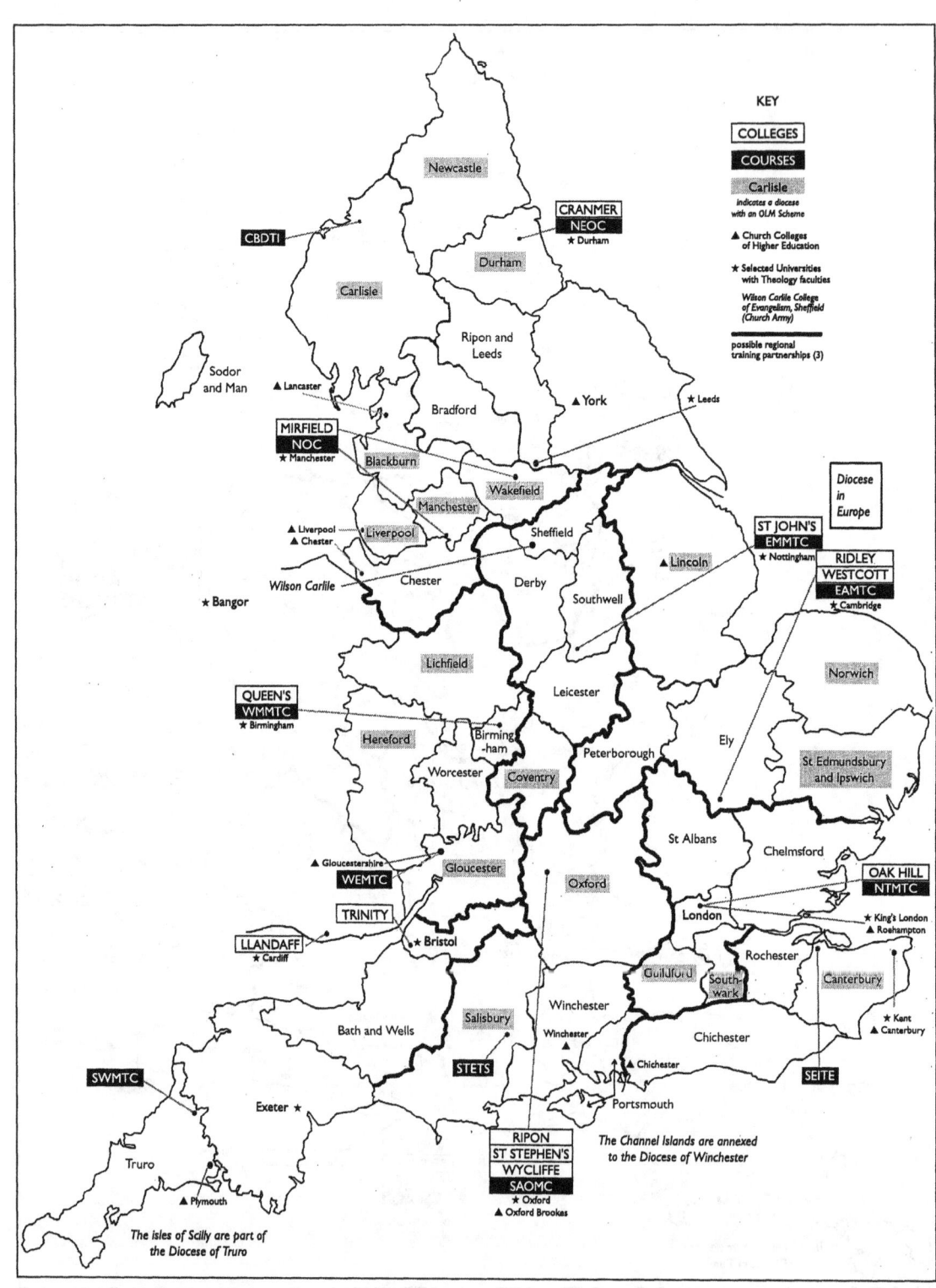

Chapter 7

Financial issues

7.1   In examining the funding of ordination training we have looked at the key drivers of the costs:

- the number of ordinands in the various types of training; the total number is driven by vocations and the split between college and course by the decisions of candidates and bishops advised by DDOs in the context of the bishops' regulations. We address in paragraph 7.10 the view that the simple solution to saving money in the area of ordination training would be a large-scale shift from college- to course-type training;

- the required ratio of staff to students in the different modes of training; the current ratios are set out in paragraph 7.6 and from an educational and formational point of view are believed to be appropriate. However we believe that savings could be achieved through operating together within RTPs as we explore in paragraph 7.11;

- the increasing impact of ICT; the potential for savings through the effective use of ICT is discussed at paragraph 7.11;

- the major impact of the cost of maintenance of ordinands, and their families, in college-type training; this is an area where we believe better value can be obtained by the Church were some of these funds redirected toward teaching resources as we explore in paragraph 7.30;

- the increasing cost of the periods of residence for course-based students; closer working with the colleges could provide helpful savings;

- the duplication of administration in the large number of institutions; this is an area with potential for real savings as we explore in paragraph 7.11;

- the subsidies to central Church funds within the existing fee system relating to some colleges and courses;

- the financial benefit flowing to the Church of the provision of buildings and other resources provided by the trusts which own the colleges. Central Church funding for ordination training does not make provision for the cost of major refurbishment which is required in many cases with older college buildings. Such refurbishment is financed in some cases by borrowing and in others by appeals.

Our work in this area has built on the recent publication and implementation of *Managing Planned Growth* (2000) and its *Supplementary Report*[60] (2001).

7.2   We believe that the ordained ministry is a distinctive gift to the Church. It follows from this that *the Church of England is right to invest significantly in high-quality and cost-effective training of the clergy*. Further, given that the clergy are a very large proportion of the deployable leadership resources of the Church, it again seems entirely right to invest substantially in their training, both initial and continuing training. Most organizations have come to the view that training should not be seen as a drain on resources, but as an opportunity for strategic investment for the sake of the organization as a whole – in our case for the good of the Church and its mission.

7.3   Again, in general, we accept the Church's current approach in which *training for ordination is a charge on the Church*, rather than, for example, on the candidate. This is because our system of reward for the clergy is one of a stipend, rather than salary.[61] Thus, by contrast, while Anglican students in the USA and elsewhere fund themselves through training, subsequent remuneration levels are normally adequate to enable clergy to repay any loans taken out to fund training. This is not a possibility in our case because of the level of the stipend.[62] In addition, our system of broadly uniform stipends has meant that it is possible for stipendiary clergy to move around the country and be genuinely deployable. Seen within this wider picture, it is appropriate for the Church to pay for the initial training of its clergy.

7.4   The Synod budget for the Central Fund for Ministerial Training (known as the Vote 1 budget) is £9,138,000 for the year 2002 and the actual expenditure during year 2001 was £8,667,000. Over the coming year this budget is expected to increase modestly to £9,175,000 in 2003, £9,411,000 in 2004, and to £9,725,000 in 2005.

The budget for the year 2002 and the actual expenditure for 2001 are analysed as follows:

Cost of	Budget Year 2002	Actual Year 2001
Colleges	6,005,658	5,645,621
Courses	2,566,032	2,480,776
OLM Schemes	278,692	249,558
University fees	247,386	265,012
Pre-theological	20,060	7,915
Mixed-mode	20,347	18,560
Total	9,138,175	8,667,442

In addition to the above, the dioceses contribute directly to the training of ordinands by making maintenance payments direct to the individuals. This is currently in the region of £3.1m. Thus the cost of training for ordination is in the region of £12.3m. However, to look at the overall cost of training to the Church, it is also necessary to take into account the estimated costs of CME 1–4 incurred by dioceses, the diocesan contribution to OLM schemes, and diocesan Reader and lay training costs which in total amount to about £3.5m per annum. This brings the total cost of training borne at central and diocesan levels to approximately £15.8m. This is analysed below in chart form.

Financial issues

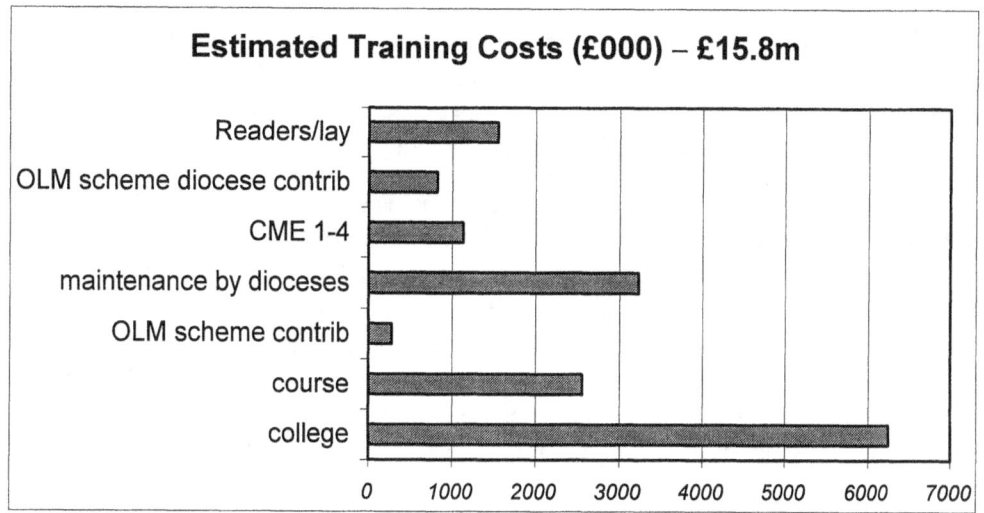

7.5 The actual training costs for the above equates to less than 2 per cent of the Church's estimated total budget which is in the region of £825m and covers stipends and housing, pensions, buildings work and repairs, church running costs and other associated expenditure. In addition, in each diocese there are a large number of parish priests who fill the role of unpaid tutors to individuals and are excluded from the above figures. The service they provide is extremely valuable to the Church as a whole.

7.6 In viewing these costs it is helpful to look at the overall financial position of the colleges and courses. For the academic year 2002/2003 this information, based on the budgets which the colleges and courses have submitted to Ministry Division, is summarized as follows:

		Colleges	Course	Total	2001/2002
Academic					
	Cost	£ 3,461,097	£ 2,205,386	£ 5,666,484	£4,981,505
	Staff numbers	84	43	128	129
Administration					
	Cost	£ 1,757,969	£ 330,973	£ 2,088,942	£ 2,189,072
	Staff numbers	55	16	71	68
Residential					
	Cost	£ 2,594,063	£ 734,818	£ 3,328,881	£ 3,231,124
Total cost		£ 7,813,129	£ 3,271,178	£ 11,084,307	£ 10,401,700
Total student numbers		796	773	1569	1588
Of which sponsored by bishops		621	586	1207	1230
Student/staff ratio					
	Academic	9	18		
	Administration	14	48		

The respective sizes of the institutions, in terms of student numbers, is set out in Appendix 3. We also comment on the student/staff ratios in paragraph 2.10 (iv) above. For colleges, 'residential' covers catering, domestic, and premises costs. For courses, this covers the costs of residential weekends and summer school or equivalent.

7.7   Costs per student in 2002/03 vary in colleges between £11,214 and £7,541 and in courses between £5,641 and £3,190. The amount charged to the Church is in many cases less than cost, because of subsidies from other income, donations or reserves. When expressed as fees per student these amounts vary between £8,919 and £7,533 for colleges (excluding Mirfield for which the fees are £4,773) and between £2,883 and £5,349 for courses. The fees for courses in particular vary because of the impact of geography and the size of the institutions. Details of costs, fees and estimated 'subsidies' for each college and course are shown in Appendix 9. As part of the existing annual budget process, the comparisons between institutions are critically reviewed and more recently the bursars are meeting regularly to identify and share best practice. We discuss in paragraphs 7.49 to 7.52 below the savings which we consider should be achieved by reducing the fixed or core costs of colleges to the level required for the number of ordinands currently training in colleges. Once the RTPs are established there should be further scope for savings in core costs.

Summary of financial proposals

7.8   In the following pages we offer a detailed account of the current situation in the financing of training and of our proposals. In this paragraph we summarize these issues for the sake of clarity. (In this paragraph we have used the current language of candidates training either at a college or on a course.) In overview:

- we assume that the Ministry Division will reduce the base on which core costs for colleges are calculated in order to reflect the current decline in the numbers in college-type training. The full amount would result in a reduction of 75 but this would leave no leeway for any rise in the number of candidates in colleges and therefore we envisage a reduction of 50;

- we assume a saving of 7.5 per cent of administrative and academic costs through the creation of the RTP, reducing costs by about £265,000 per annum;

- we propose that funding remains at a steady level for ordinands currently on courses;

- we propose that there is a movement of 75 from candidates requiring family support from colleges to courses with a view to using the amount saved to pay for our proposals with regard to continuing training in the post-ordination phase. This will produce a saving of about £1,000,000 per annum;

- we propose that half of these 75 places at colleges be used for short periods of residence during CME 1–4;

- we propose that family and personal maintenance should become part of Vote 1, which is cost neutral;

- we propose that these savings, which total about £1,265,000 per annum, should be applied in part to fund additional costs of £1 million for CME 1–4, being £700,000 for accredited training and £300,000 for residence or equivalent training, and to fund £240,000 for research.

Financial issues

- if these proposals are fully implemented there would be no change in the number of candidates being ordained and overall the saving will be in the region of £500,000 per annum.

The following table sets out the projected figures for the coming six years, on the assumption that our proposals are fully implemented by 2008. The 2008 figures represent the projected cost of ordination training for the following years and the level of saving in comparison with the current situation.

Year	Total Vote1 for existing establishment	Reduce core costs by 50 places	Effect of our proposals	Total reduction in costs	Revised total Vote 1
	£	£	£	£	£
2003	12,181,504	-52,946	0	-52,946	12,128,558
2004	12,493,053	-218,680	-120,342	-339,022	12,154,031
2005	12,884,288	-336,561	-540,734	-877,294	12,006,994
2006	13,310,949	-342,899	-621,667	-964,566	12,346,383
2007	13,740,908	-356,615	-273,471	-630,086	13,110,822
2008	14,163,791	-369,810	-128,234	-498,043	13,665,748

We turn now to the detailed discussion of these issues.

7.9 From our overview, and in the light of the work done in the *Supplementary Report*[63] of *Managing Planned Growth*, we have come to the view that the room for significant overall savings in the area of initial training is limited. We discuss these in paragraph 7.11 and in the rest of this chapter. *However, we do believe that the Church can get a higher quality of training for our investment by continuing it into CME1–4.* While quality in training cannot be attained without a proper level of investment, there are ways of improving the financial situation in the area of training.

7.10 Before we review other options, we turn to the view that the simple solution to saving money in the area of ordination training would be a large-scale shift from college- to course-type training. This would save on the level of fees to be paid and on maintenance for candidates and their dependant families. For details see paragraph 7.30 below. (The Church undertakes to provide these ordinands with a maintenance allowance, which enables the ordinands and their families to live at a basic level without the need to borrow, at a cost of approximately £3.1m, as stated in paragraph 7.4.) The scale of the saving would be directly related to the extent of the move from college- to course-type training but it could be considerable. An illustration of the financial effect of a transfer of 150 people requiring family maintenance from college- to course-type training is shown in Illustration 6 at Appendix 14. Thus if the number of ordinands who are maintained by the Church as a whole reduces even marginally the savings could be substantial. These savings could be redirected towards funding the additional educational provision recommended in this report. However, there are good reasons to be set against the view that there should be a substantial transfer from college- to course-type training:

i) For the sake of candidates and for the good of the Church, it is important for the Church to be able to offer IME that is appropriate to the range of training needs presented by candidates. Thus, the Church needs to be able to give younger and some older candidates the opportunity to immerse themselves in a college community dedicated to a common life of worship and service, while undertaking the full-time study of theology and exploration of ministry.

ii) Many young candidates trained in the colleges will go on to give lifelong service to the Church. The initial cost of their training has to be set in the context of 30 to 40 years of faithful service. Older candidates (over 50) rarely train in colleges and under the current rules may only do so if the required short period of college training costs less than the alternative longer period of course training.

iii) If the proposed RTPs are to work and to fulfil their rich potential, it is vital that the theological colleges are deeply involved in the new pattern of training and education. The colleges would bring with them their larger staff teams, their concerns for training, formation and scholarship and their buildings, libraries and other resources.

iv) The Church has invested a great deal through fees and staffing over the years in the colleges, which are, as a result, a significant theological and ministerial resource for the Church as a whole. Furthermore, the Church benefits from the financial investment which their trusts have made over the years.

v) The colleges taken together help to underpin the comprehensiveness of the theological and Church traditions of the Church of England.

Large-scale switching of candidates from colleges to courses would lead directly to the closure of colleges, with the consequent loss of these theological, educational and financial resources to the Church as a whole and an inability of the Church to offer the necessary range of training to candidates. However we are recommending a more modest switch so as to achieve savings but to minimize the loss of resources to the Church. We set out our case in paragraphs 7.45 to 7.55 below.

7.11 We turn now to areas where there may be financial adjustments or savings to be made. These fall into the following categories:

i) We believe our proposals for RTPs would offer significant benefits in the area of education and formation for ministry but they also have financial benefits. Thus, there could be significant savings in terms of financial and administrative services being located in the RTPs, rather than in individual institutions. At the moment each college and course has to employ a bursar and their own small team of administration staff or provide these services, each for a relatively small number of students. There should be real cost benefits if partnerships integrated these services. Total administrative costs for college and courses are at present about £2.2 million. Of this amount the payroll cost amounts to £940,000. As indicated in paragraph 7.6 administrative staff numbers total 71 compared to an academic establishment of 128. By bringing together the administrative arrangements within a regional structure it should be possible to make a net saving of 7.5 per cent of that figure, i.e. £70,000. This is a net saving in that there will be some additional administrative cost in the co-ordinating work of partnerships but this could be more than offset by the potential savings. There will also be one-off reorganization costs

Financial issues

in establishing regional administration which we have estimated at £10,000 per region, say £80,000. (See paragraph 7.60.)

ii) Similarly we believe that there is scope for savings on academic staff costs as a result of the synergies created by full-time, part-time, OLM, CME 1–4, Reader and lay training coming together. The total academic payroll for the colleges and courses is about £2.5 million and we consider that a saving in the order of 7.5 per cent should be achievable. This would amount to about £195,000. This represents a saving of about just over one post per region.

iii) There is also a scope for savings in the development of flexible pathways for individual candidates who might otherwise train full-time, combining part-time and full-time modes, as recommend in paragraph 8.15 below. This is partly a matter of tuition fees to be paid and partly maintenance. As we showed in paragraph 2.22 above, under our present financial arrangements, the Church of England spends about £5.3 million or 45 per cent of its total expenditure on pre-ordination training not directly on ministerial education but on the personal and family maintenance of ordinands in colleges. Of this amount £3.1 million is spent on grants for personal and family maintenance and £2.2 million is the residential element of college costs. If there was more flexibility in terms of the pathways through training, this could lead to savings. For example some candidates might be able to start or finish in a part-time mode, in addition to experiencing training in a full-time mode. We estimate that the quantum of this saving would be the equivalent of 75 ordinands requiring family maintenance moving from college- to course-type training (see paragraph 7.29).

iv) As we will argue in Chapter 8, we wish to offer all the ordained some short-term residence (or equivalent training drawing on the resources of the current colleges) to underpin the post-ordination phase of their IME and to pay for this by a modest reduction in the number of full years of college-based training, plus family maintenance, which the Church currently pays for. This proposal is intended to be cost neutral. Further, where this is practical, we would propose that RTPs should use the theological colleges in their own region for these short-term residentials.

v) There are potential savings in the area of arrangements with institutions of higher education that will allow the Church to benefit directly from public funding. This is a complex issue that we outline in the following paragraphs.

vi) Further savings should be achieved as a result of advances in ICT, which are making communication and the sharing of resource material easier and less expensive. We recommend co-operative working between the RTPs so as to maximize the benefits available from an appropriate use of ICT.

7.12   It has been suggested in the discussion of the draft final report that RTPs could result in the creation of another layer of management with resulting additional expense. We do not consider that this will be necessary but rather that the senior members of staff of the institutions which become part of the partnership (i.e. colleges, courses, OLM schemes and Diocesan CME and lay training teams) would form a partnership senior management team. This group would report to the governing body of the RTP. While the establishment of this team will initially involve more work for those concerned we believe that in the longer term this will result in considerable savings as discussed in 7.11 i) and ii) above. During the discussion of drafts of this report the assumption that modest savings in the costs of administration and academic staff can be achieved has been questioned mainly on the grounds that the experience of regional councils or regional consortia among Colleges of Further and Higher Education has not resulted in savings and has in some cases stifled initiative. We emphasize that in proposing the creation of RTPs we are dealing with institutions of a radically different size to those quoted which are vast compared to the largest RTP. At present we suffer from inefficiency because the individual institutions are so small. We set out in Appendix 7 the way in which we anticipate that the RTPs will operate and in which savings can be achieved. The RTPs, while larger than the existing colleges and courses, will still be small flexible institutions which will be needs-led and which will be able to respond creatively to new opportunities.

7.13   We anticipate that all RTPs will face common tasks, for example in seeking compliance with regulatory authorities, such as Health and Safety, and in performing common functions such as payroll, pensions and employment matters. This area may repay closer investigation in the future but we are mindful of the point that were services to be provided on a single national basis, they would become liable for VAT payment. We conclude this discussion with our next proposal:

Proposal 7

We recommend that regional training partnerships:

i) **share administrative services and academic staff with a view to making savings;**

ii) **work closely together to maximize the benefits obtained from the appropriate use of Information and Communication Technology for learning and for formation.**

Public funding for ministerial and theological education?

7.14   Public funding of higher education is handled by HEFCE, the Higher Education Funding Council for England. HEFCE funding is applicable to institutions recognized for the purposes of delivering higher education and subject to the scrutiny of the Quality Assurance Agency (QAA). It contributes funding in relation to student numbers within institutions of higher education; in addition, the institution is eligible to collect student tuition fees.

7.15   The current situation concerning the benefits of HEFCE funding are extremely complex. Some of our institutes benefit *indirectly* from their association with HEFCE-funded HEIs (higher education institutions): this can range from access to library and ICT facilities, office and teaching accommodation, to reduced rates for academic validation, in addition to the benefits of being a part of a broader community of scholarship. At the present only one of our institutions benefits *directly* (i.e. by receiving a share of the money that HEIs receive from HEFCE), and then not on a large scale. Through discussion of this subject with the theological colleges and courses it has become clear that there is scope for a much more thorough investigation of this topic and a sharing of information between the training institutions. Equally it is apparent that the possibility of HEFCE-related benefits has to be set in the context of other considerations, which we comment on further below.

7.16   One possibility in certain circumstances would be to seek direct benefit from HEFCE funding by training institutions becoming an integral part of an HEI. The Church, through the RTP, would specify its requirements in terms of the education to be offered to ordinands or to other students through a service level agreement. For these purposes there would be a distinction, as now, between the educational programme and the wider programme of formation for ministry. Thus, candidates would work towards an award in HE terms and would also be part of a community of formation. Principals and staff would continue to write reports on the candidates' preparation for ministry as a whole. The HEI could in turn bid to HEFCE for increased HEFCE numbers to take account of ordinands and other students, or it would be happy to accept such students to fill its unused current HEFCE numbers. As long as the HEFCE criteria are met by the HEI, the funding could be available to it. The HEI would receive funding to the tune of £2,770 per year for each full-time equivalent student studying for a first degree, plus £1,100 per year in student tuition fees, with part-time students counting *pro rata* on both counts. Thus a significant proportion of the cost of the educational programme would be paid for directly via HEFCE funding. The Church would pay for the student's additional tuition fee (currently £1,100 per year), plus an amount for the ministerial side of training. Such a system could reduce the total fees paid by the Church, but the extent of the saving would depend on the figures in each locality or region.

7.17　In principle the Church might be able to move all its training to this system. This would be subject to being able to come to an agreement with suitable HEIs, which in turn would need to be sure that this partnership suited their needs as well. However, given the Government's desire to raise the numbers in higher education, for example for mature students and for students recruited from the region, this is a good time to be considering this question.

7.18　Before the Church could contemplate this move it would need to be reassured that its own requirements for communities of formation can be met and that training institutions could continue to reflect the particular traditions of the Church in which they have been founded. In addition to the service level agreement, the key to an acceptable solution would be arrangements for the joint appointment of staff on behalf of the HEI and the RTP. Further, there would be no problem in the Church continuing to carry out its own quality control measures, which would be regarded as a 'professional' inspection and validation regime.

7.19　The other caveat to enter at this stage is that once a ministerial training institute is part of a university or church college, it becomes subject to the HEI's own review of its operations. Some small Theology or Religious Studies departments have been closed because they are not deemed viable on the university's terms. Further, there is no guarantee that an HEI will use the funding it has received for particular programmes to support those programmes indefinitely. Therefore, in pursuing this issue, firstly, it will be important to ensure that the relevant HEIs see ministerial and theological education as part of their mission, rather than just in terms of numbers, and, secondly, that, as we propose above, RTPs are sufficiently large in scale so that their student numbers are significant within an HEI.

7.20　Finally, we note that the pursuit of HEFCE funding will not be possible in every location and certainly not in a uniform way. Some of the traditional universities are willing to embrace ministerial training programmes but would not wish to do so if these students counted in their HEFCE numbers. (For example, a university with very high entry standards for undergraduate programmes would have to apply the same entry standards to ministerial candidates if such candidates were to be counted for HEFCE purposes.) Thus, on this subject as others, there is a need to proceed by looking at the possibility, benefits and costs of partnership. Given the complexity of the situation and the prospects of increased indirect and direct financial benefits, we would recommend that the Ministry Division's Finance Panel and the proposed RTPs continue to investigate and evaluate the possibilities of public funding.

7.21 In the light of these factors we make the following proposal:

Proposal 8

We recommend that the Ministry Division and the proposed regional partnerships should investigate further and evaluate the possibility of benefiting from HEFCE funding.

A funding framework

7.22 At present the Church funds the individual colleges and courses in relation to projected and actual student numbers. *Managing Planned Growth* instituted a system that seeks to avoid the sudden changes in the budget to the Church as a whole, brought about through the inevitable fluctuations in the number of candidates coming forward, and, further, gives a measure of stability to the colleges and courses by differentiating between core and variable costs. A financial framework for the future should build on this approach that rightly *strikes a balance between the Church valuing its theological and training resources on the one hand and being able to respond to the changes in the number and type of candidates coming forward on the other.*

7.23 Firstly, a financial framework should be consistent with and promote the reconfiguration of the Church's training resources, as proposed above. This will mean that the Church should enable the following purposes, as set out in 6.20 above, in part financed centrally and in part through individual dioceses:

i) to provide initial ministerial education for the clergy from entry into training to the end of the first training post;

ii) to develop expertise in particular areas of mission and ministry to enhance training for ordination and other ministries and types of service;

iii) to contribute to the initial training of Readers and other lay ministers and to continuing ministerial education for all ministries;

iv) to contribute to the formal theological education of the laity through the provision of programmes of Education for Discipleship;

v) to provide capacity to do research for the benefit of the Church.

Secondly, it will mean the funding of RTPs, rather than the individual institutions in the first instance. If the partnerships are to be effective, it is important that the money comes to them in the first instance as funding and financial planning should be handled for the partnership as a whole. This would also act as an incentive for developing the partnership in terms of sharing administrative and staff costs.

Thirdly, the financial framework should be designed to ensure that:

(i) the allocation of funding is 'needs led' not 'provider led';

(ii) quality is protected;

(iii) efficiencies are achieved;

(iv) the RTPs focus on the implementation of the proposals in this report;

(v) in the event of an overall reduction in Vote 1 the RTPs could reduce capacity without sacrificing quality;

(vi) if numbers in training subsequently increase the RTPs have the capacity to train those recommended.

7.24 In the light of these fundamentals we envisage a procedure in which the RTPs will bid for funding from the Ministry Division annually, covering the following three-year period for those purposes listed above which will be funded centrally (i.e. in paragraph 7.23 above i), ii), the CME 1–4 part of iii) and v)). For the sake of transparency money will be earmarked for and paid to particular institutions or purposes. Thus, for example, while budgets will be considered by the Finance Panel for RTPs as a whole, the funding agreed for the full-time and part-time training institutions will be determined separately and while colleges remain as separate legal entities payments will be made directly to them. The bids will be scrutinized and decided on by the Ministry Division's Finance Panel in the light of the General Synod's setting of the overall budget for theological training, as at present. Partnerships would be asked to give target numbers for each form of training. If they achieve these within plus or minus 5 per cent, then the budget figure stands; if they go over these limits they would not get any more funding but if they go under them money could be clawed back. Because this process would be annual, there would continue to be a regular system of monitoring numbers and of adjusting budgets in the light of the trends of candidates and other learners.

Proposal 9

We recommend that the regional training partnerships bid for funds on a three-year rolling basis from the Ministry Division.

7.25 The decision how to deploy their staff and other resources within the partnership will be taken within the RTP. However, the decisions will be subject to annual scrutiny by the Ministry Division's Finance Panel in the course of setting budgets, as at present. This work would be done on behalf of the General Synod and exercises a proper accountability for funding of training.

7.26 The precise relationship between the dioceses and the RTPs will depend both upon local negotiation and on the structure of the RTP, i.e. whether it is a unitary body, a legal grouping or a covenant. (See 6.35 above.) We therefore set out the broad principles of the ways in which we propose that the RTPs and the dioceses should initially relate to one another with regard to OLM training (where applicable), the post-ordination phase of IME, Reader training and other lay training including Education for Discipleship. We recognize that these relationships will develop over time.

7.27 With regard to OLM training, the post-ordination phase of IME for the clergy, Reader training and other lay training including Education for Discipleship, we envisage that diocesan officers would continue to be paid by their own dioceses but would be committed by their dioceses to work within the setting of the RTP for the relevant aspects of their work. (If HEFCE funding is involved, they may further have to be approved by the relevant HEI.) As the arrangements develop and as staff are replaced we propose that all new staff should be subject to selection by the dioceses involved in conjunction with the RTP, using a joint selection panel, so that both the diocese and the RTP affirm the appointment of new staff. If so desired by all the parties, staff could be transferred from the diocese to the RTP, with the dioceses undertaking to make an equivalent financial contribution in return for a service level agreement. This does not preclude the diocese's own personnel being involved in aspects of the design or delivery of programmes.

7.28 We propose that the following principles should apply to the financial relationship between a diocese and an RTP:

- for an OLM scheme the diocese should continue to meet the costs of the scheme subject to a deduction in respect of the central contribution paid to the RTP from Vote 1. Vote 1 would continue to provide for a central contribution to the cost of OLM training as at present and these grants would be paid to the RTPs;

- for what is at present CME 1–4 the overall level of each diocese's contribution to the RTP in terms of staff and financial input should be the same as that undertaken in 2002 after adjustment for any changes in the number of clergy in this category. The increased educational provision will be funded from Vote 1;

- Reader training would be funded by the diocese either by providing the staff who would operate as part of the RTP or by paying the equivalent cost;

- lay training and programmes of Education for Discipleship would be funded by the diocese either by providing the staff who would operate as part of the RTP or by paying the equivalent cost and/or by personal contributions by those attending.

7.29 We are committed to making additional investment for the post-ordination phase of IME. This additional investment is directly linked with the proposed reduction in expenditure on the pre-ordination phase of IME as a result of the introduction of flexible pathways which we estimate will have the effect of reducing the costs of pre-ordination training by the equivalent of 75 ordinands moving from full-time to part-time type training. (See 7.11 (iii)). It is difficult at this stage to prepare a definitive budget of the costs of implementing our proposals but the main additional cost will be accredited study in the post-ordination phase. Assuming that there will be 265 stipendiary and 245 non-stipendiary and OLM ordinations per annum, at any time there would be about 1,060 stipendiary clergy and 980 non-stipendiary and OLM clergy in CME 1–4. Some of these stipendiary clergy will already have achieved degree level in ministerial theology and practice but many will not. Recognizing that the average fee per person for degree level training is about £1,000 per annum, this would imply total costs in the region of £2,040,000 per annum. We focus on the degree students because of their number while recognizing that other clergy will be training at a higher level and some on non-accredited programmes. However there are a number of factors which will mitigate this cost:

i) Dioceses are already making a contribution in excess of £1,000,000 per annum to CME 1–4 training, and part of this is for degree-level training.

ii) Some people's training will cost significantly less than £1,000 per annum.

iii) The time constraints on many non-stipendiary clergy and OLMs are likely to result in only a modest proportion undertaking these studies at a full cost of £1,000 per annum.

We propose that additional budgetary provision initially in the region of £700,000 per annum should be established for CME 1–4. In addition we propose that residential training (or other training opportunity) with a value, on a full cost basis, of £300,000 be made available for people in CME 1–4, being the approximate cost of 37.5 places in residential training, being half the places vacated by students requiring family maintenance transferring to part-time training (see 7.30 below). On the basis of a 30-week academic year this represents 1,125 weeks of residential study, which is equivalent to approximately one week each two years for all stipendiary, non-stipendiary and OLM clergy involved in CME 1–4. This is a cost of £267

Financial issues

per person per week. This will make a total of £1,000,000 per annum available for CME 1–4 in addition to existing diocesan provision. The RTP in consultation with the relevant diocesan CME officer should have flexibility in the use of these funds so as to be able to ensure that they are applied fairly to the clergy in a training post in the most appropriate way for each individual. We recommend that RTPs should be allocated these funds on a three-year rolling basis.

7.30 These funds would need to be found from cost savings in the pre-ordination phase, and probably by a modest reduction in whole years of training in the colleges, as the trend continues for older candidates requiring family maintenance to train in a part-time mode. Our proposal would be that there needs to be a reduction in the number of candidates training full-time and requiring family maintenance of around 75 from the number in the 2002 budget, i.e. from 360 to 285. The approximate costs per person per annum (at 2003 levels) of full-time and part-time training are as follows:

- Full-time training
    - College core and variable costs   £8,400
    - Allowances   £1,900
    - University fees   £ 500
    - Family maintenance   £9,306
    - Single maintenance   £1,064

- Part-time training
    - Course core and variable costs   £3,865
    - Allowances   £ 516

This reduction of 75 in the number of candidates training full-time and requiring family maintenance would (at 2003 cost levels) save net costs of around £1,017,000 per annum as shown below. This consists of a reduction of £1,508,000 in the costs of people training full-time and an increase of £491,000 in the costs of people training part-time. For this purpose we have assumed that these 75 people would have trained full-time for two years and that they will train part-time for three years, thus creating an extra 112 part-time students.

			£
Savings in:			
College costs	75 people at £8,400		630,000
Allowances and university fees	75 people at £2,400		180,000
Family maintenance	75 people at £9,306		698,000
			1,508,000

Less			
Course costs	112 people at £3,865	432,880	
Allowances	112 people at £ 516	57,800	
			490,680
Net saving			1,017,320

In effect, as a Church:

i) we will be saving about £1,000,000 per annum by transferring 75 people requiring family maintenance from college-type training to course-type training;

ii) we will reinvest this amount with £700,000 going into fees and further accredited training and £300,000 to the new component of CME 1–4 (see 7.29 above);

iii) while colleges will lose funding for pre-ordination training for 75 students, being about £630,000, they should receive about half of this amount (£300,000) through providing the residential element of CME 1–4.

7.31 We would like to have been able to recommend higher budgetary provision for CME 1–4 but we recognize fully the need at least to contain costs within the present budgetary levels and if possible to make overall savings. We believe that this additional provision for CME 1–4 would represent a significant improvement in the overall quality of our ordination training. It would, of course, be possible to vary the amounts involved by:

- varying the reduction in the number of candidates requiring family support who train in colleges, either by increasing or decreasing it. We note that there is in any event a trend from colleges towards courses;

- Applying any savings on additional training in CME 1–4 towards the cost of degree-level training or vice versa.

By requiring RTPs to submit proposals relating to the proposed use of these funds before an allocation is made on a three-year rolling basis this will enable the way in which these funds are used to be monitored by the Ministry Division's Finance Panel to ensure value for money and to assess in the light of experience whether the financial provision proposed is adequate, inadequate or excessive. However the control of the use of these funds will be in the hands of the dioceses and the RTPs.

7.32 The broad principles of our approach are summed up in our next proposal.

Proposal 10

We recommend that:

i) diocesan officers for OLM training, for the post-ordination phase of IME of the clergy, for Reader and other lay theological education including Education for Discipleship should continue to be provided by their own dioceses but are committed by their dioceses to work within the regional partnership for the relevant aspects of their work;

ii) **savings initially in the region of £1,000,000 per annum should be made within Vote 1 by a reduction of about 75 in the number of people requiring family support who train on a full-time basis and that this saving be used to fund additional costs of CME 1–4, being £700,000 for accredited training and £300,000 for residence or equivalent training.**

Funding research

7.33 An important part of our proposals is that adequate funding should be provided to the RTPs to enable them to undertake research to enable the Church to think deeply and clearly about specific issues, whether these are theological or whether they initially arise out of its mission to the world. Our reasons for recommending specific funding for research are discussed in more detail in paragraphs 2.13, 2.14 and 6.13 above. We consider that an enhanced capacity to undertake research and to work closely with other parts of the Church on research projects will help revitalize the relationship between the Church and our training institutions. We recommend that the overall level of the Vote 1 budget should be adequate to enable an element of research to be undertaken within each RTP. Initially we have in mind an overall provision broadly equivalent to one post per RTP. On the assumption of eight regions this would cost about £240,000 per annum. As for other funds, the RTPs would be required to bid for these funds and the allocation between regions may vary. We recommend that this is funded out of the proposed savings totalling about £265,000, on administrative and academic staff costs outlined in 7.11 (i) and (ii) above above. Further, we hope that RTPs will also enter into partnership with institutions of higher education, other church bodies or sources of funding to build up their research bases.

7.34 **Proposal 11**

We recommend that budgetary provision initially in the region of £240,000 in total per annum should be made within Vote 1 to fund research within each regional training partnership.

Controlling the Church's expenditure on training

7.35 As a church, we have to hold together the need for future ministers, trained to a good standard, and the need to act responsibly with regard to the costs of training. The Church of England currently has two main mechanisms for controlling expenditure on training. Firstly, in an annual process, the costs, budgets and projections of theological colleges and courses are scrutinized, adjusted and approved by the Ministry Division's Finance Panel. The total budget is then further scrutinized by the Finance Committee of the Archbishops' Council. Secondly, the General Synod is asked each year to approve the budget for training for the coming year in the light of the projected number of candidates coming forward. Since the approach set out in *Managing Planned Growth* was adopted in 2000 there is proper linkage between these two processes so that the Ministry Division's Finance Panel has to work within the parameters set by the General Synod. This is a good mechanism, allowing the Synod, on behalf of the Church as a whole, both to note the trends in terms of the numbers of candidates coming forward and, in conjunction with the work done through the committees of the Archbishops'

Council, to exercise control over expenditure. The Archbishops' Council is also able to monitor the balance between the numbers of stipendiary clergy which dioceses project as needing and being able to afford, and these coming through the training to ordination. For the future, we recommend that the same processes be used, but in relation to the proposed RTPs.

Administering personal and family maintenance

7.36   At present the costs of personal and family maintenance for married and single candidates are shared by the dioceses through a combination of:

i) diocesan scrutiny of family budgets on the basis of a nationally produced *pro forma* and guidelines;

ii) an adjustment of the level of diocesan apportionment in the light of the total cost of family maintenance.

In this way the Church rightly shares the cost of personal and family maintenance so that all benefit from the supply of future clergy without penalizing financially the dioceses that produce more ordinands. We continue to support this principle, which reflects the points that the ordained ministry is a gift to the Church as a whole and that the financial cost of training is a cost on the Church as a whole.

7.37   We propose that personal and family maintenance for married and single students should continue to be administered at diocesan level, normally by the diocesan director of ordinands (DDO) in collaboration with a diocesan finance officer, but that the budget should be transferred to become part of Vote 1. This would be cost neutral so far as the dioceses are concerned as the cost of personal and family maintenance would be removed as a direct cost from diocesan budgets and the apportionment of Vote 1 would be increased by the same amount. This mechanism will enable any budgeted savings on family maintenance costs resulting from a reduction in the periods spent training in a full-time mode to be re-allocated to fund the increased expenditure on education.

7.38   It is important that the cost of personal and family maintenance should not be a completely open-ended commitment leading to the possibilities of budget overruns and of requiring a supplementary vote. Therefore we propose that the Ministry Division's Finance Panel should allocate the personal and family maintenance budget between dioceses initially on the basis of existing experience, but in future through a bidding process. DDOs, who should be familiar with the ordinands' personal circumstances, would therefore review claims for maintenance as at present. Payment would be made by the diocese who would be reimbursed by the Ministry Division on a quarterly basis, provided the expenditure is within the approved budget. In the event that the diocesan portion of the budget for a particular year has already been committed it may be necessary for a candidate to defer starting training unless additional funds become available from Ministry Division from unused allocated funds elsewhere.

Revising the scope of Vote 1

7.39   At present the use of Vote 1 is restricted to the costs of pre-ordination training. Our proposals that IME should be reconfigured as the period from entry into training to the end of the first training post and that additional provision should be made for research leads to our next financial proposal:

Proposal 12

We recommend that the scope of Vote 1 should be expanded to cover all central costs of initial ministerial education as defined in Proposal 1, including personal and family maintenance for married and single candidates and research.

Three-year Rolling Reserve

7.40 As recommended in *Managing Planned Growth*, if in any year the expenditure on Vote 1 is less than budget, the saving is held in a Three-year Rolling Reserve so as to be available to meet any overspends in subsequent years. If the saving is not used within three years it is released and is either used to increase the Training Reserve or forms a reduction of the apportionment to dioceses. The Three-year Rolling Reserve mechanism came into operation on 1 January 2001. The saving in year 2001 was £225,000. There was a further saving of about £343,000 in 2002. It also appears that the numbers in training will be below budget in 2003 thus giving rise to further saving and an increase in the Rolling Reserve. In view of the size of the balance on the reserve at 31 December 2002, the balance was reduced to £400,000 by returning £168,000 to the dioceses in the 2004 apportionment.

7.41 The purpose of the reserve is to avoid the need for a Supplementary Vote if there is a sharp upturn in the number of candidates in training for ordination. It therefore needs to be considered whether this arrangement should continue in the future if the proposals of this report are adopted. We have recommended above that once the funds are available for allocation to the RTPs there should be no provision for additional payments to the RTPs in the event that they take more candidates than budgeted. However it needs to be decided whether the amount available for allocation should be limited to the amount in the General Synod budget or whether it could include the amounts available from the Rolling Reserve.

7.42 We consider that it would be important for the Rolling Reserve mechanism to be retained so that, with the approval of Synod, it can continue to be available to smooth the impact on Vote 1 of any approved increase in the funding required to meet the training needs of the Church as a result of an increase in the number of sponsored candidates.

7.43

Proposal 13

We recommend that the Three-year Rolling Reserve mechanism be retained and that, subject to approval by Synod, any available balance may be used, as now, to smooth the impact on Vote 1 of any approved increase in the funding required as a result of an increase in the number of sponsored candidates.

The size of the Regional Training Partnerships

7.44   From the table below, the revised budget for Vote 1, excluding personal and family maintenance, would be *c.* £9.8m. To consider the potential size of the RTPs we need to add the existing £3.5m diocesan costs for the CME 1–4, OLM, Reader and lay training (see para 7.4) to give a total budget for expenses of RTPs of £13.3m. With the recommendation of there being eight RTPs this would give a typical regional budget of about £1.5m. The academic staff numbers would be about 20–25 per region.

Vote 1

7.45 We summarize below the effect on the Vote 1 forecast for 2003 of the proposals in this section, as if they had been implemented in full.

Summary of proposals

	Forecast 2003	Effect of transfer of 75 people requiring family maintenance to part-time training	Savings on administration payroll	Savings on academic payroll	Costs of CME 1–4	Costs of research	Revised Vote 1 at 2003 prices
COLLEGES	£	£	£	£	£	£	£
College core costs	4,070,230	-496,370	-48,247	-107,216	240,000		3,658,398
College variable costs	909,571	-133,630			60,000		835,941
Total	4,979,802	-630,000	-48,247	-107,216	300,000	0	4,494,339
Allowances	1,027,455	-142,702					884,753
Total colleges	6,007,257	-772,702	-48,247	-107,216	300,000	0	5,379,092
COURSES							
Course core costs	1,519,541	288,455	-21,696	-88,140			1,698,160
Course variable costs	759,137	144,425					903,562
Total	2,278,678	432,880	-21,696	-88,140	0	0	2,601,722
Allowances	304,483	57,800					362,283
Total Courses	2,583,161	490,680	-21,696	-88,140	0	0	2,964,005
CME 1–4 fees					700,000		700,000
Research						240,000	240,000
OLM schemes	279,112						279,112
University fees	264,262	-37,298					226,964
Pre-theological	16,665						16,665
Mixed mode	24,614						24,614
Total Vote 1 at present	9,175,071	-319,320	-69,943	-195,356	1,000,000	240,000	9,830,452
Personal and family maintenance	3,006,433	-698,000					2,308,433
Total Vote 1 as proposed	12,181,504	-1,017,320	-69,943	-195,356	1,000,000	240,000	12,138,886

7.46 The following table shows the projected effect on the Vote 1 forecasts for 2003 to 2008 of the proposals in this section, assuming that they are implemented over the period from 2004 to 2007 and are fully implemented by 2008.

Illustration 1a
Summarized effect of proposals

	2003	2004	2005	2006	2007	2008
	£	£	£	£	£	£
Forecast Vote 1 at present	9,175,071	9,411,459	9,725,654	10,073,349	10,422,368	10,762,288
Personal and family maintenance	3,006,433	3,081,594	3,158,634	3,237,600	3,318,540	3,401,503
Total Vote 1 as proposed	12,181,504	12,493,053	12,884,288	13,310,949	13,740,908	14,163,791
Effect of transferring to part-time training 75 people training for two years full-time and requiring family support						
change in variable costs		-54,964	-225,508	-334,679	-343,046	-351,623
change in family maintenance		-124,008	-508,434	-751,651	-770,442	-789,703
reduction in core costs		-88,355	-355,512	-537,740	-559,250	-579,942
additional part-time costs		61,151	255,638	426,967	569,293	588,144
Net effect		-206,176	-833,815	-1,197,104	-1,103,446	-1,133,124
CME 1–4 residential costs		27,501	113,208	203,721	299,040	368,460
CME 1–4 course fees		58,333	233,333	408,333	583,333	700,000
Savings of 7.5% on academic staff pay			-97,586	-202,977	-214,881	-223,114
Savings of 7.5% on administration staff pay			-35,873	-73,641	-77,518	-80,456
Research			80,000	240,000	240,000	240,000
Adjusted forecast for Vote 1	12,181,504	12,372,711	12,343,554	12,689,282	13,467,437	14,035,557
Analysis of adjusted forecast						
Full-time	9,319,231	9,265,351	8,840,578	8,746,186	9,126,275	9,474,210
Part-time	2,583,161	2,805,753	3,191,115	3,623,439	4,013,513	4,225,507
OLM	279,112	301,607	311,861	319,658	327,649	335,840
Total	12,181,504	12,372,711	12,343,554	12,689,282	13,467,437	14,035,557
Net savings	0	120,342	540,734	621,667	273,471	128,234

As approved budgets are not available beyond 2003, the projected costs for subsequent years that are set out in more detail in Appendix 10 have been prepared assuming student numbers remain at levels for 2002/03. These projections are shown until 2008 by which time, on the assumptions adopted, the proposals discussed in this report would have been fully implemented. Therefore figures for subsequent years should be comparable with 2008. Other assumptions are shown below.[64]

7.47 The changes to the projection are based on the following assumptions regarding numbers of sponsored ordinands. This table also shows the resulting numbers of future ordinations.

Illustration 1b
Ordinand numbers

	2002/03	2003/04	2004/05	2005/06	2006/07	2007/08	2008/09
	Note 1	Note 2	Note 3	Note 4	Note 5	Note 6	Note 7
Full-time	540	540	500	465	465	465	465
Full-time places for CME 1–4			9	19	28	38	38
Total full-time places used	540	540	509	484	493	503	503
Part-time	588	590	630	665	702	702	702
Total full-time and part-time ordinands	1128	1130	1130	1130	1167	1167	1167
OLM schemes	217	220	220	220	220	220	220
Overall total	1345	1350	1350	1350	1387	1387	1387
No of people ordained at year end							
Note 8							
Full-time	240	240	222	202	202	202	202
Part-time	196	197	210	222	234	234	234
OLM	72	73	73	73	73	73	73
	508	510	505	497	509	509	509

For notes 1–7 see below.[65]

7.48 As can be seen from Illustration 1a in paragraph 7.46 above:

- the financial effect of transferring 75 people requiring family maintenance from full-time training to part-time training is to produce an initial reduction of cost in excess of £1 million per annum (or about £15,100 per person per annum, a total saving of about £30,200 per two-year ordinand) once this is fully effective.

- this is offset by the additional costs of CME 1–4 training which will also amount to approximately £1 million per annum;
- a reduction of 7.5 per cent in academic staffing levels to reflect the synergies obtained through combining the activities of full-time and part-time training should by 2006 produce savings of over £200,000 per annum;
- a reduction of 7.5 per cent in the administrative staffing level to reflect the net savings achieved through creating a merged administration function for each RTP should by 2006 create savings in the order of £75,000 per annum;
- an overall net reduction in cost is projected for each year. This varies from reductions in the region of £500,000 to £600,000 for 2005 and 2006 to about £130,000 in 2008, when our proposals are assumed to be fully implemented;
- while this proposal reduces the number of full-time spaces used for pre-ordination training by 75, the effect of this is reduced by the use of up to half of these spaces for CME 1-4.
- overall the improvements in training recommended in this report are achieved for a marginally lower cost than at present. In this illustration the number of people ordained each year remains constant and thus the cost per ordinand over the seven-year initial period of training would be broadly the same as the costs for the existing two or three years prior to ordination.

It should also be recognized that the costs of achieving the reductions in core costs could delay the benefits by three to six months.

Impact of current decline in numbers training in colleges

7.49   Since the beginning of our work as a working party the number of sponsored ordinands attending courses has remained broadly steady, but there has been a steady decline in the number of sponsored ordinands training in the colleges. The numbers are as follows:

	1999/00	2000/01	2001/02	2002/03
Colleges*	628	602	589	540
Courses	589	576	576	588
Total	1,217	1,178	1,165	1,128
OLM candidates	201	209	191	217
Overall total	1,418	1,387	1,356	1,345

*The figures shown for colleges are full-time equivalent numbers

The budgeted number of candidates for 2002/03 was 571 in colleges and 559 on courses. While it is not yet entirely clear whether the significant reduction in numbers in 2002/03 is a temporary blip or a continuation of the trend of reduced numbers of sponsored candidates in colleges, it appears that this may be a trend. It should also be noted that there are a large number of people completing their training in colleges during 2002/03 and that if the number of people recruited to begin training in September 2003 is the same as in September 2002 there will be a further significant reduction in numbers in the colleges.

Financial issues

7.50 The Vote 1 budget for 2003 assumes that the existing establishment of theological colleges and courses will be maintained. The core costs are based on numbers of sponsored candidates in 1999/00, when there were in the region of 630 sponsored candidates in colleges. The budget for 2003/04 (as at January 2003) includes a reduction in core costs of £100,000 which represents a reduction in capacity of about 15 places to about 615. The variable costs are based on the assumption that college numbers of sponsored candidates would be 571 in 2002/03 and 2003/04. The funding procedure established under *Managing Planned Growth* was intended to give stability to colleges in times of fluctuating numbers, while at the same time minimizing the risk of overspend on the Vote 1 Budget. In the event of a long-term decline in numbers in the colleges, it will be necessary for Vote 1 to be reduced and this will require a reduction in core costs. The Ministry Division's Finance Panel monitors this situation and alerts the Bishops' Committee for Ministry and the Theological Education and Training Committee when it considers that action should be taken to address long-term changes.

7.51 The significant reduction in September 2002 in the numbers of sponsored candidates in the colleges from 589 to 540 gives cause for concern. While at the time of finalizing this report (in Spring 2003) it is too early to estimate the numbers likely to be in colleges in September 2004 with any accuracy, there is clearly a risk that there could be a further significant reduction in numbers which could cause numbers to fall below 500. Therefore it is in any event likely to be necessary for the funding of core costs by Vote 1 to be reduced in the near future. On the basis that the present number of sponsored ordinands in colleges is 540 and that the budget includes the core costs required to train about 615 people, this indicates a requirement for a further reduction in funding of core costs of up to 75 places. However it is also important to recognize that some capacity should be left in the system for a possible reversal of the current trend and therefore on the basis of information currently available, and before taking into account the proposals in this report, we consider that the funding of core costs needs to be reduced by about 50 places. We set out below the additional effect this would have on the budgets for 2003 to 2008 if there were to be a reduction of funding in respect of 25 places in September 2003 and a further 25 places in September 2004.

Illustration 2						
	2003	2004	2005	2006	2007	2008
	£	£	£	£	£	£
Forecast Vote 1 at present	9,175,071	9,411,459	9,725,654	10,073,349	10,422,368	10,762,288
Personal and family maintenance	3,006,433	3,081,594	3,158,634	3,237,600	3,318,540	3,401,503
Total Vote 1 as proposed	12,181,504	12,493,053	12,884,288	13,310,949	13,740,908	14,163,791
Effect of reducing full-time capacity by 50 re existing reduction in numbers	-52,946	-218,680	-336,561	-342,899	-356,615	-369,810
Net savings arising from our proposals per paragraph 7.46 above	0	-120,342	-540,734	-621,667	-273,471	-128,234
Revised total Vote 1	12,128,558	12,154,031	12,006,994	12,346,383	13,110,822	13,665,748
Overall net savings	-52,946	-339,022	-877,294	-964,566	-630,086	-498,043

7.52 As can be seen the effect of reducing the funding of core costs in respect of about 50 places is to reduce costs by about £350,000 per annum once this is fully effective. The costs of achieving these reductions could delay the realization of these savings by three to six months. On these assumptions the total reduction in costs compared with the current establishment would, in 2008 when these proposals are fully implemented, be about £500,000 as total costs reduce from £14,163,791 to £13,665,748. This results in an equivalent reduction in Vote 1 and thus a reduction in the amounts charged to dioceses.

7.53 The core costs of the individual colleges are reviewed annually by the Ministry Division's Finance Panel and the allocation of this reduction in funding to individual colleges or RTPs would be determined by the Finance Panel after obtaining the approval of the Bishops' Committee for Ministry and the Theological Education and Training Committee for any major reductions. We anticipate that the cost reductions demonstrated in Illustration 2 equivalent to the core costs for 50 full-time training places will be achieved in accordance with normal Ministry Division procedures and that as a result this lower cost base will form the starting point for the implementation of Proposal 10, the financial effects of which are shown in Illustrations 1 and 2.

7.54 The overall impact of these proposals on the number of college places for which the core costs are funded by Vote 1 is as follows:

Financial issues

Number of places for which core costs are funded in 2002	630
Reduction in funding in budget for 2003/04 (as at January 2003)	-15
Reduction to reflect current reduction in numbers in training assumed for our proposals (paragraph 7.51)	-50
Base for implementation of Proposal 10	565
Transfer of 75 people to part-time training (Proposal 10)	-75
Number of places funded for full-time training	490
Use of half of these places for short residential periods for CME 1–4 (paragraph 7.29)	38
Number of places for which core costs will be funded on the implementation of our proposals	528

7.55　A number of colleges already recruit students from other provinces and churches as well as lay students. We are proposing that RTPs should be ecumenical bodies and that they should be encouraged to recruit full-time and part-time students from a wide range of sources. This should minimize any required reduction in full-time training resources.

Impact of possible changes in the projected numbers of ordinands in training

7.56　We have also considered the impact of possible changes in the projected numbers of ordinands in training on the financial projections. These possible scenarios and the financial implications are set out in Appendices 11 to 14 as follows:

Appendix 11	*Reduction to 490 training full-time and part-time numbers stable at 590*
Appendix 12	*Reduction to 490 training full-time and part-time numbers increase by 112 to 702*
Appendix 13	*Full-time and part-time numbers stable but reduction by 50 in numbers of people requiring family maintenance*
Appendix 14	*Reduction of 150 to 390 people training full-time, reduction of capacity by 200 to 415 and increase of 201 in numbers training part-time*

Summary of considerations

7.57 The illustrations set out in paragraphs 7.45 to 7.51 and in Appendices 10 to 14 may be summarized as follows by considering the total costs in 2008, when the proposals are assumed to be fully implemented, with the numbers to be ordained in that year on these assumptions.

Comparison of costs in 2008	Total cost in 2008	Funded capacity for full-time training	No. of people ordained following full-time and part-time training
	£		
Illustration 1			
Transfer to part-time training of 75 people training for two years full-time and requiring family support reducing core capacity to 540	14,035,557	540	436
Illustration 2			
Transfer of 75 people as above and reduce core capacity by a further 50 to 490	13,665,748	490	436
Illustration 3			
Reduce full-time numbers training by 50 and capacity overall by 100 to 515 without increase in part-time training	13,849,331	515	415
Illustration 4			
Reduce full-time numbers training by 50 and capacity overall by 100 to 515 with an increase of 112 in people training part-time	14,418,021	515	452
Illustration 5			
Maintain current numbers but reduce full-time capacity by 75 to 540 and replace 50 people requiring family support with 50 single people training full-time	14,141,931	540	436
Illustration 6			
Reduce the number of people training full-time by 150 to 390, reduce capacity by 200 to 415 and increase numbers training part-time by 201	12,421,613	415	437

The approach adopted in Illustration 6 is the most cost-effective approach considered, but we have rejected this because it would lead directly to the closure of a number of colleges, with the consequent loss of these theological, educational and financial resources to the Church as a whole. The approach adopted in Illustration 2 is the next most cost-effective approach considered. This requires a reduction in full-time capacity of 125 places to 490. This includes the reduction of 75 places recommended in Proposal 10. The financial savings from the further reduction of 50 places relating to the existing reduction in numbers would form a reduction of Vote 1 and would thus be a saving passed back to the dioceses. Therefore we recommend that the approach demonstrated by Illustration 2 should be adopted. This 'middle of the road approach' results in a cost reduction in 2008 and on a continuing basis of some

£500,000 and more in some earlier years, as set out in the table shown in paragraph 7.51 above. It also moderates the loss of theological resources through reductions in full-time capacity. This reduction in capacity should be planned as part of the reorganization which we are proposing as colleges realign within the RTP structure.

Control of costs during transition to new structure

7.58   As indicated in paragraph 7.24 above we recommend that costs should be controlled by allocating funds to the RTPs on a three-year rolling basis, but that additional funds should not be made available in the event that additional ordinands are accepted. Similarly in 7.38 we have recommended that the costs of personal and family maintenance should be restricted to the amounts included in the Vote 1 budget. It should be recognized that these two provisions in effect constitute a capping mechanism so as to ensure that expenditure is within the amounts approved by Synod. Therefore it would be possible for Synod to control any increase in costs as a result of increases in numbers of sponsored candidates recommended for training. This may result in some candidates delaying the start of their training to a subsequent year when funds are available and/or it may result in some candidates training part-time rather than full-time in order to enable RTPs to operate within budget.

7.59   The existing budgetary arrangements together with the recommendations in this report create a framework which will ensure that costs are properly controlled during the transition to the new arrangements. In particular:

i) Funding is allocated to colleges and courses by the Ministry Division's Finance Panel on an annual basis, taking into account anticipated numbers in training. The Finance Panel ensures that the funding allocated is within the Vote 1 budget. In the event that numbers in training are higher than anticipated the colleges and courses only receive the variable cost and funding should be available within the Three-year Rolling Reserve to meet any such cost.

ii) We are proposing that as these proposals are introduced a similar system of control should remain in place but that if numbers in training are more than 5 per cent over budget no further funding should be available to the RTPs from the Vote 1 budget (see 7.24 above). We are further proposing that the present procedures should be refined to the effect that budgets will be approved by the Finance Panel on a three-year rolling basis, subject to an annual review.

7.60   Some transition costs will be incurred in establishing the new arrangements.

i) Initially we anticipate that this may involve the creation in each region of an informal RTP. We envisage that this would principally act as a co-ordinating body and that the existing activities of the colleges, courses, CME, Reader and lay training would continue, at least initially, to be undertaken by the existing entities. The cost of creating, say, eight informal RTPs should be minimal, since these would be established by exchanges of letters between the various legal entities involved and at this stage the RTP would not have a separate legal existence. Legal costs may be incurred in some cases amounting to, say, £10,000.

ii) The existing college structure in particular may need to remain in place in view of the complex nature of their trust arrangements. However our aim is to encourage the existing colleges, courses, OLM, Reader and lay training operations to enter structured partnerships as soon as possible so as to achieve the synergies and economies which this would achieve. Such partnerships may involve additional legal costs which could amount to £5,000 to £10,000 per region, a total of say £60,000.

iii) There may be a need for re-organization of the courses in view of changes in boundaries. These are at present nearly all constituted as companies limited by guarantee and we envisage that some or all of the existing legal entities could be used for this purpose. The costs of these changes should be very modest, say a total of £10,000.

iv) The RTPs will need to establish administrative arrangements and we envisage that they should provide an administrative service to each participant, i.e. that the colleges and courses, CME, Reader and lay theological education should handle their administration function jointly. The administration staff involved would operate under the management of a bursar appointed to serve the whole RTP and would be jointly employed by the various legal entities involved, who would bear the employment costs proportionately. This arrangement should avoid any liability to Value Added Tax on recharges between separate legal entities. Initially this may involve some set-up costs which might total £10,000 per region, giving a total of say £80,000. However we anticipate that once these arrangements are established savings in the order of £70,000 per annum should be achieved, i.e. 7.5 per cent of total administration payroll costs.

v) Thus transitional costs could amount to £160,000 made up as follows:

- Establish RTPs   £ 10,000
- College legal costs   £ 60,000
- Legal costs of reorganizing courses   £ 10,000
- Establish regional administration   £ 80,000

Risk management during transition

7.61   Any programme of change involves risk. During the course of our work we have considered carefully the risks involved both in connection with the proposals we are making and if issues which need to be addressed are not tackled. The main risks for the Church as a whole and for the institutions are set out below:

i) The financial risks for the Church as a whole have been minimized as shown in 7.58 and 7.59 above.

ii) The uncertainty created by proposals for change can create a planning blight for the institutions potentially affected. This is particularly relevant for the colleges. This depends first upon the definition of the regions and second upon the negotiation of links between the new regions and the existing colleges. This uncertainty can affect both potential ordinands and staff recruitment (in the event of vacancies) as both ordinands and staff will only wish to be part of institutions whose future is assured. It is therefore important that, if these proposals are approved by General Synod, the arrangements for the new RTPs should be established as quickly as possible.

iii) The regional courses face uncertainty until the regions are defined, but this uncertainty is less harmful as it will always be necessary to have a provision of training on courses that covers the whole country. Particular difficulties may be faced by courses which at present serve geographical areas which may be divided between more than one RTP.

iv) OLM schemes face uncertainty until the new regions are created and until it is agreed whether each of the OLM schemes will operate within an RTP and how the operations will be integrated with those of the RTP.

v) Similar considerations apply to diocesan CME, Reader and lay training.

vi) There is a risk that negotiations may not be successful to incorporate some colleges within an RTP, in which event the resources which those colleges currently provide to theological education in this country may be lost as a contribution to ordination training. However it is hoped that all colleges will wish to participate in RTPs either in their present form or through merger and that one or more may be willing to move to another geographical location.

Risks of no action

7.62   If these proposals are not approved by General Synod other risks arise. In any event, as a result of the recent decline in full-time student numbers, which now appears to be a trend rather than a temporary blip, Ministry Division faces a need to reduce the funding of college core costs for training sponsored candidates. If, as is quite possible, this decline continues this could result in the need to cease funding in the order of 100 places which would be equivalent to the need to withdraw recognition from two medium-sized colleges. Under our proposals, the effect of this change on the colleges could be alleviated by merging with courses to provide both full-time and part-time training and to participate in training throughout the redefined six-year period of initial ministerial education. The removal of this opportunity would aggravate the difficulties which will be faced by some colleges.

Chapter 8

Encouraging and managing flexibility: some further training issues

8.1   In this chapter we turn to some concrete issues about training that arise from the proposed new framework for ministerial education, regional theological training partnerships and financial framework. This will enable us to discuss the important issue of the use of 'residence' in ministerial education.

8.2   We summed up an earlier discussion by stating that ministerial formation is *a dynamic and continuing process that draws on a range of contexts, in which the candidate moves between gathered and dispersed settings of the Church's life, and, under supervision, is helped to grow towards the role of the ordained, defined above in terms of service, holiness, vocation and mission* (4.3 and 4.9 above). In the pre-ordination phase of their training all candidates for ordained ministry need to:

- develop a rule of life;
- study in faithful, lively, reflective and self-critical contexts;
- gain a wider and deeper appreciation of the Church's mission and ministry while acquiring some basic skills in ministry.

It is within this understanding of formation that we wish to turn to the question of the value of what is often called 'residence'. In the following sections we review the use of residence in the range of types of training, seeking to evaluate their positive features, as well as commenting on some strengths and weaknesses. This is with a view to outlining the types of training settings that are available to candidates and promoting their flexible use.

The college experience

8.3   We noted above that the experience of what is usually called 'residence' has changed markedly for most candidates for ordination. This is not merely numerical – though only 43 per cent of ordinands of all categories are currently training in a college setting. Rather, the nature of residence has changed because of the rising age of ordinands, the greater proportion of married candidates, who of course return to the 'private' life of the family every evening or weekend, and cultural assumptions about study, private time and leisure. Only a small proportion of ordinands now worships, studies, relaxes and sleeps in college, and this proportion will vary from college to college. Because of these changes, subtly, over the years the notion of the common life has been reduced, for most college-based ordinands, to perhaps common worship once a day, the sharing of one or two meals a day, a study programme, groups for various purposes and some social events. This is not to deny the reality of lively communities, often drawing in families and children, but it is not, in most cases, the 'full community' for which the term 'residence' used to stand.

8.4   In addition to these changes, other features of college-style training should be taken into account:

i) Colleges offer a community, located in a set of buildings and often in a particular tradition of the Church, primarily dedicated to worship, study and service for the formation of the Church's ministers.

ii) The college environment offers a range of positive opportunities:

- a common and sustained life of worship;
- formation within a particular Church tradition;
- in-depth study of the Scriptures and the Christian tradition in a dedicated setting;
- easy access to library and other information facilities;
- opportunity for belonging to a college-wide community and to groups for a variety of purposes;
- pastoral and mission experience;
- many opportunities for informal learning through working together and through friendship and conversation with staff and fellow students.

The distinctive quality of college life is the sustained nature of the experience, day by day, focused on terms, over two to three years. This could be summarized as *primarily a gathered community, with some elements of dispersal* (vacations, placements of various sorts).

iii) For most candidates attending college entails moving house and sometimes family. Thus, the candidate (and any accompanying family) is already in a transitional state from the very start of training. It is often said that this contributes powerfully to the process of formation, by the very state of transition and by freeing the candidate for the process of training by giving him or her time for it and, further, by removing the need to go out to earn a living. It is also said that the move prepares candidates for the 'apostolic' nature of ordained ministry, i.e. that stipendiary clergy are 'sent' to minister to a community in which they are initially outsiders and from which they will eventually move on. However, this argument can be overstated in that the young candidate, the natural constituency of colleges, may not yet have a settled life in the community; in fact, his or her life may already be marked by moving, from school to university or in search of a job. Further, college life may in part replicate the intense (and some might say, artificial) communal life that she or he may well have already experienced at school or university.

iv) For the older candidate, particularly one with a family, moving to college can for some be very liberating – allowing him or her to concentrate for the first time for many years on study and preparation, and now, having experienced the world of work or other responsibilities, being mature enough to value this privilege. On the other hand, it can be a frustrating transitional period dominated by the practicalities of two moves in twenty-one months, with the consequent business of making homes, finding schools for children and employment for a spouse. Thus, both with regard to younger and older candidates, a careful consideration needs to be made of the likely advantages and disadvantages of college-style training.

The regional course experience

8.5 In the regional courses the Church now also has nearly three decades of experience of the use of intense but short-term periods of residence for educational and formational purposes in the form of weekends and eight-day residential schools. These important episodes have to be set in the broader context of the experience of training in a part-time mode as a whole. Thus the candidate joins a group of peers and builds up relationships with staff and students through weeknight meetings. The residential elements are built on this base, comprising typically six weekends per year (Friday night to Sunday lunchtime) and an eight-day residential school per year for three years.

8.6   The course environment offers a range of positive opportunities:

- a periodic common life of worship;
- formation within a community that includes a wide range of Church traditions;
- a structured programme of learning including study in a part-time mode;
- many opportunities to make connections between, on the one hand, candidates' continuing experience of everyday life and, on the other, the study of Scripture and the Christian tradition and a range of models of Christian life and practice;
- some access to library and other information facilities;
- opportunity for belonging to a course-wide community and to groups for a variety of purposes;
- pastoral and mission experience;
- periodic opportunity for informal learning through working together and through friendship and conversation with staff and fellow students.

Regional courses offer a structure for learning and formation that builds on the movement between the candidate's continuing life and service in everyday life and the opportunities to worship, study and reflect together. Thus, the distinctive characteristic of this pattern of formation is the *movement between gathered and dispersed modes of the intentional community of formation*, or, to put it another way, *the movement between the life of home, work, community and parish and the intentional community of formation*. Candidates keep in touch with their own parishes and their ordinary daily occupation but are taken out of this to learn and to reflect on experience, the mission and ministry of the Church and on the contexts of its life.

8.7   For some candidates the course model offers a highly appropriate and challenging opportunity to prepare for ministry by study and by reflection on their own and others' experience in the light of their growing theological and pastoral knowledge, understanding and skills. Attention can be paid to future parochial ministry or to ministry in secular employment (MSE). For others it can be difficult to get the balance right between continuing the demands of occupation, home and study and preparation. Some respond well to the formative potential of the movement between gathered and dispersed modes of the course community, while for others personal or ministerial issues do not emerge or cannot be handled at sufficient depth within the time constraints of this form of training.

The OLM experience

8.8   More recently, the OLM schemes have developed yet further variety in the use of residence by focusing on the candidate's continuing local and Church context. Ordained Local Ministry is intended to grow out of the growth of shared or collaborative ministry in the local context. Thus, in this case the elasticity of the concept of residence extends back to a basic meaning, the place where the candidate lives permanently! A second strand within OLM-type training is the use of course-type residence, if on a smaller scale than on regional courses. OLM-type training offers a range of positive opportunities:

- a sustained opportunity to develop the understanding and practice of collaborative ministry in a particular local context;
- a periodic common life of worship;
- formation within a community that includes a wide range of Church traditions;
- a programme of learning adapted to study in a part-time mode, including structures to help make connections between the candidate's experience of the local and the wider Church;
- opportunities to study Scripture and the Christian tradition and a range of models of Christian life and practice to support the practice of ministry;
- some access to library and other information facilities;
- opportunity for belonging to a community of learning (whether just of OLMs or of OLM, Reader and other candidates) and to groups for a variety of purposes;
- pastoral and mission experience;
- periodic opportunity for informal learning through working together and through friendship and conversation with staff and fellow students.

The distinctive characteristic of this pattern of formation is attention to the growth of collaborative ministry in a local context, combined with the movement between the life of home, work, community and parish and the intentional community of formation.

8.9   It is more difficult to evaluate the strengths and weakness of OLM-type training because it is a fairly new movement and because there has been no choice for OLM candidates in terms of the place of their training. OLMs train on their own diocesan scheme. For most OLM candidates the OLM model offers a highly appropriate and challenging opportunity to prepare for ministry by attention to the growth of collaborative patterns of ministry in their own parish and local context, in dialogue with the study of theology and personal and theological reflection. We note that Stranger in the Wings raised a range of issues about training[66] and inspectors have had concerns about inadequate staffing levels. As with other forms of training in a part-time mode, it can be difficult to get the balance right between continuing the demands of occupation, home and study and preparation.

Mixed-mode training

8.10   In relation to this discussion, the current formal mixed-mode schemes in the Church of England make use of long-term placement experience or lay ministry in a parochial setting, combined with either a college-style or a course-style approach to formation and education. In the East Anglian Ministerial Training Course case, the preparation includes two year-long placements in different settings. On the St John's scheme, there is a period of at least two years of lay ministry and part-time study, followed by ordination, normally to serve in the same parish, and continued part-time study.

8.11   The review of mixed-mode training that has recently been completed comes to very positive conclusions, though it notes that so far only strong candidates have been attracted to the schemes and that they are few in number. Nonetheless, the review reports a high quality of training in both the educational and formational aspects, which should encourage a growth in this form of training.[67]

Encouraging and managing flexibility

8.12   This brief survey highlights again that the Church is currently making use of a variety of patterns of common life for the purposes of learning and formation. In the current situation it is better to talk of such intentional, transitional communities, than of 'residence'. They are 'intentional' in that they are communities formed for the purpose of formation for ministry and 'transitional' in that candidates are intended to pass through them, with the result that they are formed and re-formed on an annual basis, with the governors and staff, at different levels, providing continuity and challenge as required.

8.13   Like the report of 1990 on 'residence',[68] as a working party we continued to be convinced of the value of these patterns of common life for the purposes of learning and formation. However, in line with our comments above, we would challenge the Church to develop these patterns, and not to restrict them to the current strict alternatives of college, course or scheme. Thus, we would encourage:

i)   the creation of opportunities for candidates to combine part-time and full-time modes of training;

ii) the possibility of combining study from home, for example at a local university or Church college, with a period of training in the RTP. While this needs to be handled with care, because of the integrative intent of study within ordination training and the concern with formation, some greater freedom to use locally available educational resources should be encouraged;

iii) the provision of periods of residence for all categories of ministers in the pre- and post-ordination phase of IME, to reflect on ministry itself within a community of learning;

8.14   Our proposals would change the nature of college-, course- or OLM-type communities. We have already noted that they are transitional but they would now be asked to accept learners for shorter periods of time and to be more flexible. To some extent this is already happening with the growth in the range of types of candidate. However, if a diversity of pathways is to be encouraged, our communities of formation would need to focus further on the particular contribution they can make to the dynamic and continuing process of formation commented on above (8.2). Thus, while some candidates would continue to have two or three years within one training institution, others would benefit from a shorter period in college, in combination with another form of training. The experience of being in a changing community could in turn help our future ministers to serve in a world which has to come to terms with increasingly fast-changing and complex communities. Finally, our proposals for the development of partnerships should give a new framework for developing opportunities for candidates and students on a variety of pathways to learn together and from each other. While there are difficult issues to be worked at here, there is also potential for a much richer context for training that we hope our institutions will wish to develop.

8.15   New arrangements will be needed to support those candidates and students who seek to realize the flexibility implicit in the proposals for a formational framework and the RTPs. As exemplars of new demands, we might consider a Cumbrian shepherd or a nurse in Canterbury. How might the proposed new framework facilitate their development of vocation? For such individuals, time, place and pace of study are critical issues and in the new institutional arrangements that are proposed it should be possible to ease the transition into part-time or full-time modes of training. We envisage the formational and learning needs of candidates being assessed first in the diocese, through the national selection system that sometimes identifies training needs, and then in the forum of the relevant RTP in which diocese and trainers are represented. The presence in each regional partnership of both full-time and part-time modes of training promote the use of a range of possibilities:

- college-type training;
- course-type training;
- OLM-type training;
- course-type training plus a period (a month, term or year) in a college setting;
- formally approved mixed-mode training (e.g. St John's mixed-mode or EAMTC or new schemes with formal approval);
- individually tailored training plans for candidates drawing on a range of resources. Individual training programmes might include full- or part-time study from home on a locally available educational programme, at a university or Church college or other appropriate resource, combined with a period of college-, course- or OLM- type training;

8.16   It is important to clarify that the phrase 'individual training plan' ought not to be taken to imply that decisions about training should be driven by individual candidates or that training should be 'individualized'. We have stated earlier that as training is for the Church's ministry it is essential that the Church makes those decisions. Further, our reflections on formation indicate that we believe that is vital for training to take place in community. The need for individual training plans arises out of the range of candidates' backgrounds and out of the proper desire to offer training that will enable candidates to take part in training to the full. Finally, it will be incumbent on those putting together training plans for individuals that the plans are shaped by the necessary focus on formation.

Recognition of prior learning

8.17   While the Church already has some experience of APL (the accreditation of prior learning, i.e. of certificated learning) and APEL (the accreditation of prior experiential learning), further benefit could be derived by more systematic use of these procedures. APL/APEL would enable the applicants, working with their dioceses, to present any learning achieved at the initial point of exploring vocation and to calibrate this against the learning outcomes that are expressed in the Statement of Expectations for Ministerial Education (paragraph 5.17). Normally the assessment of these outcomes would be undertaken by means of a reflective written piece of work. For example, a candidate who had undertaken 90 credits of studies under the Education for Discipleship initiative or another programme might find that 60 of those credits can be counted directly in his or her training for ordination. If these were in Biblical Studies and the candidate had a particular interest in this area, he or she could take higher-level modules on biblical subjects during training.

Changes in circumstance and geography

8.18   Traditionally, candidates for ministry have started and completed this ministerial journey in a single institution. This can create substantial pressure for some candidates. Examples include: a candidate's partner has an employment opportunity in another part of the country; family pressures, such as care for the elderly, trigger a move; or the birth of a child to a candidate or spouse provokes a desire to shift from a full-time to a part-time mode of training. The proposed new partnerships should be able to assist individuals through these and other life transitions. This could be facilitated by credit recognition agreements between the different institutions. This would require substantial discussion and detailed work. In principle, however, an individual ordinand should be able to transfer credit from institution A to institution B with minimum loss of time or credit. Arrangements would be needed to transfer *specific* credit – where learning outcomes in different institutions are closely matched - and *general* credit, where the *level* is appropriate but where there are gaps in the specified *content* of learning outcomes – gaps that must be addressed. External support for developing such arrangements to the satisfaction of diverse partner learning institutions can be found in universities and Church colleges.

Developing the curriculum

8.19   We propose above (4.20), that initial ministerial education be reconfigured as the period from entry into training to the end of the first training post. This proposal would bring with it many possibilities for the development of the curriculum. While we have not drawn up proposals in this area, we would have the following aims in mind:

i) to make use of the entire period from entry into training to the end of the first training post. This would allow patterns of training to be planned with the full six years in mind. Further, it could give a significant impetus to the continuity of ministerial education and formation across the pre- and post-ordination phases of IME, as a contribution to establishing patterns of lifelong learning;

ii) to give the opportunity for creative development of patterns of training, i.e. new combinations of full-time and part-time modes, or new mixed-mode schemes. Thus, there could be more use of formal schemes of mixed-mode training and different combinations of theological study, practical experience and reflection.

iii) to have a Church-wide agreement that part-time study and ministerial development will be a formal expectation of ministers during the first training post;

iv) to relieve the pressure on the curriculum for pre-ordination training by allowing the timetabling of some theological and ministerial studies in the post-ordination phase;

v) to ensure that contextual and reflective learning continues to be given its proper emphasis throughout the whole period of training, but is now better related to the candidate's continuing engagement with the Scriptures and the Christian tradition;

vi) to enable the continued learning and ministerial development of ministers in their first post to be assessed formally and for ministers to gain an appropriate academic award for their learning, where this is appropriate. This would be the normal expectation, candidates working to degree or a postgraduate level, as appropriate. While all would be expected to continue to study, for a few the academically accredited route may not be appropriate, either because it would inhibit learning because it is too technically demanding or because the candidate already has a range of academic awards, including one in the ministerial field. Also some candidates might continue with accredited studies but at the same level at which they completed the pre-ordination phase.

In terms of new developments, while it is essential that our structures encourage new developments to arise out of the life of the Church, they need to be co-ordinated and related to our training provision as a whole, to avoid the continuing proliferation of small institutions. We envisage the local RTPs as the context within which such new developments in training can find a home.

8.20   In the consultation on the interim report, there was some misunderstanding that the proposals for the reconfiguration of IME and for the use of a Statement of Expectations for Ministerial Education were in fact a proposal for a national curriculum. This was not and is not the case. The framework for ministerial education, as a broad statement of desired outcomes in candidates, is an element of agreed policy within which each institution or partner will be required to work, in order that there are Church-wide standards in terms of attainment. However, we envisage the proposed RTPs continuing to be responsible for developing programmes and the curriculum, subject to the approval of the Ministry Division as at present. What will, however, be necessary will be some broad parameters for the curriculum so that candidates who train up to ordination in one region can make use of the post-ordination phase of a curriculum designed in the region in which they will serve their title. (For some candidates it may be appropriate for them to have components of their post-ordination phase of IME outside of the region, but others will pick the programme of their new diocese and its CME and therefore relate to the local RTP.) These parameters for the curriculum could be developed from the broad parameters set in ACCM 22, and already employed in *Mission and Ministry* and *Mind the Gap*: Interpretation of the Christian Tradition for Today; the Formation of Church life; Addressing Situations in the World.

Communities of learning in the post-ordination phase

8.21   Our proposals will have significant implications for both the pre-ordination phase and the post-ordination phases of training. The current strengths of this latter phase, the current CME 1–4, includes the opportunity for the recently ordained and licensed to:

i)   reflect together, in formal and informal ways, on the practice of ministry;

ii)   engage in experiential and contextual learning clearly related to the immediate contexts for ministry;

iii)   relate to the personnel, structures and policies of the diocese in which they serve.

These strengths are clearly related to a particular community of learning, the group of ministers in a diocese involved in the CME 1–4 programme.

8.22   To the strengths of the current CME 1–4 we now wish to add the continuation and completion of programmes of theological and ministerial learning. Given the range of ability and of achievement by the time of ordination, it is inevitable that ministers will require programmes at different academic levels. Some will be topping up a diploma to degree level, some will undertake higher-level awards, while some will be on non-accredited programmes. This new situation will require careful handling of the issue of the communities of learning and formation to which candidates will belong. We envisage that ministers in this phase of development will belong both to a diocesan group, similar to the current CME 1–4 arrangements, and to a cohort of those studying on a particular programme. For some the two aspects of continuing training will be closely related, for example, for those who trained before ordination within the local RTP and are now completing a related award. For others it will be appropriate for them to pursue a theological and ministerial award outside the region. In either case it is important for these two aspects of continuing training to enrich each other and not to be undertaken in isolation. For this approach to work well it will require:

i) good liaison between the candidate/minister and all those responsible for the pre- and post-ordination phases;

ii) clarity about expectations with regard to attendance, hours to be devoted to learning of various types and deadlines for the production of assignments of various types;

iii) good procedures for resolving issues relating to both sides of the overall programme of learning.

While this is a more complex task than at present, it will require exactly the same commitment to negotiation and partnership which will be required for the flourishing of the RTPs.

Church-wide standards

8.23 As a Church we have valued having broadly common standards in ordination training, while at the same time honouring a diversity of approach. This has been achieved by giving the responsibility initially to theological educators in each institution and then for the training offered to be inspected and approved on behalf of the Church. This work is carried out by:

i) bishops' inspections of the training institution as a whole every five years;

ii) validation of training programmes by the Ministry Division's Educational Validation Panel every five years and subsequent annual moderation.

If IME is reconfigured to cover the period from entry into training to the end of the first training post, it will be appropriate for the Church's means for checking on standards to be extended to the newly defined IME as a whole. Secondly, the proposed RTPs should be subject to these processes, rather than the individual institutions. These issues will need to be worked through in detail but overall the load on the individual institutions of the partnerships should be reduced, as should the number of inspections and validation events that need to be carried out. One issue to be reviewed is whether the current form of the Church's processes is appropriate for the proposed regional structure.[69] The overall aim should be that the Church has mechanisms in place to ensure that the training it offers to its ordinands and clergy is appropriate to its task and of a good quality.

Validating training programmes

8.24 Currently the content, level and balance of training programmes are scrutinized by the Ministry Division's Educational Validation Panel. These programmes consist of the entire training package offered to ordinands, i.e. the educational programme, such as a degree or diploma, in the context of the formation and practical training on offer. If approved, these programmes are regarded as 'validated routes' that are deemed to be within the current bishops' regulations and can be paid for out of central funds. For the future, the concept of validated routes will continue to be valuable within the new framework for:

i) standard training programmes within a college, course or OLM scheme, plus the post-ordination phase of IME;

ii) new standard training programmes that will be devised by RTPs, drawing on the available range of full-time or part-time educational and formational resources, including the post-ordination phase.

In addition to validating training programmes, a new approach will be needed to approve the 'individual training plans' drawn up for candidates whose particular needs would not be met by these standard training programmes (see 8.15 above). These individual training plans should be approved in order to maintain a proper comparability in the standards of training for all candidates.

Regulating the pathways for individual candidates

8.25 We turn now to the wider issue of how the training pathways for individual candidates are to be decided. A 'pathway' in this sense will include decisions about:

- the mode of training (college, course, scheme, mixed-mode, combinations of these, individual training plan);
- the length of training;
- the training programme (i.e. the educational award within the whole formational and training package).

Before we move to proposals for the regulation of the choice of pathways for individual candidates we need to outline the current situation and to establish its underlying values.

The current approach

8.26 Under our current approach pathways for candidates are regulated by a number of factors, some of which belong to the Church's understanding of itself, and its ministry, and some of which are organizational matters. In the former category belong the points that bishops have a special responsibility for ministry and for ordination and that, in the Church of England, they exercise that charge having received advice from a range of parties. It is helpful to distinguish between two types of episcopal authority:

i) the action undertaken by an individual bishop, on behalf of the Church as a whole, for example, the decision whether or not to ordain a candidate;

ii) the actions of bishops, acting corporately, through the House of Bishops, for example agreeing a Church-wide policy about training. Thus the current bishops' regulations for training have been agreed and revised from time to time by the House of Bishops. This also has a financial dimension in that central Church funds may only be used for the training of candidates within bishops' regulations.

8.27 As an organizational matter the House of Bishops asks the Ministry Division to carry out various executive functions. These include administering selection conferences that advise bishops, approving the curriculum and budgets of training institutions, and paying for the cost of training within bishops' regulations. In the area under consideration two areas of work are relevant:

i) For candidates following standard educational and formational programmes leading to ordination, the Ministry Division's Educational Validation Panel scrutinizes and approves 'validated routes', ensuring that they adequately prepare candidates for ordination. Programmes that are approved in this way are deemed to be within bishops' regulations;

ii) Where it may be appropriate for candidates to train outside of bishops' regulations, the Ministry Division's Candidates Panel reviews the candidate's case, and advice is given to the bishop. Examples of the type of case reviewed include requests for an extra year in college-type training to allow a candidate over 30 to complete a degree while in training.

Where pathways through training are approved, through the two procedures outlined here, the training is paid for from the central fund for ministerial training.

8.28   With regard to individual candidates, bishops sponsor candidates for selection conferences and make decisions about whether to send candidates into training (having received advice from Diocesan Directors of Ordinands). Similarly they make decisions about whether or not, and when, to ordain candidates, having received advice from DDOs and principals of training institutions. With regard to pathways through training, under the current agreement of the House of Bishops, the length and mode of training (i.e. college, course or OLM) is determined by bishops' regulations. Thus, a candidate who is under 30 and is not a theology graduate will train for three years in a theological college and this training will be funded out of central Church funds. (For a summary of the regulations and the choices for candidates, see paragraph 2.18 above.) Where the pathway indicated by bishops' regulations is not appropriate for an individual candidate the bishop asks for advice from the Ministry Division, working through its Candidates Panel. Here it is important to use the distinction made above: it is a bishop's decision whether and when a candidate should be ordained, whereas the bishops have collectively decided to adopt bishops' regulations for training and to ask the advice of the Ministry Division about variations in training. In the case of additional training, positive advice from the Candidates Panel is required if central funds are to be used for training. In these ways the Church has acted corporately in this matter. The underlying values of this approach are:

- Church-wide standards can be maintained in terms of the programmes for formation and education offered to candidates;

- candidates are dealt with fairly in terms of the amount of training offered to them and paid for by the Church;

- the money which is raised from dioceses (and ultimately parishes) to fund training is spent in a controlled and accountable way;

- dioceses can have confidence that candidates coming to them from other dioceses have received training to a common standard.

Regulating the choice of pathways for candidates: a new approach

8.29   We have argued above that the time has come to move to a more flexible approach to the training of candidates. In Proposal 2 we recommend that bishops' regulations should be replaced by a statement of the qualities and learning expected in candidates at various stages in their formational journey (para. 5.19). Thus, in future, bishops and training institutions could take into account a candidate's prior learning or particular needs, rather than just allocating them two or three years of training according to the current rules. However, our Proposal 2 only deals with assessing candidates' progress towards ordination and beyond. It does not help with the decisions to be made about how long training should be or whether it should be in college, course or scheme, some combination of them or another pattern of training. As a result, we will require a new process for making these decisions. A complete deregulation of these decisions could undermine confidence in Church-wide standards in training, lead to inequality of opportunity among candidates and to poor financial management. A better approach would be to clarify the *organizational framework* within which decisions would be made and to develop *criteria* to inform the decisions that need to be made.

The organizational framework for deciding on candidates' pathways

8.30   Initial reflections on training proposals for candidates will take place probably from early on in the process of exploring a possible vocation to ordained or other ministry. Certainly this will be the case once the candidate's educational aspirations and abilities have been assessed by the DDO. This will include an exploration of what elements of learning may be appropriate under the Education for Discipleship initiative in this phase (see 5.22–4 above). Once a candidate has been to a selection conference and the bishop has decided to send him or her into training, the bishop and DDO will need to take the initiative in putting forward an initial plan for training.

8.31   As training is a partnership between the sponsoring diocese and the training institutions, it will be appropriate for the initial plan to be further discussed and reflected on within the relevant RTP. The training institutions' particular contribution here will be their knowledge and expertise in the whole range of types of training on offer. Thus, for this purpose, the RTP will act as a forum for testing and developing the initial training proposal. In the cases of candidates training within the region, the diocese and the training institutions will be directly represented in this forum. As a result the dioceses and the training institutions can work very directly with each other to come to decisions about training pathways. When candidates train out of the region, the diocese will need to make its initial proposal to the relevant RTP. It will be valuable to have this discussion and agreement with the relevant RTP so that all the training possibilities are explored and so that all candidates are dealt with on an equal basis.

8.32   The discussion of candidates' pathways will need to take note of:

- the diocese's view of the candidate and his or her proposed pathway towards ordination and beyond;
- the candidate's aspirations, abilities and needs;
- the possibilities for the various forms of training, the range of validated training programmes and the possibility of an 'individual training plan' for the candidate;
- the training institutions' expertise in training and in the particular characteristics of the various forms of training;
- the range and flexibility of resources within the region and the range of possibilities outside of the region;
- the cost and practicality of the various options.

8.33   In most cases agreement will be reached on the pathway for the candidate through this procedure of the diocese making the initial proposal which is then refined in the relevant RTP. In terms of policy it is appropriate that as training is a partnership between the bishop, advised by the DDO, on the one hand, and the training institute on the other, these two parties should come to an agreement on the pattern of training. Where agreement cannot be reached or where it would be helpful to seek further advice, the candidate's case should be remitted to the Ministry Division. As now, where routes for training are approved in this way, the training will be paid for from the central fund for ministerial training.

Criteria to inform decisions about training pathways

8.34 If decisions are to be reached which continue to command Church-wide confidence, there will need to be a common set of criteria against which these discussions will take place. The overarching question is how can the Church best prepare the candidate for his or her future service to the Church and the world. Thus, ultimately the Church should decide the form of training because the preparation is for the Church's ministry, not career or personal development. At the same time the Church needs to provide training that will best equip the candidate and that will enable the candidate to engage with training, taking into account the candidates' abilities, needs and personal circumstances. In the light of these general statements we propose the following criteria:

A. Development in Christian discipleship and towards a ministerial role

B. Personal maturity

C. Life situation – employment, domestic situation, communal and social support, need for personal and/or family maintenance

D. Access to educational and training institutions – transport, any issue of disability

E. Ability to benefit from a particular type of training – educational potential and need

F. Level of prior learning, both general and specific to ministerial theology and practice

G. Timing and mode of training – when is the best time to engage in the various training possibilities (full-time, part-time, mixed-mode)?

H. Category of sponsorship and potential years of ministerial service

In these paragraphs we have dealt with the way the Church should determine the pathways of individual candidates. We now review the question of the total numbers in the various forms of training.

Regulating overall numbers in training on the various pathways

8.35 In our current approach we only track the total number of candidates in training and where they are training. In the future it will be helpful to set out projections for the various types of training and to make a regional allocation in the light of these projections. This would be a replacement for the Bishops' Agreed Maximum for theological colleges, a quota system that currently applies only to the colleges. The chart below sets out the types of training and the projected numbers of candidates in each year in both the pre- and post-ordination phases. The types of training include the familiar college, course and OLM scheme but also make provision for individual training plans (candidates combining some college-type and course-type or a full-time student studying from home on a course or in a college, and so on).

	Year 1	Year 2	Year 3	Ordination	Year 4	Year 5	Year 6
college type							
course type							
OLM type							
mixed mode							
individual training plan							
research students							

This use of such a matrix could be part of a planning process. It will allow a linkage to be established between the budget set by General Synod, the allocation of student numbers to the RTPs and the numbers of candidates coming forward. Further it could allow the Church to relate the number of candidates in training to deployment needs.

8.36 These reflections on encouraging and managing flexibility lead us to sum up with our next proposal:

Proposal 14

We recommend that:

i) **flexible pathways through training are developed, drawing on college, course and OLM types of training and other resources, in order to meet the training needs of candidates;**

ii) **the current approach to validating routes for ordinands on standard programmes be continued and be extended to the pre- and post-ordination phases of IME as defined in this report;**

iii) **the sponsoring diocese initiates the discussion about the appropriate pathway through training for individual candidates and that the final decision is made through agreement between the sponsoring bishop, advised by the DDO, and the relevant regional training partnership;**

iv) **an appropriate procedure be devised for the Ministry Division to scrutinize and approve the individual training plans of candidates training on non-standard programmes, and to give advice on the training of candidates not agreed under iii) above.**

Chapter 9

List of proposals and outlook

9.1   As we have indicated, as a working party we have benefited greatly from the many people who have read, debated and responded to our interim and draft final reports. In the light of three rounds of consultation we have been able to develop our report and its proposals in ways that we hope will commend themselves to the Church and other interested parties. Our report is intended to give a clear statement of the general direction in which ministerial and theological education in the Church of England should develop, while allowing for local and regional development to take place within a well-coordinated framework.

Future work, timetable for approval, implementation

9.2   This report has been considered and endorsed by the Archbishops' Council and the House of Bishops. If the proposals are approved by the Church, the next phase of work will include:

i) devising and agreeing a programme and a timetable for implementation, in consultation with all affected parties;

ii) implementation in stages over the following five years.

While there are many interlocking issues to resolve, priority should be given to determining the boundaries of the proposed RTPs. Without this work in place, it will be difficult to proceed very far on other issues of implementation. We envisage that this work should be completed within six months to a year of the approval of the report. In more general terms, the implementation phase will require the setting-up of an implementation group and/or a series of smaller task groups at a national level and in each of the regions. The process will best be served by a combination of regional co-operation, creativity and initiative on the one hand and national co-ordination and oversight on the other.

Proposal 15

We recommend that appropriate arrangements be made for the implementation of this report at the national and regional levels.

List of proposals made in this report

9.3   We conclude our report by collecting together the proposals in this paragraph and then by reflecting on our hopes for the Church, its ministry and for the society which it seeks to serve. Having sought the mind of the Church through extensive consultation, we are bringing forward a new framework to provide for high-quality training for the clergy and to strengthen lay theological education. In the light of these aims we make the following proposals.

Proposal 1

We recommend that initial ministerial education be reconfigured as the period from entry into training to the end of the first training post. (4.20)

Proposal 2

We recommend that the current bishops' regulations for training be replaced by a framework for ministerial education, based on:

i) agreed phases of development in a formational journey, and

ii) statements indicating the qualities and learning expected of candidates at key points in that journey. (5.19)

Proposal 3

We recommend that:

i) opportunities for learning, under the general title of Education for Discipleship, are offered on a Church-wide basis for a range of students, which might include lay people seeking to deepen their Christian discipleship, trainee Readers and other lay ministers and potential candidates for ordination;

ii) prospective ordinands are encouraged to engage in such preliminary studies before they enter training;

iii) for prospective ordinands the amount and level of such studies should be decided in the light of the candidate's abilities, needs and circumstances, with the guideline that candidates with no prior formal learning in theology for ministry are encouraged to attain 60–120 credit points at Level 1, or its equivalent. (5.28)

Proposal 4

We recommend, as a series of norms, that:

i) candidates for ordained ministry should have successfully achieved a minimum of diploma level in ministerial theology and practice before ordination;

ii) they continue with further learning at an agreed level according to their ability in the post-ordination phase of IME;

iii) typically, those who are to hold posts of responsibility (for example, team vicars, some chaplains or incumbents) achieve a minimum of degree level in ministerial theology and practice, or its equivalent, by the time of appointment to a post of responsibility. (5.34)

Proposal 5

We recommend the creation of new institutional arrangements for training through structured and effective partnerships, drawing on diocesan training establishments (including OLM schemes), theological colleges and courses, in collaboration both with other churches and with UK higher education. The purposes of the new training partnerships should be:

i) to provide initial ministerial education for the clergy from entry into training to the end of the first training post;

ii) to develop expertise in particular areas of mission and ministry to enhance training for ordination and other ministries and types of service;

iii) to contribute to the initial training of Readers and other lay ministers and to continuing ministerial education for all ministries;

iv) to contribute to the formal theological education of the laity through the provision of programmes of Education for Discipleship;

v) to provide capacity to do research for the benefit of the Church. (6.20)

Proposal 6

We recommend:

i) the creation of regional theological training partnerships, with each partnership offering the range of training and education listed in Proposal 5;

ii) that the House of Bishops grants its recognition for ordination training to these regional training partnerships. (6.28)

Proposal 7

We recommend that regional training partnerships:

i) share administrative services and academic staff with a view to making savings.

ii) work closely together to maximize the benefits obtained from the appropriate use of Information and Communication Technology for learning and for formation. (7.13)

Proposal 8

We recommend that the Ministry Division and the proposed regional partnerships should investigate further and evaluate the possibility of benefiting from HEFCE funding. (7.21)

Proposal 9

We recommend that the regional training partnerships bid for funds on a three-year rolling basis from the Ministry Division. (7.24)

Proposal 10

We recommend that:

i) diocesan officers for OLM training, for the post-ordination phase of IME of the clergy, for Reader and other lay theological education including Education for Discipleship should continue to be provided by their own dioceses but are committed by their dioceses to work within the regional partnership for the relevant aspects of their work;

ii) savings initially in the region of £1,000,000 per annum should be made within Vote 1 by a reduction of about 75 in the number of people requiring family support who train on a full-time basis and that this saving be used to fund additional costs of CME 1–4, being £700,000 for accredited training and £300,000 for residence or equivalent training. (7.32)

Proposal 11

We recommend that budgetary provision initially in the region of £240,000 in total per annum should be made within Vote 1 to fund research within each regional training partnership. (7.34)

Proposal 12

We recommend that the scope of Vote 1 should be expanded to cover all central costs of initial ministerial education as defined in Proposal 1, including personal and family maintenance for married and single candidates and research. (7.39)

Proposal 13

We recommend that the Three-year Rolling Reserve mechanism be retained and that, subject to approval by Synod, any available balance may be used, as now, to smooth the impact on Vote 1 of any approved increase in the funding required as a result of an increase in the number of sponsored candidates. (7.43)

Proposal 14

We recommend that:

i) flexible pathways through training are developed, drawing on college, course and OLM types of training and other resources, in order to meet the training needs of candidates;

ii) the current approach to validating routes for ordinands on standard programmes be continued and be extended to the pre- and post-ordination phases of IME as defined in this report;

iii) the sponsoring diocese initiates the discussion about the appropriate pathway through training for individual candidates and that the final decision is made through agreement between the sponsoring bishop, advised by the DDO, and the relevant regional training partnership;

iv) an appropriate procedure be devised for the Ministry Division to scrutinize and approve the individual training plans of candidates training on non-standard programmes, and to give advice on the training of candidates not agreed under iii) above. (8.36)

Proposal 15

We recommend that appropriate arrangements be made for the implementation of this report at the national and regional levels. (9.2)

Our hopes for the future

9.4   In setting out on our task, we indicated that our aim was to provide high-quality training for the clergy that will equip them to offer vibrant and collaborative spiritual leadership, to empower a vocationally motivated laity and, thereby, to promote and serve God's mission in the world (1.1 above). In reviewing our thinking, we conclude by outlining what we hope the Church will gain by approving and implementing these proposals.

i) For the Church, we hope for:
- a decisive stimulus to lifelong learning in the clergy, leading to a deeper discipleship of Jesus Christ and a more effective leadership of the Church's mission;
- a well-coordinated and country-wide provision for theological education, available to lay and ordained alike;
- a framework for learning and for ministerial education that will enhance the mission of the Church by releasing the gifts of lay and ordained;
- the benefits of a research capability which can be responsive to the needs of the Church.

ii) For the ordained ministry, we hope for:
- a training that will prepare and equip them well for the demanding role of ordained ministry, both in its initial phase and as a stimulus to, and resource for, lifelong learning;
- a clear pathway through initial exploration and study, via selection and initial training to later ministry, that is flexible enough to meet the needs of the range of those coming forward for ministry and demanding enough to maximize each person's potential;
- a standing that combines their roles as spiritual leaders of communities and as people who serve both the Church and the wider society in which it is set to a good standard.

iii) For the Church's training establishment, we hope for:
- a new institutional base that will enable it to carry out its tasks, properly equipped and in a way that clearly serves the mission of the Church;
- a range of staff expertise, covering all the appropriate theological and ministerial aspects and with a secure research element;
- a maximizing of the potential of the partnership with universities and church colleges of higher education, enabling students and staff to derive full benefit from these arrangements and for the Church to contribute substantially to the study of Christian theology as a witness to the faith.

iv) For the wider community, we hope for:
- a better-informed and a more spiritually dynamic contribution to society from the Church and its leadership, lay and ordained;
- a more mature and mutually beneficial partnership between the Church's ministerial and lay training establishment and UK higher education.

Thus, while our proposals would require a significant rethinking and reorganizing of our training establishment, and of patterns of training and education in the Church, we believe that they offer substantial benefits for the Church and for its mission in the world – and specifically for the formation of ministers within a learning Church.

Appendix 1

Terms of reference and membership of the working party on the structure of funding of ordination training

A. Terms of reference

i) Building on the work of the Vote 1 review group, to consider and advise on the wider issues identified in that report concerning the funding and structure of initial training for ordination.

ii) To review the training needs of the Church in the light of developing patterns of ministry and the Church's future needs in ministry.

iii) To comment on the specific areas listed by the Vote 1 report:

- Diversification by colleges and courses – wider issues
- Exploring the different types and length of training
- Funding of research in colleges and courses
- Impact of lay ministry and other authorized ministries on the number of stipendiary clergy needed
- Incorporation of pooling costs within the apportionment
- Possible economies of scale through fewer institutions
- Sponsorship category for ordained ministry (stipendiary and non-stipendiary)
- Ways of working with the wider church to reduce overheads.

B. Membership – follows on the next page

Membership of the working party on structure and funding of ordination training

Chairman	The Rt Revd John Hind	Bishop of Gibraltar in Europe; now Bishop of Chichester
Member of the House of Bishops	The Rt Revd Dr Peter Forster	Bishop of Chester
Ministry expertise	The Revd Canon Keith Lamdin	Director of the Board of Stewardship, Training, Evangelism and Ministry – Diocese of Oxford
	The Revd Canon June Osborne	Treasurer, Salisbury Cathedral; Bishops' Inspector
	The Revd Canon Dr Robin Greenwood	Ministry Development Officer – Diocese of Chelmsford; now, as an Observer, Provincial Officer for Ministry, Church in Wales
Training expertise	The Revd Dr Richard Burridge	Dean, King's College, London; Member of Vote 1 Working Party; member of General Synod
	The Revd Dr Judith Maltby	Chaplain – Corpus Christi College, Oxford
Finance expertise	The Revd Barry Nichols (Vice Chairman)	Chairman – Vote 1 Working Party; Retired partner – Ernst & Young
	Mr Richard Finlinson	Chairman – Canterbury DBF
Training institutions	The Revd Dr Jeremy Sheehy	Principal, St Stephen's House, Oxford
	The Revd Canon Dr David Hewlett	Principal, South West Ministry Training Course; Director of the Queen's Foundation, Birmingham from April 2003
	The Revd Canon Wendy Bracegirdle	Principal, Manchester OLM Scheme (until December 2002)
Diocesan	Mr Phil Hamlyn-Williams	Reader; Lincoln Diocesan Secretary; Member of Vote 1 Working Party; Member of Archbishops' Finance Committee
	Mr Anthony Archer	St Albans Diocese; member of General Synod
Church Colleges of Higher Education	Professor Dianne Willcocks	Principal of York St John College, formerly the College of Ripon and York St John
Ecumenical members	The Revd Don Pickard	Formation in Ministry Office, Methodist Church
	The Revd Roy Lowes (from February 2002)	Secretary for Training, United Reformed Church
Assessors	Mr Richard Hopgood (until July 2002)	Archbishops' Council: Director of Policy
	The Ven Dr Gordon Kuhrt	Director of Ministry
Secretaries	Mr David Morris	Archbishops' Council Ministry Division: Finance & Administrative Secretary
	The Revd Dr David Way	Theological Education Secretary
	Miss Sarah Evans	Secretariat

Appendix 2

List of those who contributed to the consultation process

The main phases of the consultation process were:

A. an *initial request* for views in the light of our terms of reference (Appendix 1) in January–April 2001;

B. regional meetings and a request for written comments on our *interim report* (February–July 2002);

C. regional meetings and a request for written comments on our *draft final report* (November 2002)

The working party is grateful for all those who took part in this consultation process. Listed below are those who corresponded with the working party, with an indication of the phase of the process to which they contributed.

bishops and retired bishops	Initial	Interim	Final
Bishop of Beverley *	✓		
Bishop of Birmingham *	✓		
Bishop of Bristol *	✓		
Bishop of Dudley		✓	
Bishop of Grantham		✓	
Bishop of Leicester *	✓		
Bishop of Liverpool *	✓		
Bishop of Ludlow	✓	✓	
Bishop of Newcastle *		✓	
Bishop of Norwich *	✓		
Bishop of Penrith	✓		
Bishop of Portsmouth *		✓	✓
Bishop of Ripon and Leeds *	✓		
Bishop of Salisbury *		✓	
Bishop of Southampton		✓	
Bench of Bishops, Wales		✓	
Bishop of Warwick	✓		
Bishop of Willesden		✓	
Bishop of Worcester *	✓		

deans and provosts	Initial	Interim	Final
Dean and Chapter Lincoln	✓		
Dean of Norwich *	✓	✓	
Dean of Ripon *	✓	✓	
Dean of Truro	✓		
Dean of Wakefield *	✓		
Chancellor of York inster		✓	

archdeacons	Initial	Interim	Final
Archdeacon of Halifax	✓		
Archdeacon of Norwich *	✓		
Archdeacon of West Ham *	✓		

dioceses	Initial	Interim	Final
Bath and Wells Diocese	✓	✓	
Regional consultation organized by: Birmingham Diocesan Office			✓
Birmingham Diocesan Secretary	✓		
Birmingham Diocese		✓	✓
Blackburn Diocese		✓	
Bristol Diocese		✓	
Canterbury Diocese	✓	✓	
Standing Committee of DBF Carlisle	✓		
Chelmsford Diocese			✓
Chester Diocese		✓	
Chichester Diocese		✓	
Coventry Diocese – CME Adviser	✓	✓	
Coventry Diocesan Secretary	✓	✓	
Derby Diocese – East Midlands Regional Meeting		✓	
Derby Diocese – Warden of Readers/Laity Development Adviser		✓	
Durham Diocese, Board of Ministries and Training		✓	
Ely Diocese		✓	
Diocese of Europe		✓	
Exeter Diocese		✓	
Gloucester Diocese – Readers Committee		✓	
Guildford Diocese			✓
Hereford Diocese	✓	✓	

Appendix 2

dioceses (cont.)	Initial	Interim	Final
Lichfield Diocese	✓	✓	
Lichfield Diocese – Bishop's Council		✓	
Lincoln Diocese	✓	✓	
Liverpool Diocese	✓		
Liverpool Diocesan Secretary	✓		
London Diocese		✓	
Manchester Diocese – Board of Ministry		✓	
Newcastle Diocese		✓	
Norwich Diocese – Bishop's Staff		✓	✓
Norwich Diocese – Course Management Committee		✓	
Oxford Diocese – Stewardship, Training, Evangelism & Ministry		✓	
Portsmouth Diocese	✓		
Ripon and Leeds Diocese		✓	
Rochester Diocese		✓	
Sheffield Diocese		✓	
Sheffield, Diocesan Board of Finance		✓	
Sheffield Diocesan Secretary		✓	
Southwell Diocese		✓	
Southwark Diocese – Ministry & Training Policy Committee		✓	
Wakefield Diocese		✓	✓
Worcester Diocese	✓		
York Diocese		✓	

other clergy	Initial	Interim	Final
The Revd Michael Ainsworth *	✓	✓	
The Revd J. L. Alderton-Ford *	✓		
Sister Mary Angela *	✓		
The Revd Paul Ayers *	✓		
The Revd Canon Peter Ballard	✓		
The Revd Caroline Baston		✓	
The Revd Dr Ian Bell			✓
The Revd Prof Nigel Biggar *	✓		
The Revd Dr Alan Billings	✓		
The Revd Canon Lesley Bentley	✓		
The Revd J. R. Bowen		✓	

other clergy (cont.)	Initial	Interim	Final
The Revd W. Bowen		✓	
The Revd Chris Bracegirdle	✓		
The Revd Canon Robin Brown	✓		
The Revd David Butterfield *	✓	✓	
The Revd Graeme Buttery *	✓		
The Revd Canon G. Chesterman	✓		
The Revd Daniel Clark	✓		
The Revd Canon Ronald Coppin		✓	
The Revd Steven Croft		✓	
The Revd Dr Stephen Dawes	✓		
The Revd Canon Adrian Dorber	✓		
The Revd Canon Carol Farrer	✓		
The Revd Michael Foster		✓	
The Revd Canon Richard Franklin		✓	
The Revd Richard Franklin		✓	
The Revd Canon Tim Gouldstone	✓		
The Revd Canon Terence Grigg	✓		
The Revd Canon John Hall	✓		
The Revd Prof Daniel Hardy	✓	✓	✓
The Revd Alan Hargrave *	✓		
The Revd Crispin Harrison	✓		
The Revd Simon Heathfield			✓
The Revd Canon Dr David Hewlett		✓	
The Revd Tim Hillier		✓	
The Revd Toddy Hoare	✓	✓	
The Revd Canon Michael Hodge	✓		
The Revd Canon Douglas Holt	✓		
The Revd Lawrie Jenkins		✓	
The Revd Terry Joyce	✓		✓
The Revd Chris Key		✓	
The Revd Canon Michael Kitchener	✓	✓	
The Revd Colin Lawlor		✓	
The Revd Christopher Lindlar		✓	
The Revd Barry Linney		✓	
The Revd Colin Lunt			✓

Appendix 2

other clergy (cont.)	Initial	Interim	Final
The Revd Canon Ralph Mallinson	✓		
The Revd Dr Jeremy Morris		✓	
The Revd David Neno	✓		
The Revd T. Newcombe *	✓		
The Revd Canon Prof Edward Norman			✓
The Revd Canon Gordon Oliver			✓
The Revd Catherine Packer	✓		
The Revd Canon Trevor Page	✓		
The Revd Colin Patterson	✓		
The Revd Brian Pettifer		✓	
The Revd John Richardson *	✓		
The Revd Peter Robinson	✓	✓	
The Revd Prof Canon Christopher Rowland		✓	
The Revd Canon Stanley Royle	✓		
The Revd Canon John Salter	✓		
The Revd Canon Mark Sanders	✓		
The Revd Prof Bernard Silverman *	✓		
The Revd Mark Sowerby		✓	
The Revd Canon Beaumont Stevenson		✓	
The Revd Mair Talbot	✓		
The Revd Prof Anthony Thiselton *	✓	✓	
The Revd Richard Paul Thomas *	✓		
The Revd Dr M. Thompson			✓
The Revd Canon John Thomson		✓	
The Revd Nicholas Vesey		✓	
The Revd Canon Michael Walters *	✓		
Canon Michael Warner			✓
The Revd Michael Warren		✓	
The Revd Canon Jim Wellington *	✓		
The Revd Canon Vernon White (as Chancellor of Lincoln)	✓		

lay people	Initial	Interim	Final
Ms Gill Ambrose *	✓		
Mrs Lynn Anderson *	✓		

Formation for ministry within a learning church

lay people (cont.)	Initial	Interim	Final
Mr Edward Armistead	✓		
Ms Sallie Bassham *		✓	
Mr Mark Birchall		✓	
Dr David Bowen *	✓		
Dr Patricia Bracegirdle	✓		
Ms Beatrice Brandon *	✓		
Mrs Elizabeth Bridger *	✓	✓	
Mr Chris Chapman		✓	
Prof Michael Clarke	✓		
Judge T.A.C. Coningsby *	✓		
Ms Joanna Cox	✓		
Mr Jim Drennan	✓		
Mr Stephen Dunham *	✓		
Mr David Edwards	✓		
Mr Michael Evans	✓		
Mr Stuart Evans	✓		
Mr Nigel Feilden	✓		
Prof Alan Ford	✓		
Prof David Ford	✓		
Mr Philip Gray		✓	
Mrs Faith Hanson *	✓		
Mr George Hext		✓	
Mr Michael Hodge	✓		
Ms Sue Howard	✓		
Mr Frank Knaggs *	✓		
Mrs M. Langham	✓		
Prof Paul Light		✓	
Dr Edmund Marshall *	✓		
Mr John Munns		✓	
Mr David Munro	✓		
Mrs J. Park	✓		
Mr Chris Peck	✓		
Ms Brenda Pitton		✓	
Mr Julian Pykett	✓		
Mr Timothy L. F. Royle *	✓		
Mr Michael Selby	✓		
Ms Judi Shepherd	✓		
Mr Colin Slater *	✓		
Mr Neil Smart		✓	
Mr Ian R. Smith *	✓		
Miss Olive Stephens		✓	

Appendix 2

lay people (cont.)	Initial	Interim	Final
Mr Barry Stewart	✓		
Prof E. Stuart	✓		
Mr Brian Strand	✓		
Ms Margaret Townsend *		✓	
Prof Keith Watson	✓		
Mr Robin Wootton			

theological colleges, courses & OLM	Initial	Interim	Final
Canterbury OLM		✓	
Carlisle & Blackburn Diocesan Training Institute	✓	✓	
Carlisle & Blackburn Diocesan Training Institute Council		✓	✓
College of the Resurrection, Mirfield	✓	✓	
College of the Resurrection, Mirfield, Common Room		✓	
College of the Resurrection, Mirfield – Council		✓	
Cranmer Hall, Durham	✓	✓	
East Anglia Ministerial Training Course		✓	
East Midlands Ministerial Training Course			✓
Gloucester OLM scheme		✓	
Guildford OLM scheme		✓	✓
Hereford OLM scheme	✓		
Lichfield OLM scheme		✓	
Liverpool OLM scheme	✓	✓	
Manchester OLM scheme		✓	
North East Oecumenical Course		✓	
North East Oecumenical Course students		✓	
North Thames Ministerial Training Course	✓		
North Thames Ministerial Training Course Council		✓	
Norwich OLM	✓	✓	
Nottingham University		✓	
Oak Hill Theological College	✓	✓	
Queen's Foundation (The)		✓	
Queen's students		✓	
Ridley Hall, Cambridge – common room		✓	✓
Ripon College, Cuddesdon	✓		✓
Ripon College, Cuddesdon – governing body		✓	

theological colleges, courses & OLM (cont.)	Initial	Interim	Final
St Albans and Oxford Ministry Course	✓		
St Albans and Oxford Ministry Course students		✓	
St Edmundsbury & Ipswich OLM scheme		✓	
St Johns College, Durham		✓	
St Johns College Nottingham		✓	✓
St Johns Nottingham Council		✓	
St Johns Nottingham students		✓	
St Martin's College, Lancaster		✓	
St Michael's College, Llandaff		✓	
St Stephen's House	✓	✓	
St Stephen's House Council		✓	
St Stephen's House students		✓	
Salisbury OLM		✓	✓
Sarum College, Salisbury			✓
South East Institute for Theological Education	✓		✓
South East Institute for Theological Education – governing body		✓	
Southern Theological Education and Training Scheme	✓		
Southern Theological Education and Training Scheme, Board of Governors	✓	✓	✓
Southern Theological Education and Training Scheme – 3rd year students		✓	
Southern Theological Education and Training Scheme – 1st year students		✓	
South West Ministerial Training Course Council		✓	
Southwark OLM		✓	
Trinity College, Bristol – Council		✓	
Wakefield OLM		✓	
West of England Ministerial Training Course	✓		
West of England Ministerial Training Course – governing body		✓	
West of England Ministerial Training Course – student on governing body		✓	
Westcott House, Cambridge			✓
Westcott House, Cambridge – Chaplain		✓	
Westcott House, Cambridge – group of ordinands		✓	
Wycliffe Hall, Oxford	✓	✓	✓

Appendix 2

corporate responses	Initial	Interim	Final
Anglican CME Officers of West Midlands & ecumenical colleagues		✓	
Association of Ordinands & Candidates for Ministry		✓	
Baptist College, Bristol		✓	
Board of Mission, Church House		✓	
Bristol Baptist College - Christopher Ellis		✓	
Cambridge Federation	✓		
Cambridge Theology Foundation		✓	
Canterbury Christ Church – University College		✓	
Cardiff University		✓	
Central Readers Council		✓	
Cheltenham & Gloucester College	✓		
Chester College, Department of Theology and Religious Studies			✓
CHRISM		✓	
Church Army, Wilson Carlile College, Sheffield	✓	✓	
Church Pastoral Aid Society			✓
CME Panel, Ministry Division	✓	✓	
Committee for Minority Ethnic Anglican Concerns	✓	✓	✓
Connected Community Learning, Peterborough			✓
Cornhill Training Centre	✓		
DRACS, Ministry Division		✓	
Durham University, Theology Department		✓	
East Midlands Consortium for Training and Education for Ministry		✓	
East Midlands Regional Meeting		✓	
Elland Society	✓		
Evangelical Council of (The C of E)		✓	
Finance Committee - Archbishops' Council			✓
Gloucestershire University (formerly Cheltenham and Gloucester College)		✓	
Guildford Community Family Trust		✓	
Inspection Working Party, Central Secretariat of the Archbishops Council		✓	
Kent University - Prof. Robin Gill		✓	
King Alfred's College, Winchester		✓	
Leeds University		✓	
NW Regional Group, CME Officers		✓	

corporate responses (cont.)	Initial	Interim	Final
Oxford, Theology Faculty Centre		✓	
Reader Training Panel, Ministry Division		✓	
Regent's Park College, Oxford		✓	
Rochester Readers		✓	
Scottish Episcopal Church – General Synod Office			✓
St Mark and St John College, Plymouth	✓		
Southern Regions Institute		✓	
Trans-Atlantic & Pacific Alliance of Churches		✓	
Vocation, Recruitment and Selection Committee, Ministry Division		✓	
The Church in Wales, Council for Mission/Ministry		✓	
Whitelands College and University of Surrey Roehampton		✓	
United Reformed Church		✓	
United Reformed Church Training Committee		✓	
University of Wales, Bangor – Theology and Religious Studies Department		✓	
York St John (formerly Ripon and York)	✓		✓

* Member of General Synod

Appendix 3

Total number of ordinands in training 2002/2003

	1	2	3	4	5	6	7	Other full-time students 2002/03
	Sponsored Students: 2002/2003						2001/02	
	Men		Women		Lay			
Theological colleges	Stip/NSM	Perm NSM	Stip/NSM	Perm NSM	Stip/NSM	**TOTAL:**	*TOTAL:*	
Cranmer Hall	31	5	29	1	0	66	65	29
Mirfield	28	0	0	0	0	28	36	12
Oak Hill	54	1	1	0	0	56	54	42
Queens Birmingham	10	0	11	0	0	21	16	19
Ridley Hall	37	0	18	0	0	55	58	3
Ripon College	30	2	24	0	0	56	68	5
St John's Nottingham	35	0	21	3	0	59	73	8
St Stephen's Oxford	18	2	2	0	0	22	37	9
Trinity College	44	0	20	0	0	64	73	39
Westcott House	28	1	27	1	0	57	60	8
Wycliffe Hall	48	0	17	0	0	65	70	32
TISEC	0	0	0	0	0	0	0	
Llandaff	1	0	4	0	0	5	4	
TOTAL COLLEGES	**364**	**11**	**174**	**5**	**0**	**554**	*614*	**206**
Regional courses								
Carlisle & B'burn	3	4	3	2	0	12	11	13
East Anglian	16	6	22	14	0	58	66	7
East Midlands	3	5	9	8	0	25	33	45
North East	10	9	15	9	0	43	36	8
Northern	26	12	30	20	0	88	81	16
North Thames	16	6	11	8	0	41	32	11
St Albans/Oxford	10	10	21	17	1	59	59	1
STETS	10	18	14	40	1	83	84	26
SEITE	14	20	18	26	0	78	85	14
South West	4	2	6	16	0	28	24	12
West Midlands	2	7	7	19	0	35	31	26
West of England	6	4	17	11	0	38	36	9
Other training establishments	0	1	0	0	0	1	0	0
TOTAL COURSES	**120**	**104**	**173**	**190**	**2**	**589**	*578*	**188**
TOTAL COLLS & CRSES	**484**	**115**	**347**	**195**	**2**	**1143**	*1192*	**394**
OLM schemes (see next table)	0	90	0	127	0	217	*191*	0
TOTAL in training	**484**	**205**	**347**	**322**	**2**	**1360**	*1383*	**394**

The figures above include 9 college students whose training is being funded totally from other sources *as well as* those paying reduced fees. The figures therefore show total student numbers and not just those who count towards the Bishops' Agreed Maximum. The number of college students who count towards the BAM is 537.

Sponsored OLM candidates training on schemes recognized by the House of Bishops 2002/03

Diocese	Men	Women	Total	2000/01
Blackburn	2	4	6	5
Canterbury	7	10	17	15
Carlisle	1	3	4	3
Coventry	2	2	4	2
Gloucester	3	2	5	5
Guildford	6	9	15	12
Hereford	4	2	6	3
Lichfield	8	4	12	13
Lincoln	1	4	5	1
Liverpool	1	5	6	6
Manchester	7	11	18	18
Newcastle	1	1	2	2
Norwich	8	13	21	21
Oxford	9	9	18	16
St Eds and Ips	7	7	14	7
Salisbury	6	16	22	28
Southwark	12	18	30	27
Truro	0	0	0	2
Wakefield	5	7	12	5
TOTAL	90	127	217	191

Appendix 4

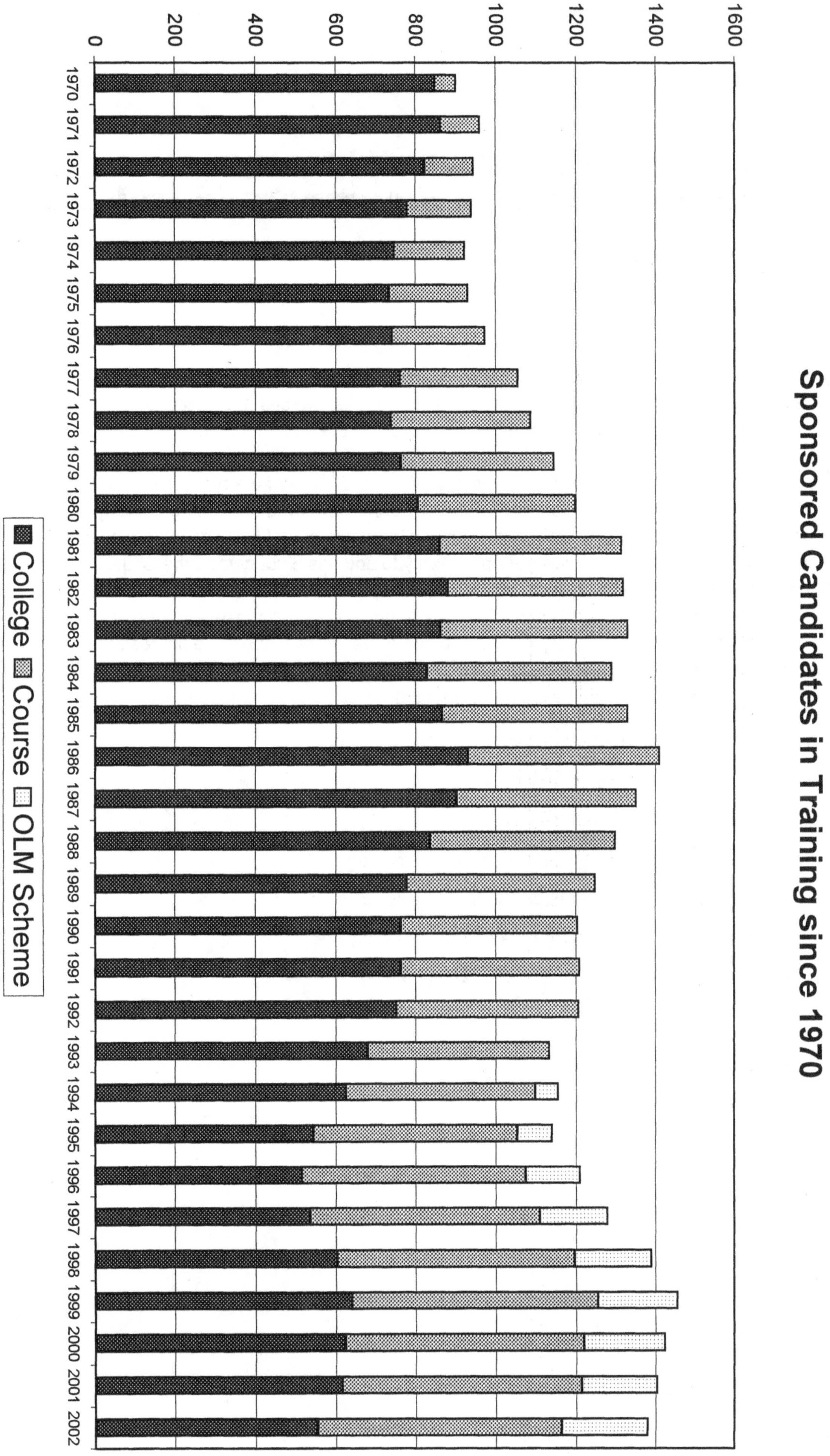
Sponsored Candidates in Training since 1970
0
200
400
600
800
1000
1200
1400
1600
1970 1971 1972 1973 1974 1975 1976 1977 1978 1979 1980 1981 1982 1983 1984 1985 1986 1987 1988 1989 1990 1991 1992 1993 1994 1995 1996 1997 1998 1999 2000 2001 2002
College
Course
OLM Scheme

Appendix 5

Training institutions used by the Methodist Church and numbers in training

February 2003

In accordance with the *Principles for Theological Education* (approved by Conference 1997) and, in particular, (f) 'Theological Education should be ecumenical, wherever possible', the Methodist Church works with the Ministry Division, with the courses and colleges approved by the Church of England for training and is represented on the monitoring bodies of the Education Validation Panel and the Inspections Working Party. The information below is provided to illustrate the current closeness of working and some of the resources available for closer working in future, and as a signal of an intention to work with the Church of England and the United Reformed Church in implementing the outcomes of the present review, as far as possible. Since the review was set up explicitly to address a concern of the Church of England the giving of this information cannot be taken to imply that the Methodist Church, though represented on the Working Party, will take up as policy all those recommendations. The table below sets out the position as at the end of December 2002. The figures are to be used with care: the patterns of training in the Methodist Church and ways of recording statistics differ from those of the Church of England.

In the table below, columns A – H show

- A   Foundation students in part-time training
- B   foundation students in full-time training
- C   Student ministers in part-time pre-ordination training
- D   Student ministers in full-time pre-ordination training
- E   Student deacons in part-time pre-ordination training
- F   Student deacons in full-time pre-ordination training
- G   Total number of students
- H   Notional 'full-time' capacity of institution, where applicable (based on tutorial supervision)

Appendix 5

Training institution	A	B	C	D	E	F	G	H
Bangor, Centre for Ministry Studies	1	-	-	-	-	-	1	
Carlisle and Blackburn Diocesan Training Institute	1	-	1	-	-	-	2	
Cliff College, Derbyshire	2	2	-	-	-	-	4	
East Anglian Ministerial Training Course	5	-	2	1	-	-	8	
East Midlands Ministry Training Course	5	-	4	-	-	-	9	
Partnership for Theological Education Manchester, NOC	9	-	9	-	1	-	19	
North Bank Centre for Christian Living	3	-	-	-	-	-	3	
North Thames Ministerial Training Course	7	-	5	-	-	-	12	
Partnership for Theological Education Manchester, Hartley Victoria College	25	4	4	7	-	1	41	30
Queen's Foundation Birmingham (inc WMMTC)	18	4	6	7	-	3	38	
South East Institute for Theological Education	8	-	3	-	-	-	11	
St Albans and Oxford Ministry Course	-	-	-	-	-	-	-	
St Michael's College, Llandaff	-	4	-	3	-	-	7	10+
Southern Theological Education and Training Scheme	10	-	7	-	-	-	17	
South West Ministerial Training Course	5	-	8	-	-	-	13	
Theological Institute for the Scottish Episcopal Church	1	-	-	1	-	-	2	
Urban Theology Unit, Sheffield	4	2	1	3	-	-	10	20
West of England Ministerial Training Course	4	-	-	-	-	-	4	
Wesley College, Bristol	3	10	1	15	-	4	29	40+
Wesley House, Cambridge	2	8	2	8	-	-	20	30
Wesley Study Centre, Durham	6	12	2	10	-	-	30	20+
Westminster Institute, Oxford	9	-	1	1	-	-	11	
York Institute of Community Theology	9	1	1	-	-	-	11	
Training entry deferred/ not yet allocated	1	1					2	
Totals	138	48	57	56	1	8	308	

Total full-time students 112   Total foundation students 186

Total part-time students 196   Total pre-ordination students 122

The outcome of selection conferences would suggest that about 260 of these students in training would eventually be ordained (235 presbyteral, 25 diaconal). The Methodist Church in 2002 agreed to discontinue the use of categories for selection and training

As at the end of December 2002, a further 95 students awaited allocation into foundation training, most of whom were to begin training in September 2003.

Appendix 6

Training institutions used by the United Reformed Church and numbers in training

February 2002

Queen's College, Birmingham

Westminster College, Cambridge

Mansfield College, Oxford working in partnership with Regent's Park College

The Partnership for Theological Education, Manchester

Scottish United Reformed and Congregational College, Glasgow

East Anglian Ministerial Training Course

East Midlands Ministerial Training Course

North East Oecumenical Course

St Albans and Oxford Ministry Course

South East Institute for Theological Education

South West Ministerial Training Course

Southern Theological Education and Training Course

West Midlands Ministerial Training Course

St Michael's College, Llandaff

Students in training in the 2001/2002 year were:

Stipendiary ministry	68
Church-related Community Workers	5
Non-stipendiary Ministry	38
Total	111

Appendix 7

A possible structure for Regional Training Partnerships

1. As indicated in paragraph 6.35 the model of regional training partnerships (RTPs) may vary from region to region. The models could include:

    - A covenant between separate and distinct entities, with protocols for
    - co-operation.
    - One legal entity providing ordination training, with a covenant relationship with dioceses and other churches relating to Reader and lay theological education.
    - One legal entity where all resources are organizationally subsumed under one legal framework

    We envisage that the creation of RTPs will often involve a process of growing together and that an individual partnership may initially come into being as a covenant and then move forward over a period of years to become one legal entity.

A. Illustration of a covenant relationship

2. In order to demonstrate the way in which an RTP may be established in the first place we detail below the way in which we envisage that the loosest arrangement, i.e. a covenant between separate and distinct entities, might operate.

3. Let us suppose a region comprising:

    Dioceses A, B, C and D

    A Methodist and a URC district

    A Church of England college of 60 places and six academic staff

    A Methodist college of 20 places and two academic staff

    Two courses each of 60 places and each with three academic staff

    An OLM scheme in dioceses B and D each with nine places each

    The four dioceses each with one to two full-time people dealing with lay and Reader theological education and either a full post or half a post each dealing with CME 1 – 4. These too will be contributed to the RTP.

4. From this is created an RTP which offers:

    70 places full-time pre-ordination training
    135 places in part-time pre-ordination training
    18 places in OLM training

Appendix 7

324 places of post-ordination training, including a number of weeks of residential training *(based on the following number of ordinations each year: Church of England full-time – 22, part-time – 45, OLM – 6, Methodist full-time – 8, giving a total of 81. Over 4 years this generates 324 places for CME 1–4)*
Involvement in Reader and lay theological education

In the colleges the equivalent of 5 places would be filled by deacons and priests undertaking week-long residential periods.

Governance of the RTPs

5   The governing body of the RTP would include representatives of both users and suppliers, being the dioceses (the diocesan bishop or someone appointed by him), the Methodist and URC districts and students (the users), the trustees of the full-time training institutions, and the trustees of the part-time training institution and staff (the suppliers). The chair would be elected from among the representatives of the dioceses and Methodist and URC districts. At this stage the governing body would not be a separate legal entity. All the members would be members of the governing bodies of either or both the college and the part-time training institution (see paragraph 7 below).

6   The Anglican and Methodist theological **colleges** would continue as separate legal entities and would offer full-time training both to people from the region and also from other regions. The funding for full-time students would not depend on where the student comes from in the country. Colleges could also offer part-time training in liaison with the part-time training institution. They would participate in the post-ordination phase of IME both on a residential and a non-residential basis. The colleges could maintain their distinctive traditions. Staff would be appointed by the colleges but with a representative from the RTP on any selection panels. Bishops and Methodist and URC authorities would be free to arrange for ordinands who are to train on a full-time basis to train either at the colleges within their RTP or at any other college. As part of their commitment to the RTP, the colleges would invite a representative of the regional part-time training institution (see 7 below) to be a member of the governing body of the college.

7   The regional **courses** would, in this example, be reconstituted as one legal entity offering part-time training in four or more locations so as to provide accessible training throughout the region. It will be important that this be established and perceived as an entirely new entity and not as the successor of one or other of the existing courses. However in legal terms this could probably be achieved most conveniently by changing the membership and detailed objectives of one of the existing courses which exists as a company limited by guarantee so as to meet the new requirements. The new part-time training institutions (PTTI) would provide IME covering the full period of IME as reconstituted. This would be delivered by the staff of the PTTI in co-operation with the staff of the colleges, the diocesan OLM schemes and the diocesan CME officers. The PTTIs would also co-operate with and be a resource for the diocesan Reader and lay theological education teams.

8   The governing bodies of the PTTIs would include representatives of the dioceses, the Methodist and URC districts and the colleges as well as staff and student representatives. The chair would be elected from among the representatives of the dioceses and the Methodist and URC districts.

9   It should be noted that as a mark of the covenant relationship between the colleges and the PTTIs within the RTP it is proposed that the colleges should appoint a representative of the PTTI as a member of the governing body of the college and that the PTTI should appoint a representative of the college as a member of its governing body. Further convergence of membership of the respective governing bodies could occur at a later point.

10 While establishing this arrangement the existing courses within a region will probably need to operate in tandem for a period while shadow governing bodies, management teams and methods of operation for the PTTI are established and while any new appointments are made.

Management of the RTPs

11 The executive management of the RTP would be in the hands of the 'senior managers' being the principals of the colleges and the PTTI, together with the Directors of Ministry (or equivalent) from each diocese (i.e. one person from each diocese). If the extent of Methodist or URC participation in the activities of the RTP warrants it they would also be entitled to have a representative on the senior management team, as they would in our example. The bursar would normally attend meetings of the team. In this example this group would consist of six to eight people who should work in partnership to ensure that the colleges, the PTTI, the four dioceses and the other participating denominations work closely together. We propose that this group should be chaired by one of their number and that this chair-person should be appointed by the representatives on the governing body of the dioceses and the Methodist and URC districts. (In principle it seems right that this appointment is made by the churches, rather than by the practitioners.) This appointment should be for a fixed period of one to three years and should be reconsidered at the end of that period. It is hoped that in this way the most suitable person for the role would be appointed, whatever their main responsibility. We would expect this senior management group to meet regularly, say once a month.

12 There would then be a wider management team, including the senior managers and the principals or vice-principals responsible for full-time and part-time ordination training and OLM training, the diocesan CME officers and Reader and lay training officers and the bursar responsible for the finances of the RTP. This wider management team would meet less regularly, say three times a year. It would include a total of 34 people as shown in Appendix 8. Other smaller ad hoc meetings would take place as required to deal with particular issues.

13 This management structure is illustrated in Appendix 8 Example 1.

14 There are at present twelve courses and therefore twelve course principals and twelve course vice-principals. There is also a minimum staffing requirement of three academic staff for each course. If it is accepted that there should be eight regions (and there may be fewer than eight), it should be possible to save costs

Appendix 7

by reducing the number of principals by four. Assuming the cost of a principal is £36,000 per annum this would result in savings of £144,000 per annum. So far as vice-principals are concerned we assume that their time will continue to be required in the new PTTIs. We recognize that part of each principal's time is allocated to teaching and that there will be an increase in the administrative load on the principals of the PTTIs as a result of the proposed changes. Therefore within existing cost levels there is the opportunity for each PTTI to appoint an additional half member of academic staff, i.e. four in total (at a cost of about £30,000 per annum per full-time person).

15 The academic staffing costs of the constituent elements of the RTP described in paragraph 3 above, before and after the change, are illustrated below. The staffing changes in the PTTI are set out in the preceding paragraph. Through sharing expertise between the college and the PTTI it is possible to reduce the staffing of the college by 0.5. As a result of these changes, overall staffing levels are reduced by one, with a total saving in this example of £36,000.

Current academic staff costs			
	No.	Costs per staff member	Total cost
Church of England college		£	£
Principal	1.0	36,000	36,000
Other staff	5.0	30,000	150,000
Methodist college			
Principal	1.0	36,000	36,000
Other staff	1.0	30,000	30,000
Course 1			
Principal	1.0	36,000	36,000
Other staff	2.0	30,000	60,000
Course 2			
Principal	1.0	36,000	36,000
Other staff	2.0	30,000	60,000
	14.0		444,000

Future academic staff costs			
	No.	Costs per staff member	Total cost
Church of England college		£	£
Principal	1.0	36,000	36,000
Other staff	4.5	30,000	135,000
Methodist college			
Principal	1.0	36,000	36,000
Other staff	1.0	30,000	30,000
PTTI			
Principal	1.0	36,000	36,000
Other staff	4.5	30,000	135,000
	13.0		408,000

16   It has been suggested in the discussion of the draft final report that the creation of RTPs will lead to another layer of management, but we do not consider that this should be the case. This illustration shows a saving of at least 7.5 per cent can be made on these academic staffing costs. If the two courses were to continue operating separately but within the management structure of the RTP it would still be necessary to have a principal for each course but it should be possible to reduce other staff numbers by 0.5 between the two courses, thus reducing overall staff numbers by one and staff costs by a total of £30,000 instead of £36,000 as shown in the above example. The savings on administration staff costs would be achieved on a similar basis. There should also be further savings available to be made within diocesan OLM, CME and Reader and lay training budgets as a result of efficiencies achieved by working within the RTP structure. Initially these may be offset by time taken to negotiate and develop the new operating arrangements.

17   We envisage that once the RTP is established the academic posts could increasingly become joint appointments between the college and the PTTIs so as to establish a good spread of specialisms within the staff of the RTP as a whole.

Administrative arrangements

18   We recommend that one bursar and administrative support team should serve the RTP, so as to achieve economy, efficiency and co-ordination within the RTP as a whole. The staff should be employed jointly by any separate legal entities involved, normally the college and the PTTI, and the costs should be shared proportionally to the activities involved. If administration services are also offered to any of the dioceses they should also join in the joint employment arrangements

Appendix 7

for the relevant staff. This arrangement, which is similar to that adopted by the National Church Institutions, should avoid additional costs resulting from VAT on cross charges. Ideally the administrative staff would all be based in the same location, but in some circumstances this may not be suitable and it may be preferable for them to be located partly in the college and partly in the main office of the PTTI. The administrative unit would provide accounting services, academic administration, personnel services, ICT and a secretariat.

Arrangements for OLM schemes

19   OLM staff would continue to be appointed by the diocesan bishop, but this would follow participation by representatives of the RTP on the selection panel. OLM staff would be paid by the diocese. The scheme would continue to receive a contribution from Vote 1 as at present. It is proposed that the OLM team would work within the RTP using the resources of the RTP to the maximum extent possible. Any savings would accrue to the diocese concerned. It would also be open for the diocese to 'buy-in' part or all of its OLM training from the PTTI.

Arrangements for further investment of £1 million per annum in the post-ordination phase of IME

20   The additional budgetary allocation totalling £1 million for the post-ordination phase of IME is divided into two parts and it is proposed that these parts should be managed in different ways.

21   The £700,000 to be made available for further training will be allocated by the Ministry Division Finance Panel to dioceses following a bidding process. This is likely to be allocated broadly *pro rata* to the number of people in their first four years after ordination. The control of the use of this will be in the hands of dioceses (i.e. probably their CME officers) in consultation with the RTP. Much of this training will probably be provided by the RTP. However the funds may be used for external courses where this is more appropriate for the individuals concerned. Dioceses will be reimbursed for this expenditure by Ministry Division on a termly basis. Any overspend on this budget would need to be borne by the diocese concerned. Any underspend would form a reduction of expenditure on Vote 1 and, if not required for the Three-year Rolling Reserve, would be returned to dioceses as a whole as a reduction of apportionment.

22   The £300,000 to be made available for short-term residential blocks of training will be allocated by the Ministry Division Finance Panel to colleges within an RTP following a bidding process. This is also likely to be allocated broadly *pro rata* to the number of people in their first four years after ordination. We anticipate that colleges will negotiate appropriate packages of residential experience with the diocesan CME officers and submit bids for funds to the Finance Panel. It is intended that these funds be made available to the colleges provided the users (i.e. the diocesan CME officers) are satisfied. If diocesan CME officers are not satisfied with the packages offered, the CME officers will be able to apply to the Finance Panel for the appropriate proportion of the funds to be made available to them for alternative formation/training experiences. Any overspend on this budget would need to be borne by the diocese concerned. Any underspend

would form a reduction of expenditure on Vote 1 and, if not required for the Three-year Rolling Reserve, would be returned to dioceses as a whole as a reduction of apportionment.

Arrangements for the post-ordination phase of IME

23   The oversight of candidates continuing training during the first four years after ordination (CME 1–4) will continue to be the joint responsibility of the diocesan CME officer and the training incumbent. However the diocesan CME officer should work closely with the other staff of the college or PTTI, as appropriate, to ensure that there is proper continuity between the pre- and post-ordination phases of ordination training. Many of these clergy will continue to undertake structured training within the RTP, but some will study elsewhere. Where people move on ordination from one region to another there will inevitably be a change in responsibility for their oversight. In these situations the CME officer will need to consult the staff of the institution in which the individual undertook their pre-ordination training to ensure that there is as much continuity as possible between the pre- and post-ordination phases of formation.

Arrangements for Reader and lay theological education

24   It is hoped that dioceses will wish to operate their Reader and lay theological education within the overall framework of the RTP so as to strengthen the resources available both to the Reader and lay education teams and to the RTP. This would also assist the development of Education for Discipleship programmes. This arrangement will need to be negotiated separately between each diocese and each RTP. While we hope that the advantages of operating within the RTP will be significant and will be recognized, dioceses will nevertheless, of course, be free to develop or to continue diocesan Reader and lay education initiatives outside the activities of the RTP should they so wish.

Co-ordinated delivery of training

25   We envisage that in most situations, wherever the syllabus covers the same ground in the same depth, part-time ordination training (for stipendiary, non-stipendiary and OLM ministry) and Reader and lay theological education should be delivered together. We should seek to avoid the existing situation in some places where similar material is delivered separately by courses, OLM schemes and Reader and lay theological education teams. In this way all those studying the same subject in the same location at the same depth could do so together. This would enable the RTP to view the staffing as a whole in terms of specialisms and could enrich the experience of all the students.

26   The candidate's point of view is important. A lay person seeking to undertake a course of Education for Discipleship would have that provided by the RTP. This training would be delivered locally and arranged by the officer with responsibility for that diocese with the help of part-time tutors, in line with the current pattern in many places. Reader training might be delivered similarly but with sessions,

Appendix 7

perhaps together with ordinands, taught by staff, mainly occupied in full-time or part-time training. An ordinand could be training part-time or full-time in the region or full-time in another region at the direction of the bishop. Nevertheless this illustration is of a region which has the capacity to offer training to candidates for this full range of vocations.

Allocation of funds to RTPs

27   As mentioned in paragraph 7.24 we envisage a funding procedure in which RTPs will bid for funding from the Ministry Division annually, covering the following three years. Funding will be agreed for each constituent element of the RTP, i.e. the amounts payable to the college and the PTTI will be identified separately. However it will be open to the RTP to transfer funding between the college and the PTTI where this is agreed (by the two entities concerned) to be more effective. Where such a transfer takes place (for example, where it is agreed that an educational programme originally intended to be taught by a PTTI would be better delivered by a college, or vice versa), equivalent adjustments should be made to the budget so that the RTP is not disadvantaged when actual performance is compared with budget for claw back purposes (see paragraph 28 below).

Controls to ensure costs savings are achieved

28   It is important to recognize that under these proposals the existing rigorous controls over the use of Vote 1 will be continued and indeed to some extent strengthened. At present the Ministry Division Finance Panel, using the procedures established under *Managing Planned Growth*, allocates funding of core and marginal costs to colleges and courses. The Finance Panel ensures that the total amount allocated is within the Vote 1 budget. If college or course actual numbers vary from those in the agreed budget, the core costs (currently 80 per cent for colleges and 65 per cent for courses) are paid on the basis of budgeted numbers and variable costs are paid on the basis of actual numbers. Therefore the only way in which an overspend could arise on the Vote 1 budget would be if actual numbers were to exceed budgeted numbers. In this situation the additional amount payable from Vote 1 would be limited to the variable costs, i.e. 20 per cent in the case of colleges and 35 per cent in the case of courses. The Vote 1 Three-year Rolling Reserve should normally be adequate to meet this additional cost.

29   We are proposing that this arrangement be strengthened further, on a basis consistent with HEFCE funding arrangements, so that if target numbers are achieved within plus or minus 5 per cent then the budget figure stands. If these numbers are exceeded no additional funding would be made available, but if the numbers are lower by more than 5 per cent the variable costs, on any reduction of more than 5 per cent, would be clawed back. This has the effect of removing the remaining possibility of funding paid to RTPs being greater than the amounts agreed by the Finance Panel.

30   Similarly, so far as the ability to ensure that cost savings are achieved is concerned, this can be ensured by this mechanism. If the Finance Panel reduced

RTP funding by say 7.5 per cent as proposed in respect of academic and administrative staff costs this can be enforced by eliminating these amounts from the agreed budget. It will then be a matter for the RTP to ensure that it operates within the funds which will be made available to it. Thus the responsibility for implementing the savings in the RTP rests with the RTPs. Experience shows that in the past colleges and courses have been able to achieve significant cost savings when this has been necessary and when the central budgetary mechanism has enforced this. We believe that these modest cost savings are soundly based in principle and can be enforced in practice.

Other possible developments

31 In some regions it is possible that an existing course might merge with an existing college to create a combined full-time and part-time training institution, while another existing course within the region might continue a separate existence as part of the RTP. This could prove to be an acceptable arrangement as an initial step towards convergence.

B. Possible future developments

An RTP as one legal entity

32 As a further step towards convergence, in some regions it may be possible for the RTP to become one legal entity either from inception or in due course. This could occur either if the only college and course in a region are already part of the same legal entity or in the fullness of time if the relevant college or colleges in a region agree to merge with the regional PTTI. When the RTP becomes one legal entity, the governance and management would be simplified in that there would then be one governing body (with membership as described in paragraph 5 above) and one principal with oversight of the delivery of all full-time and part-time ordination training in the region. The senior management team would continue to operate as described in paragraph 11 above. At this stage some part of CME 1–4 and Reader and lay theological education would continue to be delivered by diocesan staff working in co-operation with the RTP. The detailed relationship between diocesan education teams and the RTP would be a matter for regional negotiation and decision from time to time. The objectives would include the desire to achieve quality and efficiency through co-operation and participation in the RTP but without stifling local initiative or restricting the ability of dioceses and other churches to develop local training initiatives within their own area of responsibility. A suggested organization chart is shown at Appendix 8 Example 2.

One legal entity where all the resources are subsumed under one legal framework

33 As a final step towards convergence, in the fullness of time, in order to achieve further efficiencies, dioceses and other churches may decide to transfer all their

Appendix 7

Reader and lay training to the RTP. In this event we envisage that the diocesan and other church members of the senior management team would continue to be appointed and paid by dioceses and other churches with RTP representation on selection panels and they would continue to be jointly responsible to their dioceses or churches and to the RTP. Other staff would be appointed by the RTP with appropriate church representation on selection panels. The governing body and the senior management team would continue to be appointed and to operate as described in paragraphs 5 and 11 above. Each diocese and other church would purchase the CME, Reader and lay theological education activities transferred from diocesan staff to RTP staff. A suggested organization chart is shown at Appendix 8 Example 3.

Appendix 8

Illustrative organizational charts
Example 1

Regional training partnership
Possible organization chart
Covenant relationship

Legal entity	C of E College	Methodist College	PTTI	Diocese A	Diocese B	Diocese C	Diocese D	Other Churches
Senior Management	College Principal (1)	Principal (1)	Principal (1)	Ministry Director (0.5)	Ministry Director (0.5)	Ministry Director (0.5)	Ministry Director (1)	Other Churches' Representative (0.5)
Finance and Administration	Bursar Finance and Admin Staff							
	Vice-principal (1) Other staff (3.5)	Other staff (1)	Vice-principal (1) Other staff (3.5)	Officers for CME (0.5) Reader (0.5) Lay (0.5)	Officers for OLM (1) CME (1) Reader (0.5) Lay (0.5)	Officers for CME (0.5) Reader (0.5) Lay (0.5)	Officers for OLM (1) CME (1) Reader (0.5) Lay (1)	Training Officers (say 1.5)
Numbers of academic staff (FTE)	5.5	2	5.5	2	3.5	2	4.5	2

Total numbers of academic staff	No.	FTE
Senior management	8	6
Other staff	26	21

166

Appendix 8

Illustrative organizational charts
Example 2

Regional training partnership
Possible organization chart
With diocesan and other church training being distinct

		Diocese A	Diocese B	Diocese C	Diocese D	Other Churches
Legal entity	RTP					Other Churches'
Senior Management	RTP Principal (1)	Ministry Director (0.5)	Ministry Director (0.5)	Ministry Director (0.5)	Ministry Director (1)	Representative (0.5)
Finance and Administration	Bursar Finance and admin staff					
Other staff	Vice-principals (3) Other staff (9)	Officers for CME (0.5) Reader (0.5) Lay (0.5)	Officers for OLM (1) CME (1) Reader (0.5) Lay (0.5)	Officers for CME (0.5) Reader (0.5) Lay (0.5)	Officers for OLM (1) CME (1) Reader (0.5) Lay (1)	Training Officers (say 1.5)
Numbers of academic staff (FTE)	13	2	3.5	2	4.5	2

Total numbers of academic staff

	No.	FTE
Senior management	6	4
Other staff	28	23

This takes no account of possible further savings through convergence

Appendix 8

Illustrative organizational charts
Example 3

Regional training partnership
Possible organization chart
For RTP as one legal entity

Incorporating diocesan and other church training

Legal entity	RTP						RTP
Senior Management	RTP Principal (1)	RTP Ministry Director (0.5)	RTP Ministry Director (0.5)	RTP Ministry Director (0.5)	RTP Ministry Director (0.5)	RTP Ministry Director (1)	Other Churches' Representative (0.5)
Finance and Administration	Bursar Finance and admin staff						
Other staff	Vice-principals (3) Other staff (9)	Officers for CME (0.5) Reader (0.5) Lay (0.5)	Officers for OLM (1) CME (1) Reader (0.5) Lay (0.5)	Officers for CME (0.5) Reader (0.5) Lay (0.5)	Officers for OLM (1) CME (1) Reader (0.5) Lay (1)		Training Officers (say 1.5)
Numbers of academic staff (FTE)	13	2	3.5	2	4.5		2

Total numbers of academic staff

	No.	FTE
Senior management	6	4
Other staff	28	23

This takes no account of possible further savings through convergence

168

Appendix 9

College and course budgeted expenditure, fees and estimated subsidies in 2002/03

COLLEGES	Budgeted expenditure per head 2002/03	Agreed Fee 2002/03	College 'subsidy' per head 2002/03	Budgeted number of sponsored students 2002/03	Total budgeted fees 2002/03	Total estimated 'subsidy' 2002/03
	£	£	£		£	£
Cranmer Hall, Durham	7,541	7,533	8	65	489,645	499
College of the Resurrection, Mirfield	9,762	4,773	4,989	34	162,282	169,642
Oak Hill Theological College	10,305	8,178	2,127	55	449,790	116,999
Queen's College, Birmingham	10,123	8,421	1,702	20	168,420	34,046
Ridley Hall, Cambridge	8,831	8,310	521	57	473,670	29,724
Ripon College, Cuddesdon	8,760	8,235	525	68	559,980	35,700
St John's College, Nottingham	9,540	8,595	945	82	704,790	77,507
St Stephen's House, Oxford	11,214	8,100	3,114	36	291,600	112,099
Trinity College, Bristol	8,376	8,190	186	74	606,060	13,751
Westcott House, Cambridge	9,214	8,919	295	56	499,464	16,547
Wycliffe Hall, Oxford	10,075	8,319	1,756	69	574,011	121,173
St Michael's College, Llandaff		8,442		4	33,768	0
				620	5,013,480	727,688

COURSES	Budgeted expenditure per head 2002/03	Agreed fee 2002/03	Course 'subsidy' per head 2002/03	Budgeted number of sponsored students 2002/03	Total budgeted fees 2002/03	Total estimated 'subsidy' 2002/03
	£	£	£		£	£
Carlisle and Blackburn Diocesan Training Institute	4,314	4,449	-135	8	35,592	-1,080
East Anglian Ministerial Training Course	4,495	3,969	526	61	242,109	32,086
East Midlands Ministry Training Course	3,190	2,883	307	37	106,671	11,369
North East Oecumenical Course	4,496	3,498	998	40	139,920	39,920
Northern Ordination Course	3,738	3,630	108	84	304,920	9,072
North Thames Ministerial Training Course	4,457	4,245	212	35	148,575	7,408
St Albans and Oxford Ministry Course	4,761	4,056	705	58	235,248	40,889
Southern Theological Education and Training Scheme	4,230	3,981	249	87	346,347	21,663
South East Institute for Theological Education	3,983	3,816	167	82	312,912	13,694
South West Ministry Training Course	5,641	5,349	292	24	128,376	7,008
West Midlands Ministerial Training Course	3,658	4,146	-488	31	128,526	-15,128
West of England Ministerial Training Course	3,828	3,819	9	40	152,760	360
				587	2,281,956	167,261

Notes to Appendix 9

1. Budgeted expenditure per head is based on budgets submitted to Ministry Division by the colleges and courses for funding approval purposes. Total expenditure has been divided by the estimated number of full-time equivalent students.

2. College and course subsidies per head represent the difference between the budgeted expenditure per head and the agreed fee computed for funding approval purposes.

3. The budgeted number of sponsored students represents the number of students included in the budgets prepared by each college and course.

4. The total budgeted fees represents the amounts payable to the colleges and courses if they achieve budgeted numbers. If actual numbers vary the amounts payable are reduced or increased by the variable costs for the change in student numbers, being 20 per cent in the case of colleges and 35 per cent in the case of courses.

5. The total estimated 'subsidy' represents expenditure covered by other income, donations or reserves.

6. Queen's College, Birmingham and the West Midlands Ministerial Training Scheme are both constituent parts of the Queen's Foundation, Birmingham. The negative subsidy of £15,128 to West Midlands MTC should therefore be netted against the Queen's College subsidy of £34,046.

Appendix 10

Forecast Vote 1 at present (January 2003)

	2002	Forecast 2003	Forecast 2004	Forecast 2005	Forecast 2006	Forecast 2007	Forecast 2008
COLLEGES							
College core costs	3,935,577	4,070,230	4,075,392	4,231,735	4,409,468	4,585,847	4,755,523
College variable costs	980,470	909,571	1,033,577	1,059,633	1,086,124	1,113,277	1,141,109
Total	4,916,047	4,979,802	5,108,968	5,291,368	5,495,592	5,699,124	5,896,632
Allowances	1,089,611	1,027,455	976,816	1,001,235	1,026,266	1,051,922	1,078,220
Total colleges	6,005,658	6,007,257	6,085,784	6,292,603	6,521,858	6,751,046	6,974,852
COURSES							
Course core costs	1,459,591	1,519,541	1,427,615	1,482,478	1,552,154	1,622,001	1,686,881
Course variable costs	780,198	759,137	948,866	972,586	996,901	1,021,823	1,047,369
Total	2,239,789	2,278,678	2,376,481	2,455,064	2,549,055	2,643,825	2,734,250
Allowances	326,243	304,483	329,463	338,016	346,466	355,128	364,006
Total courses	2,566,032	2,583,161	2,705,944	2,793,080	2,895,522	2,998,953	3,098,256
CME 1–4 fees							
Research							
OLM Schemes	278,692	279,112	301,607	311,861	319,658	327,649	335,840
University fees	247,386	264,262	279,779	288,172	295,376	302,761	310,330
Pre-theological	20,060	16,665	12,917	13,239	13,570	13,909	14,257
Mixed mode	20,347	24,614	25,428	26,699	27,366	28,051	28,752
Total Vote 1 at present	9,138,175	9,175,071	9,411,459	9,725,654	10,073,349	10,422,368	10,762,288
Personal and family mtce	3,153,328	3,006,433	3,081,594	3,158,634	3,237,600	3,318,540	3,401,503
Total Vote 1 as proposed	12,291,503	12,181,504	12,493,053	12,884,288	13,310,949	13,740,908	14,163,791
Analysis of forecast							
Full-time	9,446,779	9,319,231	9,485,502	9,779,347	10,095,770	10,414,306	10,729,694
Part-time	2,566,032	2,583,161	2,705,944	2,793,080	2,895,522	2,998,953	3,098,256
OLM	278,692	279,112	301,607	311,861	319,658	327,649	335,840
Total	12,291,503	12,181,504	12,493,053	12,884,288	13,310,949	13,740,908	14,163,791

Appendix 10

Assumptions for Forecast Vote 1 at present

(i) Basic core cost increases for 2003/04 for colleges will be 3.2 per cent, for 2004/05 3.4 per cent, for 2005/06 and 2006/07 4.2 per cent and for 2007/08 and subsequent years 3.7 per cent. This includes the assumption that academic staff will continue to be paid at current levels adjusted by inflation and does not take into account any additional costs arising from the implementation of 'Generosity and Sacrifice'.

(ii) £100,000 has been deducted from college core costs in 2003/04 representing a reduction in capacity of about 15 places.

(iii) Basic core cost increases for courses will be 3.1 per cent for 2003/04, 3.4 per cent for 2004/05, 4.7 per cent for 2005/06 and 2006/07 and 4 per cent for 2007/08 and subsequent periods.

(iv) Variable costs, student allowances and personal and family maintenance to follow RPI inflation of 2.5 per cent for 2004 and thereafter.

(v) Personal and family maintenance based on actual cost in 2001 of £3,146,000 adjusted pro-rata for changes in numbers of sponsored candidates at colleges.

(vi) Numbers in colleges and on courses and OLM schemes continuing at 2002/03 actual levels.

Appendix 11

Reduction to 490 training full-time and part-time numbers stable at 590

Impact of possible changes in the projected numbers of ordinands in training

1 We note that over the last two years the numbers of ordinands in the colleges has declined and that this may continue with the intake for September 2003. If there is a further reduction of 50 in September 2003 in the numbers in full-time training (of whom 30 are assumed to be people requiring family maintenance) without a change in numbers in part-time training the effect on the numbers in training and on future ordinations would be as set out below.

Illustration 3a Continuation of current trend							
	2002/03	2003/04	2004/05	2005/06	2006/07	2007/08	2008/09
	Note 1	Note 2	Note 3	Note 4	Note 5	Note 6	Note 7
Full-time	540	490	490	490	490	490	490
Full-time places for CME 1–4			9	19	28	38	38
Total full-time places used	*540*	*490*	*499*	*509*	*518*	*528*	*528*
Part-time	588	590	590	590	590	590	590
Total full-time and part-time ordinands	1128	1080	1080	1080	1080	1080	1080
OLM schemes	217	220	220	220	220	220	220
Overall total	1345	1300	1300	1300	1300	1300	1300
No. of people ordained at year end							
Note 8							
Full-time	240	218	218	218	218	218	218
Part-time	196	197	197	197	197	197	197
OLM	72	73	73	73	73	73	73
	508	488	488	488	488	488	488

2 If a similar approach to the reduction in funding of core costs is adopted to that proposed in paragraph 7.51, whereby funding of core costs is provided for 25 more places than currently anticipated as required in the longer term (so as accommodate a modest reversal of the current trend), this would require funding of core costs to be reduced to fund 515 places (490 plus 25). As from 2003/04 the Vote 1 budget (as at January 2003) includes funding of

Appendix 11

core costs for 615 places. Therefore a further overall reduction in funding of 100 places is required. This could be regarded as being the 'transfer' of 75 places proposed in this report plus a further reduction of 25 places. If this approach is adopted the effect on the Vote 1 budgets for 2003 to 2008, assuming a reduction of 25 places in September 2003, 40 places in September 2004 and 35 places in September 2005, is estimated to be as set out in Illustration 3b below.

Illustration 3b

Effect of treating proposed reduction in full-time training as reflected in existing trend, without an increase in part-time numbers.

	2003	2004	2005	2006	2007	2008
	£	£	£	£	£	£
Forecast Vote 1 at present	9,175,071	9,411,459	9,725,654	10,073,349	10,422,368	10,762,288
Personal and family maintenance	3,006,433	3,081,594	3,158,634	3,237,600	3,318,540	3,401,503
Total Vote 1 as proposed	12,181,504	12,493,053	12,884,288	13,310,949	13,740,908	14,163,791

Effect of continuing trend reducing full-time training by 50 people training for two years of whom 30 require family support

	2003	2004	2005	2006	2007	2008
change in variable costs	-68,240	-211,841	-217,286	-222,718	-228,286	-233,993
change in family maintenance	-104,536	-307,991	-315,690	-323,583	-331,672	-339,964
reduction in core costs	-52,946	-220,888	-344,044	-358,493	-372,833	-386,628
additional part-time costs		0	0	0	0	0
Net effect	-225,722	-740,720	-877,020	-904,794	-932,792	-960,585
Effect of reducing full-time capacity by a further 50 re existing reduction in numbers		-33,133	-183,490	-358,493	-372,833	-386,628
CME 1–4 residential costs		27,501	113,208	203,721	299,040	368,460
CME 1–4 course fees		58,333	233,333	408,333	583,333	700,000
Savings of 7.5% on academic staff pay			-91,698	-186,442	-194,278	-201,703
Savings of 7.5% on administration staff pay			-33,898	-68,474	-71,306	-74,003
Research			80,000	240,000	240,000	240,000
Adjusted forecast for Vote 1	11,955,782	11,805,034	12,124,723	12,644,799	13,292,072	13,849,331

Analysis of adjusted forecast

	2003	2004	2005	2006	2007	2008
Full-time	9,093,509	8,756,752	8,876,974	9,142,986	9,554,200	9,919,498
Part-time	2,583,161	2,746,675	2,935,888	3,182,156	3,410,223	3,593,993
OLM	279,112	301,607	311,861	319,658	327,649	335,840
Total	11,955,782	11,805,034	12,124,723	12,644,799	13,292,072	13,849,331
Net savings	225,722	688,019	759,565	666,150	448,836	314,460

Appendix 11

On this basis the overall costs would be some £185,000 higher than those shown in paragraph 7.51 but the number of people ordained at the end of each year would be some 21 lower, being 488 in 2006/07 and subsequent years rather than 509.

3   The following further points should be noted in relation to Illustration 3:

- The reduction in variable costs is lower in this illustration (by 33 per cent or some £117,000 in 2008) as it relates to a further reduction of 50 people training full-time (down from 540 to 490) rather than 75 as assumed in Illustrations 1 and 2.

- The reduction in family maintenance is lower in this illustration (by 57 per cent or some £450,000 in 2008) as it relates to a reduction of 30 people requiring family maintenance and 20 people requiring single maintenance rather than 75 requiring family maintenance as assumed in Illustrations 1 and 2.

- There are no additional costs of part-time training as it is assumed that these numbers will not increase. This reduces costs by £588,000.

- The reduction in core costs declines by 20 per cent or £193,000 in 2008 because it relates to 100 places rather than 125.

Overall total costs in 2008 when these proposals are fully implemented are estimated at £13,849,331, which is about £300,000 less than the costs of the current establishment which are projected as £14,163,791.

Assumptions adopted for Illustrations 3a and b

Ordinand numbers – 3a

1. 2002/03 — Based on current numbers

2. 2003/04 — Assume reduction of 50 at colleges and no increase in courses, caused by current trend

3. 2004/05 — Assume no change in full-time or part-time numbers
   Assume CME 1–4 residential training for one year group

4. 2005/06 — Assume no change in full-time or part-time numbers
   Assume CME 1–4 residential training for two year groups

5. 2006/07 — Assume no change in full-time or part-time numbers
   Assume CME 1–4 residential training for three year groups

6. 2007/08 — Assume no change in full-time or part-time numbers.
   Assume CME 1–4 residential training for four year groups

7. 2008/09 — Assume no change in full-time or part-time numbers

8. For the calculation of numbers ordained at the year end assume that in 2002 and subsequent years 1/3rd full-time people train for three years and 2/3rds train for two years. Assume all part-time and OLM people train for three years

Financial illustration – 3b

1. The change in family maintenance assumes that of the reduction of 50 full-time candidates 30 would have been entitled to family maintenance grants and 20 to single maintenance grants.

2. The first line showing a reduction in core costs relates to a reduction of 50 places for candidates training full-time. (25 from September 2003 and 25 from September 2004)

3   There are no additional part-time costs as part-time numbers are assumed not to increase.

4   The second line showing a reduction of core costs relates to the further reduction of costs for 50 places which are funded but unused in 2002/03. (15 from September 2004 and 35 from September 2005)

5   CME 1–4 residential and training costs are phased in commencing in September 2004 and are assumed to apply to those ordained in 2004 and subsequent years.

6   Savings of 7.5 per cent on academic and administration staff pay are assumed to commence in September 2005.

7   Payments of grants for research are assumed to commence in September 2005.

Appendix 12

Reduction to 490 training full-time and part-time numbers increase by 112 to 702

Impact of possible changes in the projected numbers of ordinands in training

1   If the number of people training full-time reduces to a constant level of 490 and the numbers training part-time were to increase in subsequent years to the levels assumed in Illustration 1, the effect on the numbers in training and on future ordinations would be as set out below.

Illustration 4a

Increased part-time numbers

	2002/03	2003/04	2004/05	2005/06	2006/07	2007/08	2008/09
	Note 1	Note 2	Note 3	Note 4	Note 5	Note 6	Note 7
Full-time	540	490	490	490	490	490	490
Full-time places for CME 1–4			9	19	28	38	38
Total full-time places used	540	490	499	509	518	528	528
Part-time	588	590	630	665	702	702	702
Total full-time and part-time ordinands	1128	1080	1120	1155	1192	1192	1192
OLM schemes	217	220	220	220	220	220	220
Overall total	1345	1300	1340	1375	1412	1412	1412
No. of people ordained at year end							
Note 8							
Full-time	240	218	218	218	218	218	218
Part-time	196	197	210	222	234	234	234
OLM	72	73	73	73	73	73	73
	508	488	501	513	525	525	525

2   The effect on the financial projections is shown in Illustration 4b below.

Illustration 4b

Effect of treating proposed reduction in full-time training as reflected in existing trend, with an increase in part-time numbers.

	2003	2004	2005	2006	2007	2008
	£	£	£	£	£	£
Forecast Vote 1 at present	9,175,071	9,411,459	9,725,654	10,073,349	10,422,368	10,762,288
Personal and family maintenance	3,006,433	3,081,594	3,158,634	3,237,600	3,318,540	3,401,503
Total Vote 1 as proposed	12,181,504	12,493,053	12,884,288	13,310,949	13,740,908	14,163,791

Effect of continuing trend reducing full-time training by 50 people training for two years of whom 30 require family support

	2003	2004	2005	2006	2007	2008
change in variable costs	-68,240	-211,841	-217,286	-222,718	-228,286	-233,993
change in family maintenance	-104,536	-307,991	-315,690	-323,583	-331,672	-339,964
reduction in core costs	-52,946	-220,888	-344,044	-358,493	-372,833	-386,628
Net effect	-225,722	-740,720	-877,020	-904,794	-932,792	-960,585
Additional part-time costs		61,151	255,638	426,967	569,293	588,144
Effect of reducing full-time capacity by a further 50 re existing reduction in numbers		-33,133	-183,490	-358,493	-372,833	-386,628
CME 1–4 residential costs		27,501	113,208	203,721	299,040	368,460
CME 1–4 course fees		58,333	233,333	408,333	583,333	700,000
Savings of 7.5% on academic staff pay			-95,006	-197,600	-209,288	-217,314
Savings of 7.5% on administration staff pay			-34,712	-71,221	-75,001	-77,846
Research			80,000	240,000	240,000	240,000
Adjusted forecast for Vote 1	11,955,782	11,866,186	12,376,239	13,057,862	13,842,660	14,418,021
Analysis of adjusted forecast						
Full-time	9,093,509	8,756,752	8,869,947	9,121,519	9,512,677	9,870,938
Part-time	2,583,161	2,807,826	3,194,431	3,616,686	4,002,334	4,211,243
OLM	279,112	301,607	311,861	319,658	327,649	335,840
Total	11,955,782	11,866,186	12,376,239	13,057,862	13,842,660	14,418,021
Net savings/(additional costs)	225,722	626,868	508,049	253,087	-101,752	-254,230

Appendix 12

The following points should be noted in relation to this illustration:

- this adds a further £570,000 to the overall budget by 2008 being the additional part-time costs net of additional savings on academic and administration staff pay;
- The numbers ordained increase by 37 (compared with Illustration 3) from 488 to 525 in 2006/07 and subsequent years and are 16 more than the numbers assumed for Illustrations 1 and 2 (509);

Overall total costs in 2008 when these proposals are fully implemented are estimated at £14,418,021, which is some £255,000 above the costs of the current establishment which are projected as £14,163,791.

Assumptions adopted for Illustrations 4a and b

Ordinand numbers – 4a

1. 2002/03 Based on current numbers

2. 2003/04 Reduction of 50 in part-time

3. 2004/05 Assume no change in full-time numbers
   Assume increase of 40 part-time candidates
   Assume CME 1–4 residential training for one year group

4. 2005/06 Assume no change in full-time numbers
   Assume further increase of 35 part-time candidates
   Assume CME 1–4 residential training for two year groups

5. 2006/07 Assume no change in full-time numbers
   Assume further increase of 37 part-time candidates
   Assume CME 1–4 residential training for three year groups

6. 2007/08 Assume no change in full-time or part-time numbers
   Assume CME 1–4 residential training for four year groups

7. 2008/09 Assume no change

8. For the calculation of numbers ordained at the year end assume that in 2002 and subsequent years 1/3rd full-time people train for three years and 2/3rds train for two years. Assume all part-time and OLM people train for three years

Financial illustration – 4b

1. The change in family maintenance assumes that of the reduction of 50 full-time candidates 30 would have been entitled to family maintenance grants and 20 to single maintenance grants.

2. The first line showing a reduction in core costs relates to a reduction of 50 places for candidates training full-time. (25 from September 2003 and 25 from September 2004)

3. Additional part-time costs relate to increases of part-time numbers of 40 in September 2004, a further 35 in September 2005 and a further 37 in September 2006.

4. The second line showing a reduction of core costs relates to the further reduction of costs for 50 places which are funded but unused in 2002/03. (15 from September 2004 and 35 from September 2005)

5. CME 1–4 residential and training costs are phased in commencing in September 2004 and are assumed to apply to those ordained in 2004 and subsequent years.

6   Savings of 7.5 per cent on academic and administration staff pay are assumed to commence in September 2005.

7   Payments of grants for research are assumed to commence in September 2005.

Appendix 13

Full-time and part-time numbers stable but reduction by 50 in numbers of people requiring family maintenance

Impact of possible changes in the projected numbers of ordinands in training

1   If full-time and part-time numbers were to remain at the existing levels of 540 and 590 respectively, but the number of ordinands requiring family maintenance fell by 50 and without an increase in part-time numbers, the effect on numbers in training and on future ordinations would be:

Illustration 5a

Maintain current numbers but reduce core costs to this level

	2002/03	2003/04	2004/05	2005/06	2006/07	2007/08	2008/09
	Note 1	Note 2	Note 3	Note 4	Note 5	Note 6	Note 7
Full-time	540	540	540	540	540	540	540
Full-time places for CME 1–4			9	19	28	38	38
Total full-time places used	*540*	*540*	*549*	*559*	*568*	*578*	*578*
Part-time	588	590	590	590	590	590	590
Total full-time and part-time ordinands	1128	1130	1130	1130	1130	1130	1130
OLM schemes	217	220	220	220	220	220	220
Overall total	1345	1350	1350	1350	1350	1350	1350
No. of people ordained at year end							
Note 8							
Full-time	240	240	240	240	2405	240	2405
Part-time	196	197	197	197	197	197	197
OLM	72	73	73	73	73	73	73
	508	510	510	510	510	510	510

2   The effect on the financial projections is shown in Illustration 5b below.

Illustration 5b

Maintain current numbers but reduce core costs and replace 50 people requiring family maintenance with 50 single people training full-time

	2003	2004	2005	2006	2007	2008
	£	£	£	£	£	£
Forecast Vote 1 at present	9,175,071	9,411,459	9,725,654	10,073,349	10,422,368	10,762,288
Personal and family maintenance	3,006,433	3,081,594	3,158,634	3,237,600	3,318,540	3,401,503
Total Vote 1 as proposed	12,181,504	12,493,053	12,884,288	13,310,949	13,740,908	14,163,791

Effect of maintaining current numbers but replacing 50 people requiring family maintenance with 50 single people training full-time

	2003	2004	2005	2006	2007	2008
change in variable costs	0	0	0	0	0	0
change in family maintenance	-144,072	-422,410	-432,971	-443,795	-454,890	-466,262
reduction in core costs		0	0	0	0	0
additional part-time costs		0	0	0	0	0
Net effect	-144,072	-422,410	-432,971	-443,795	-454,890	-466,262
Effect of reducing full-time capacity by 75 re existing reduction in numbers		-88,355	-355,512	-537,740	-559,250	-579,942
CME 1–4 residential costs		27,501	113,208	203,721	299,040	368,460
CME 1–4 course fees		58,333	233,333	408,333	583,333	700,000
Savings of 7.5% on academic staff pay			-94,279	-191,819	-199,870	-207,503
Savings of 7.5% on administration staff pay			-35,059	-70,894	-73,823	-76,613
Research			80,000	240,000	240,000	240,000
Adjusted forecast for Vote 1	12,037,433	12,068,122	12,393,009	12,918,755	13,575,448	14,141,931
Analysis of adjusted forecast						
Full-time	9,175,160	9,021,913	9,154,213	9,434,938	9,861,995	10,240,910
Part-time	2,583,161	2,744,602	2,926,935	3,164,160	3,385,805	3,565,181
OLM	279,112	301,607	311,861	319,658	327,649	335,840
Total	12,037,433	12,068,122	12,393,009	12,918,755	13,575,448	14,141,931
Net savings	144,072	424,931	491,279	392,194	165,460	21,860

The following points should be noted in relation to this illustration:

- this position could arise if there is an increase in vocations among single people but a capping of the number of ordinands requiring family support who train full-time. Any increase in vocations is likely to result in an increase in both single ordinands and in those

Appendix 13

requiring family support in which event additional part-time costs could arise as illustrated in Illustration 4.

- the reduction in core costs amounts to £580,000 in 2008 as capacity is assumed to be reduced by 75 (re the existing decline in numbers) to 540 rather than by 100 (as compared with Illustration 4), consisting of 50 in respect of the existing reduction in numbers and 50 in respect of an assumed further reduction;

- the main further reduction in cost compared with the present position relates to family maintenance and amounts in 2008 to £466,000, by assuming that 50 students training on a full-time basis and requiring family maintenance which in 2003 costs about £9,306 per family are replaced by 50 people eligible for single maintenance grants which in 2003 average £1,064 per person, a reduction in 2003 of £8,242 per candidate;

- the numbers ordained remain broadly as at present;

- overall total costs in 2008 when these proposals are fully implemented are estimated at £14,141,934, which is marginally below the costs of the current establishment which are projected as £14,163,791.

Assumptions adopted for Illustrations 5a and b

Ordinand numbers – 5a

1. 2002/03   Based on current numbers

2. 2003/04   Assume no change in full-time or part-time numbers

3. 2004/05   Assume no change in full-time or part-time numbers
   Assume CME 1–4 residential training for one year group

4. 2005/06   Assume no change in full-time or part-time numbers
   Assume CME 1–4 residential training for two year groups

5. 2006/07   Assume no change in full-time or part-time numbers
   Assume CME 1–4 residential training for three year groups

6. 2007/08   Assume no change in full-time or part-time numbers
   Assume CME 1–4 residential training for four year groups

7. 2008/09   Assume no change

8. For the calculation of numbers ordained at the year end assume that in 2002 and subsequent years 1/3rd full-time people train for three years and 2/3rds train for two years. Assume all part-time and OLM people train for three years

Financial illustration – 5b

1. The change in family maintenance assumes that 50 full-time candidates requiring family support are replaced by 50 single students.

2. The reduction in core costs is shown separately below. See note 4.

3. Part-time numbers are assumed to continue as in 2002/03.

4. The second line showing a reduction of core costs relates to the reduction of costs for 75 places which are funded but unused in 2002/03. (40 from September 2004 and 35 from September 2005)

5. CME 1–4 residential and training costs are phased in commencing in September 2004 and are assumed to apply to those ordained in 2004 and subsequent years.

6 Savings of 7.5 per cent on academic and administration staff pay are assumed to commence in September 2005.

7 Payments of grants for research are assumed to commence in September 2005.

Appendix 14

Reduction of 150 to 390 people training full-time, reduction of capacity by 200 to 415 and increase of 201 in numbers training part-time

Impact of possible changes in the projected numbers of ordinands in training

1   We have also considered, but rejected for the reasons set out in 7.10 above, the possibility of proposing a much more major shift of people requiring family maintenance from full-time to part-time training. Assuming that 100 people training full-time for two years and 50 people training full-time for three years, all of whom require family maintenance, transfer to part-time training for three years the effect on the numbers in training and on future ordinations would be as follows:

Illustration 6a

Ordinand numbers

	2002/03	2003/04	2004/05	2005/06	2006/07	2007/08	2008/09
	Note 1	Note 2	Note 3	Note 4	Note 5	Note 6	Note 7
Full-time	540	540	473	406	390	390	390
Full-time places for CME 1–4			9	19	28	38	38
Total full-time places used	540	540	482	425	418	428	428
Part-time	588	590	657	724	791	791	791
Total full-time and part-time ordinands	1128	1130	1130	1130	1181	1181	1181
OLM schemes	217	220	220	220	220	220	220
Overall total	1345	1350	1350	1350	1401	1401	1401
No. of people ordained at year end							
Note 8							
Full-time	240	240	210	180	173	173	173
Part-time	196	197	219	241	264	264	264
OLM	72	73	73	73	73	73	73
	508	510	503	495	510	510	510

2   The effect on the financial projections is shown in Illustration 6b below.

Illustration 6b

Transfer to part-time training 100 people training for two years full-time and 50 people training for three years full-time and requiring family maintenance and reduce capacity by a further 50 re existing reduction in numbers

	2003	2004	2005	2006	2007	2008
	£	£	£	£	£	£
Forecast Vote 1 at present	9,175,071	9,411,459	9,725,654	10,073,349	10,422,368	10,762,288
Personal and family maintenance	3,006,433	3,081,594	3,158,634	3,237,600	3,318,540	3,401,503
Total Vote 1 as proposed	12,181,504	12,493,053	12,884,288	13,310,949	13,740,908	14,163,791

Effect of transferring to part-time training 100 people training for two years full-time and 50 people training for three years full-time and requiring family maintenance full-time

change in variable costs	0	-93,897	-387,592	-621,204	-686,093	-703,245
change in family maintenance	0	-212,722	-873,137	-1,396,067	-1,540,885	-1,579,407
reduction in core costs		-147,995	-614,462	-998,762	-1,118,499	-1,159,884
additional part-time costs		102,428	422,749	767,068	1,021,677	1,055,508
Net effect	0	-352,186	-1,452,441	-2,248,965	-2,323,800	-2,387,028
Effect of reducing full-time capacity by a further 50 re existing reduction in numbers	-52,946	-218,680	-344,044	-358,493	-372,833	-386,628
CME 1–4 residential costs		27,501	113,208	203,721	299,040	368,460
CME 1–4 course fees		58,333	233,333	408,333	583,333	700,000
Savings of 7.5% on academic staff pay			-90,703	-187,279	-198,846	-206,522
Savings of 7.5% on administration staff pay			-32,335	-64,765	-67,871	-70,460
Research			80,000	240,000	240,000	240,000
Adjusted forecast for Vote 1	12,128,558	12,008,022	11,391,306	11,303,501	11,899,931	12,421,613
Analysis of adjusted forecast						
Full-time	9,266,285	8,859,385	7,708,761	6,977,940	7,035,387	7,309,660
Part-time	2,583,161	2,847,031	3,370,684	4,005,904	4,536,895	4,776,113
OLM	279,112	301,607	311,861	319,658	327,649	335,840
Total	12,128,558	12,008,022	11,391,306	11,303,501	11,899,931	12,421,613
Net savings	52,946	485,031	1,492,982	2,007,448	1,840,977	1,742,178

Appendix 14

3   In this projection we have also assumed that there is a further reduction in capacity of 50 places as a result of the current reduction in numbers, thus reducing funded capacity by a total of 200 (150 people 'transferred' plus 50 re existing reduction in numbers) from 615 to 415 and leaving 25 funded spaces for expansion.

The following points should be noted in relation to this illustration:

- By 2008, if these proposals are fully implemented this would produce an overall cost reduction of over £1.7 million per annum, reducing the projected costs from £14,163,791 to £12,421,613.

- However the effect on the capacity of full-time provision required would be very significant. This reduction of 200 spaces would be partly offset by funding of nearly 40 spaces for CME 1–4, but a net reduction of 160 spaces could result in the Church ceasing to use up to three of the existing colleges for full-time training.

- The overall effect in 2008, on the assumptions adopted, of the transfer of 150 people to part-time training would be to reduce costs by £2,387,028, a saving of £15,913 per person per annum or £30,000 for a two-year ordinand and £54,000 for a three-year ordinand.

Assumptions adopted for Illustrations 6a and b

Ordinand numbers – 6a

1. 2002/03   Based on current numbers

2. 2003/04   Assume no change in full-time or part-time

3. 2004/05   Assume 67 new candidates requiring family maintenance 'transfer' to part-time (50 for 2 years & 17 for 3 years)
Assume CME 1–4 residential training for one year group
Part-time numbers increase by 67 transferred from full-time

4. 2005/06   Assume 67 further new candidates requiring family maintenance 'transfer' to part-time (50 for 2 years & 17 for 3 years). This give an increase of 75 part-time
Assume CME 1–4 residential training for two year groups

5. 2006/07   Assume 16 candidates requiring family maintenance complete third year of training and are not replaced
Assume CME 1-4 residential training for three year groups
Assume part-time numbers increase by 67 as all people transferring from full-time train for 3 years not 2

6. 2007/08   Assume no change in full-time numbers
Assume CME 1-4 residential training for four year groups

7. 2008/09   Assume no change

8. For the calculation of numbers ordained at the year end assume that 1/3rd full-time people train for three years and 2/3rds train for two years. Assume all part-time and OLM people train for three years

Financial illustration 6b

1   The change in family maintenance assumes that the reduction of 150 full-time candidates would all have been entitled to family maintenance grants.

2   The first line showing a reduction in core costs relates to a reduction of 150 places for candidates transferring to part-time training.

3   Additional part-time costs are for the 150 people transferring from two or three years full-time training to three years part-time training, thus increasing part-time numbers by 201.

4   The second line showing a reduction of core costs relates to the further reduction of costs for 50 places which are funded but unused in 2002/03 (25 from September 2003 and 25 from September 2004).

5   CME 1–4 residential and training costs are phased in commencing in September 2004 and are assumed to apply to those ordained in 2004 and subsequent years.

6   Savings of 7.5 per cent on academic and administration staff pay are assumed to commence in September 2005.

7   Payments of grants for research are assumed to commence in September 2005.

Notes

Chapter 1

1 p. 30.

2 *Theological Training. A Way Ahead. A Report to the House of Bishops of the Church of England on Theological Colleges and Courses* [= the 'Lincoln report'], 1992; *Theological Colleges – The Next Steps. Report of the Assessment Group on Theological Colleges* [= the 'Hereford report'], 1993.

3 See the discussion of the development of this policy in G. W. Kuhrt, *Issues in Theological Education and Training*, ABM Ministry Paper no. 15, 2nd edition, 1998, pp. 7–8.

4 Level 1 is equivalent to first-year undergraduate studies. On educational use of 'levels', see para. 5.3 below, and for a glossary of educational terms, see p. 54.

Chapter 2

5 *Eucharistic Presidency. A Theological Statement by the House of Bishops of the General Synod*, CHP, 1997.

6 *A Time to Heal. A Contribution towards the Ministry of Healing. A Report for the House of Bishops on the Healing Ministry*, CHP, 2000.

7 *The Way Ahead. Church Schools in the New Millennium*, CHP, 2001.

8 These are the latest figures available. The figure for ordinands refers to 2002–03. The Reader figure is taken from the Central Readers' Council Annual Report for 2002.

9 These figures are for 2001–02. The Ministry Division does not keep detailed figures for staff numbers for OLM schemes as the financial contribution to diocesan OLM budgets is based on a basic grant plus a *per capita* sum per ordinand.

10 In the interim report, we did not take proper account of the sharing of staff expertise that does occur in some settings and which means that the range of expertise available in those settings is much greater than might be suggested by the numbers on the staff in individual institutions. We are grateful to those who made this point.

11 There are instances of courses and schemes sharing staff but they are rare. In addition to the Queen's Foundation noted above, examples would include STETS and Salisbury OLM which have a joint member of staff and the arrangement to share facilities and some teaching between NOC and Mirfield. A further example of partnership would be the consortium between a group of OLM schemes, EAMTC and the University of Wales, Bangor, which includes a small but valuable element of shared teaching.

12 For this purpose, the number of OLM candidates have been divided by 17 schemes, not 19, as Durham is not yet fully operational, while the dioceses of Carlisle and Blackburn train their candidates together through one regional course.

13 *Eucharistic Presidency*, p. ix.

14 'We invite the Church to consider what long-term role the Church colleges might have in the pre- and post-ordination training of the clergy.' *The Way Ahead. Church of England Schools in the New Millennium*, CHP, 2001, para. 9.40.

15 The figures for 2002 are £5.3m for maintenance out of a total expenditure of £11.9m. This total sum is made up of the General Synod Vote 1 and diocesan support for family maintenance. Of the £5.3m for personal and family maintenance, £3.1m is for family maintenance. (The only sums that are not included are the amounts that individual dioceses put into their own OLM schemes and voluntary giving through the Train-A-Priest fund. The figures do include the amounts the central Church contributes to OLM training.)

Chapter 3

16 'Kingdom, Church and Ministry' in *The Historic Episcopate*, ed. Carey K. M. (ed.), Dacre Press, Westminster 1954, p.15.

17 Summary of the report of the working party on theological education, commissioned by the Anglican Primates' meeting, Kanuga, North Carolina, USA, March 2001, p. 3.

18 *Education for the Church, Ministry* = ACCM 22, p. 23.

19 *Mission and Ministry*, p. 51.

20 Despite abuses and misunderstandings of this model (especially in the interests of 'integrist' and top-down structures of Church organization), the language and imagery of the Body can, with these safeguards, reinforce both the christological and pneumatological nature of ministry as well as drawing attention to its corporate (and hence collaborative) character.

21 See, among many publications, *The Priesthood of the Ordained Ministry*, Board of Mission and Unity, London, 1986; *Eucharistic Presidency*.

22 'It is evident unto all men diligently reading holy Scripture and ancient Authors, that from the Apostles' time there have been these Orders of Ministers in Christ's Church: Bishops, Priests, and Deacons.' The Preface to The Form and Manner of Making, Ordaining, and Consecrating Bishops, Priests, and Deacons according to the Order of the Church of England.

23 Canon C15.1, reproduced in *Common Worship*, p. xi.

24 *Laws of Ecclesiastical Polity*, Book 7.

25 This has been a major theme of the ecumenical agreements, for example *Baptism, Eucharist and Ministry* [The Lima Text], Faith and Order Paper 111, World Council of Churches, 1982 and the series of bilateral texts listed, among other places, in *Eucharistic Presidency* (CHP 1997), pp. 68–9.

Chapter 4

26 *Mind the Gap*, p. 31.

27 Summary of the report of the working party on theological education, commissioned by the Anglican Primates' meeting, Kanuga, North Carolina, USA, March 2001, p. 3.

28 *Theological Colleges for Tomorrow*, CIO, 1968, chp. 1. The report on *Residence – an Education* (ACCM Occasional Paper no. 38, 1990) deals helpfully with many related topics, such as community, spiritual formation and personal development.

29 Cf. the remarks on 'directional learning' in the Kanuga report, p. 19: 'Consideration needs to be given to the living traditions of meaning as renewed in each context, and how this embodies the "directional learning" that is the ongoing dynamic of Church life in every situation'.

30 p. 41.

31 p. 39.

32 See *Reader Ministry and Training* (2000), chapter 4 and *Mind the Gap* (2001), chapters 1–2.

33 Gordon Oliver, 'A Local Success that Reveals a Major Structural Failure', *British Journal of Theological Education*, 12.1 (2001), 25–35.

34 In October 2000 the House of Bishops confirmed that curates should normally serve four years before they take on posts of incumbent status but never less than three years.

35 The language of 'training post' and 'first curacy' is not entirely applicable to OLMs as they will continue as 'curates' and in the same parish after the first years of ordained ministry.

36 While we continue to use this term, we note the development of new patterns of supervision, where the supervisor is not necessarily an incumbent, and the range of types of first post, not all of them in parochial ministry.

37 p. 50.

Chapter 5

38 To give examples of possible misunderstandings, not all stipendiary clergy will hold posts of responsibility, while some permanent non-stipendiary will, while some PNSM candidates will be more academically able than some SM/NSM candidates. Further, while the charts are split into ministerial, vocational and educational columns, in preparation for ministry the three strands of course have to be intertwined.

39 The UK government agreed to the targets about accreditation set in the European Declaration of Bologna 1999.

40 Foundation degrees are suitable pathways for auxiliary professionals, who will gain a foundation degree by covering a broader range of material at Level 2, rather than progressing to the intellectually more demanding Level 3 studies.

41 See the paper, 'Accrediting prior learning and experience within initial training for ordained and Reader ministry' (July 2001), available from the Ministry Division.

42 *The Report of a Working Party on Criteria for Selection for Ministry in the Church of England*, ABM Policy Paper no. 3A, 1993, pp. 101–2; reproduced as a separate leaflet by the Ministry Division.

43 *Mission and Ministry*, pp. 41–2.

44 *Beginning Public Ministry*, pp. 12–13.

45 *Mind the Gap*, ch. 4.

46 *Preparing for Ordained Ministry. Good Practice in Assessment and in Reporting on Candidates within Initial Training*, Ministry Division, 2002.

47 The Quality Assurance Agency (QAA) for Higher Education's subject benchmark statement for Theology and Religious Studies is available at www.qaa.ac.uk/crntwork/benchmark/theology.pdf

48 A focus for this learning on 'exploration of vocation to discipleship, ministry and mission' was suggested by one of the contributors to the consultation on our interim report.

49 The most recent publication in this area is *A Review of Pre-Theological Education, January 1997–December 1999*, CHP, Archbishops' Council, 2001.

50 *Foundation Training. Handbook for Applicants*, Methodist Church, Formation in Ministry Office.

51 In this report we have used the phrases 'theology for ministry' and 'ministerial theology and practice' in nearly synonymous ways. Both refer to the study that arises out of the faith and life of the Church and its ministry. The latter phrase is useful to make it clear that the learning encompasses reflection on the practice of ministry.

Chapter 6

52 The work of the dioceses is summarized in *Shaping Ministry for a Missionary Church. A Review of Diocesan Ministry Strategy Documents 1997,* ABM, 1998; while the views of the training institutions are to be found in their responses to ACCM 22 and *Mission and Ministry*.

53 In the consultation on the interim report, some respondents from university departments have put the opposite case, i.e. that consolidating Church student numbers in the stronger departments would weaken theology in the UK because it might lead to withdrawal from weaker university departments. We note this point but would want to reply that to get the benefit from studying in university departments, ordinands need to be in strong and lively departments with a range of expertise that is directly relevant to their needs and, where possible, that is complemented by relevant expertise in other subject areas. In practice, where the Church's students are actually being taught by university staff, this is already the case. By contrast, some validation arrangements are with small departments or with HEIs with no faculty of theology.

Notes

54 On this point we note the call for 'a national centre for urban training and theology' contained in the report of the Urban Bishops' Panel, 'The Urban Renaissance and the Church of England', GS 1446, 2002, p. 11.

55 For example, the former Southern Dioceses Ministerial Training Scheme, a regional course sponsored by seven Church of England dioceses, has been superseded by the Southern Theological Education and Training Scheme, in a partnership between eight dioceses and the Methodist and United Reformed Churches. In an earlier period, the current Trinity College, Bristol resulted from the merger of three former colleges.

56 See note 2, and paragraphs 1.20 and 2.16 above.

57 The exception would be the north-west region where there is currently no Anglican theological college. We address this in paragraph 6.34 below.

58 These figures are arrived at by adding the actual number of current college staff in a region to figures based on the following assumptions: one CME officer and one adult education officer per diocese; one and a half members of staff per OLM scheme for each diocese that has a scheme; and an average figure of five and a half for staff to offer training in a part-time mode (i.e. the total number of staff on the current regional courses divided by eight).

59 In regions where it may be necessary to reconstitute the regional course because of changes to the boundaries of the region, the shadow management and staff must play a full role in the planning process for the regional training partnership.

Chapter 7

60 *Managing Planned Growth. Supplementary Report*, Ministry Division, 2001.

61 For the recent report on this issue, see *Generosity and Sacrifice*, CHP, 2001.

62 *Supplementary Report*, p. 20.

63 Paragraph 3.3.

64 Assumptions adopted for Illustration 1a – Summarised effect of proposals

    1   The change in family maintenance assumes that the reduction of 75 full-time candidates would all have been entitled to family maintenance grants.

    2   The reduction in core costs relates to a reduction of 75 places.

    3   Additional part-time costs are for the 75 people transferring from two years full-time training to three years part-time training, thus increasing part-time numbers by 112.

    4   CME 1–4 residential and training costs are phased in commencing in September 2004 and are assumed to apply to those ordained in 2004 and subsequent years.

    5   Savings of 7.5 per cent on academic and administration staff pay are assumed to commence in September 2005.

    6   Payments of grants for research are assumed to commence in September 2005.

65 Assumptions adopted for Illustration 1b – Ordinand numbers

1	2002/03	Based on current numbers
2	2003/04	Assume no change in full-time or part-time
3	2004/05	Assume 40 new candidates requiring family maintenance 'transfer' to part-time. Assume CME 1–4 residential training for one year group Part-time numbers increase by 40 transferred from full-time
4	2005/06	Assume 35 further new candidates requiring family maintenance 'transfer' to part-time. This gives an increase of 75 part-time Assume CME 1–4 residential training for two year groups
5	2006/07	Assume no change in full-time numbers Assume CME 1–4 residential training for three year groups Part-time numbers increase by 37 as 75 people transferring from full-time train for 3 years not 2
6	2007/08	Assume no change in full-time numbers. Assume CME 1–4 residential training for four year groups
7	2008/09	Assume no change
8		For the calculation of numbers ordained at the year end assume that in 2002 1/3rd full-time people train for three years and 2/3rds train for two years. Following transfer of 75 two year people to part-time training this will change to 39 per cent for three years and 61 per cent for two years. Assume all part-time and OLM people train for three years

Chapter 8

66 *Stranger in the Wings*, ABM Policy Paper no. 8, GS Misc 532, 1998. The recommendations in this area are focused on the adequacy of doctrine and biblical studies; spiritual nurture; preaching, communication and liturgy; and the value of placements.

67 'A Review of Mixed-Mode Training', Ministry Division, February 2003, chaired by the Revd Canon Leslie Morley.

68 *Residence – an Education*, ACCM Occasional Paper no. 38, 1990.

69 It is worth noting that the current framework for inspection and Church validation has been successfully used to inspect and validate institutions that include a college and a course (e.g. the college and course within the Queen's Foundation). Thus, in principle, the Church's processes for accountability and quality could be used and developed for the proposed new partnerships.

www.ingramcontent.com/pod-product-compliance
Lightning Source LLC
Chambersburg PA
CBHW081420300426
44110CB00016BA/2327